AF698494

From Rage to Reason

From Rage to Reason

Why We Need Sex Crime Laws Based on Facts, Not Fear

Emily Horowitz

BLOOMSBURY ACADEMIC
NEW YORK • LONDON • OXFORD • NEW DELHI • SYDNEY

BLOOMSBURY ACADEMIC
Bloomsbury Publishing Inc
1385 Broadway, New York, NY 10018, USA
50 Bedford Square, London, WC1B 3DP, UK
29 Earlsfort Terrace, Dublin 2, Ireland

BLOOMSBURY, BLOOMSBURY ACADEMIC and the Diana logo
are trademarks of Bloomsbury Publishing Plc

First published in the United States of America 2023

Copyright © Emily Horowitz, 2023

Cover image: © Carlos J. Flores. On the Bleachers, 2014.
Pen and marker on paper. 8 1/4 x 5 3/4 in.

All rights reserved. No part of this publication may be reproduced or transmitted in any form or by any means, electronic or mechanical, including photocopying, recording, or any information storage or retrieval system, without prior permission in writing from the publishers.

Bloomsbury Publishing Inc does not have any control over, or responsibility for, any third-party websites referred to or in this book. All internet addresses given in this book were correct at the time of going to press. The author and publisher regret any inconvenience caused if addresses have changed or sites have ceased to exist, but can accept no responsibility for any such changes.

Library of Congress Cataloging in Publication Control Number: 2023014177

ISBN: HB: 978-1-4408-7939-5
ePDF: 978-1-4408-7940-1
eBook: 979-8-216-17160-7

Typeset by Amnet ContentSource
Printed and bound in the United States of America

To find out more about our authors and books visit
www.bloomsbury.com and sign up for our newsletters.

For Marina & Juliet & Elroy & Pebbles

Contents

Preface: Worse Than Murder

There's a strange feeling of solitude when you know something is objectively true and most others are utterly convinced it's untrue. There are times when the feeling is even more intense. You express your convictions, which you know to be based in fact, only to be met with rage because what you say undermines so many core, entrenched beliefs. Most alienating is when the arguments you bring forth are called not only false but equivalent to endorsing the worst type of evil.

Almost everyone will disagree with the thesis of this book. It argues that endless punishment and abuse toward those convicted of sex offenses is wrong and destructive. The experience of being branded a "sex offender" is horrendous, and those living with this label are subject to unending cruelty and revulsion from almost all sides. This group is often excluded even by those—such as religious and spiritual leaders and organizations, criminal justice reformers, and advocates for social justice—who, on principle, support and forgive those who have made terrible mistakes.

There are two aspects to this excessive treatment: the public sex-offense registry itself, which formally creates a set of pariahs banished from society and blocked from ever fully engaging in it, and the informal, personal microlevel realities of being objects of moral disgust. These dimensions are interrelated. Being publicly listed on a sex-offense registry and branded with the official "sex offender" status creates stigma and colors all interpersonal relationships.

The underlying and unofficial societal revulsion toward those with sex-offense convictions cuts more deeply than the registry itself. The most obvious example is the well-documented vicious treatment that those with sex offenses face in prison, a reality that predates the registry. While those on registries outside of prison don't primarily experience overt ostracization or physical violence, they are still viewed with loathing and fear. Society is both uncomfortable and enraged by their very presence and existence.

Society bases viewing those on registries with unique revulsion on two factors. First, society fears this population due to the false but pervasive belief that all those convicted of sex offenses are similarly predatory, uncontrollable, and unable ever to stop offending. Therefore, they must be punished and subject to permanent surveillance because, unlike all other humans, they are uniquely impervious to change.

Second, society loathes this population on the basis that sexual harm crosses a line. Sexual harm is held to be of a nature and magnitude unlike virtually any other injury, including murder or any other form of physical assault or abuse. This level of intense societal aversion can be attributed to three interrelated factors. First, the idea that sexual harm is an experience from which one can never recover and that all forms of sexual harm are equally traumatic. Second, because almost all victims of sexual harm are women and children, those labeled as perpetrators of sexual harm are viewed as having injured those who are most innocent and vulnerable. Third, and most notably, the fact that the harm is sexual taps into our deepest social taboos and personal sense of shame; despite the sexual revolution of the 1960s, sex is still tinged with embarrassment, morality, confusion, secrecy, and disgust.

A body of well-founded and indisputable data shows that these attitudes are rooted in myths and irrationality. Those who commit sex offenses are not all the same, and regardless of the particular sex-offense subcategory, recidivism rates are far lower than those for almost any other crime. There is no evidence that those on registries are a distinct breed of person, unresponsive to punishment and treatment, or that subjecting them to lifelong banishment and humiliation makes them less likely to reoffend. Sexual harm is profound, but no evidence suggests that excessive and draconian punishment resolves the pain and trauma of those hurt any more than do ordinary criminal-legal sanctions or other forms of accountability.

My work is not intended to add to the irrefutable body of evidence that registries and other special sex-offense laws are ineffective and unnecessary. Rather, I hope to convey the cruelty inherent in our policies and perceptions and the societal impact of tolerating and even celebrating this excessive treatment. Denying those who have been punished the opportunity to repent and reenter society creates new harm while undermining philosophical, religious, spiritual, and ethical principles of forgiveness and redemption. Yet, when it comes to those convicted of sex offenses, we often abandon the grace and understanding we may readily offer to others.

Thus, one goal of this book is to share, in detail, the nightmarish reality of living as a hated pariah in the modern world. Those I interviewed helped me understand what it's like to exist in a half-free, half-alive state of existence, and I hope to highlight the torture inflicted by ill-conceived laws that function solely to name and shame. The broader goal is to force us to confront our own complicity in this regime and to ask what drives our fear, our hatred, and our unwillingness to forgive and accept. Even if registries disappear, as they should, we must actively recognize the causes and consequences of our destructive impulses and willingness to create monsters and destroy human lives.

Ultimately, I seek to humanize and unearth empathy for those our society has thoroughly dehumanized and discarded *after* punishment. This is not because I have a "soft spot" for those convicted of sex offenses or that I minimize the trauma of sexual harm or question the extent of sexual violence. Those who tolerate this treatment are largely motivated by misunderstandings, even myths, regarding this issue. We must devise reasonable, just, evidence-based policies, while de-escalating panic-driven attitudes that result in the needless and brutal exile of an entire class of people—something that affects even their closest relatives and friends, who accompany them in the simplest daily aspects of life, yet to whom society attaches some strange, metaphysical guilt by association. In short, I hope to change hearts and minds so that our laws, and attitudes, are reflective of the respect and justice deserved by all human beings.

Acknowledgments

This book is dedicated to all those impacted by conviction registries, who are denied the dignity and opportunity to rebuild their lives after punishment. It is also dedicated to those who recognize the irrationality and cruelty of this regime and bravely fight, often at personal and professional risk, for laws based reason and justice.

I am greatly indebted to all those who helped me write and edit this book. Alan Astro, most notably, helped me think about this issue in a far more nuanced way and as always helped me with all aspects of writing and presentation and argument, and I cannot thank him enough for this and everything else. Many others also helped with research and editing and reading early drafts, including Bruno Chaouat, Natasha Frid, Victoria Maxham, and Shawn Rolfe.

I am also indebted to those fearless organizations that helped me by promoting my study, giving me opportunities to present my research, and helping me access members of the registrant community, including the Alliance for the Constitutional Reform of Sex Offense Laws, the National Association for the Reform of Sex Offense Laws, Texas Voices, Florida Action Committee, the Chicago 400, Women Against the Registry, United Voices 4 Sex Offense Reform, and the Restorative Action Alliance. These organizations, as well as the smaller grassroots organizations and individual advocates and activists, work every day to help those suffering from unjust policies.

The process of writing this book was a particularly challenging one, and I am so lucky to have colleagues who are also among my closest friends, who were always there for me personally and professionally, especially in trying times. I thank Athena Devlin, John Edwards, Kathleen Gray, Jenny Labendz, Jennifer Lancaster, Nickie Phillips, Eric Platt, Sara Rzeszutek, Scott Weiss, and Jennifer Wingate.

I want to thank my mentors/close friends Ira Ellman and Tara Ellman, Judith Levine, Debbie Nathan, Laurie Jo Reynolds, and Lenore Skenazy for always helping me with all things—personal and political. I thank Catherine Carpenter, Jay Rice, and Amber Vlangas for helping me better approach organizing and collaborating. I thank all those who shared their lives and experiences with me and helped me better understand what it's like to live in this world in this way, including Carlton, Chance, Derek, Doyle, Jay, Jeff, and Willie, who went far beyond what I asked of them and I am truly humbled by how much they shared with me. I thank Carlos for his willingness to share and donate his art. I thank E for everything and more, but most especially for making sure neither distraction nor hunger delayed the completion of this project.

Introduction

This book explores how and why those convicted of sex offenses are viewed differently from and as far worse than those convicted of any other crimes. I analyze the consequences of permanently punishing and publicly branding this group in harsh and distinct ways. This set of policies has contributed to a dangerous intensification of rage and misinformation—on the left and on the right—regarding the extent, pervasiveness, and reality of sexual violence. Liberal activists argue the problem is ignored and underpunished by a sexist and misogynist culture that doesn't care about women and children and that tolerates harassment. Conservatives, too, claim the phenomenon is greater than realized and insufficiently sanctioned, but with a slightly different emphasis: the responsibility lies with an anticarceral and sexually permissive culture.

I ultimately argue that most sex offenses are caused and characterized by the same factors attached to most crime. Those convicted are almost always dealing with such things as untreated mental illness, substance use and abuse, brain injuries, untreated trauma, abuse or neglect, or post-traumatic stress disorder (PTSD) resulting from military service or other painful past experiences. As in the case of most transgressions, committing a sex offense is almost never a premeditated or carefully executed decision, where one weighs risks and consequences, but a crime of impulse and opportunity. Most incidents occur during times of extreme personal stress, when individuals aren't addressing or acknowledging long-standing mental, psychological, and emotional issues. It is also worth noting that minorities are disproportionately represented on registries, consistent with similar patterns throughout the criminal-legal system. One exhaustive study found that African Americans are more likely to be listed on public registries in every U.S. state with the exception of Michigan (Ackerman & Sacks, 2018).

Thus, I base my position that eliminating special, lifetime, public punishment for this population on decades of clear and consistent research about sex-offense recidivism, and see this as crucial to developing a society with frank and realistic—and effective—approaches to prevention, treatment, and punishment. As always, reasonable punishment, treatment, and reentry opportunities are effective ways to limit reoffense.

There is a wealth of research and data about the uselessness of our sex-offense policies from the standpoint of preventing new sex offenses. My 2015 book, *Protecting Our Kids? How Sex Offender Laws Are Failing Us*, presents the reasons why our current laws have failed and reviews the extensive body of supporting research and related data. That work is part of a far larger body of literature that has emerged since the start of our current, post-1994 sex-offense legal regime.

The purpose of the current book is to describe and analyze what these laws have done to the targeted individuals. I started this project with the aim of exploring how the generally growing violence of our political and cultural climate was impacting those convicted of sex offenses. I sought to explore the impact of such phenomena in the context of the increasing frequency of using terms such as "pedo" and "groomer" against ideological foes in social media and political discourse amid the increasing belief in conspiracies, such as PizzaGate and QAnon, which posit elite involvement in child sex rings and trafficking.

This book is grounded on three interrelated ideas. First, research on and evidence against excessive punishment for sex offenses (and crime in general) is becoming evermore extensive and irrefutable. Second, rage and misinformation about sexual violence are, alas, increasing simultaneously. Third, those convicted of sex offenses are the human casualties of this disconnected reality because they are subject to growing legal surveillance and control, social isolation, and a general normalization of violence.

I have interviewed those on registries to determine the extent to which the political and cultural context has changed their day-to-day lives. My project developed as I came to a far deeper understanding of the realities of living life in a state of banishment. I had conducted interviews for my first book, and through my subsequent deepening engagement with advocacy efforts, I already knew many experiencing life on the registry. However, this new round of conversations transformed my understanding of the stakes. I started to see the need for a book that details the realities of life when someone is viewed as subhuman and has no choice but to partake of a largely hidden but officially sanctioned postprison subculture. This book can be most succinctly characterized as an effort to communicate the true human and societal impact of laws and attitudes that are driven by hatred and misinformation.

Unique Challenges of Studying Sex Offenses

It is also crucial here, at the onset, to state that my work is premised on the fact that sexual harm is traumatic for those personally impacted, as well as a profound and pervasive social problem. Those who experience sexual victimization of any kind are deeply harmed, and perpetrators should be punished and held accountable. The purpose of this book is not to downplay the harm caused by sexual violence or to justify or excuse the actions of those who do damage, but to reveal the extent and damage of cruel and unusual responses.

I'd also like to address a unique challenge of researching sex-offense law and policy. First, studying this issue is different from working on other topics related to social problems or criminal justice. If one studies, say, serial killers or those convicted of homicide or physical violence, one does not have to clarify that they oppose murder or assault. Yet those who study this topic must assert their opposition to sexual violence and the harm it causes, as there is an assumption that advocating for rational sex-offense policy is motivated by a tolerance for sexual abuse or a failure to grasp the extent of trauma experienced by victims.

Almost all social scientific and legal writing on this topic includes such a caveat at the start, and it is also frequently voiced by advocates and others testifying for rational sex-offense policy. Many, for instance, preface their comments by sharing their personal experiences of sexual harm. This is due to the historical context of current laws. First is the understandable societal rage at our past indifference in the face of sexual violence, our skepticism about the depth of the pain experienced by those harmed, and the historical lack of formal and informal sanctions for sexual abusers. Second, during the period when feminists fought to bring attention to the problem of sexual violence, a cycle of sex panics, beginning with the day care panic of the 1980s, started to grip our culture. This combination, in the context of tough-on-crime policies and a growing victim-rights movement, led not only to our current sex-offense policies but also a climate where it became problematic to voice even the slightest concern that extreme punitive measures may be unjustified.

The need to state that one recognizes the harm and existence of sexual violence while critiquing certain legal, civil, and social responses to sexual violence go beyond the areas of scholarship and advocacy. Anyone failing to personally reject those on registries, including one's relatives, partners, employers, and friends, are also subject to the accusation that they tolerate sexual violence. This charged climate contributes to unjustifiably vexed experiences of those convicted of sexual violence, such as I seek to convey in this book.

Sociologist Loïc Wacquant offers the best analysis of why studying sex offenses is not only difficult but also essential. He views our current policies as rooted in an overall societal descent into what he calls "penalization," or the growing use of the criminal-legal system to respond to all social problems and "contain" populations damaged by neoliberal economic and social welfare policies. In his insightful *Punishing the Poor: The Neoliberal Government of Social Insecurity*, he explains that it is:

> imperative that we adopt a rigorously analytical attitude and avoid echoing the shrill rhetoric of the entrepreneurs in morality who have latched onto sexual lawbreakers as the heinous incarnation of criminal depravity. We must insist that the latter be treated like any other problem category handled by the penal arm of the state. This entails taking pains to recognize gradations in types of offenses and to describe sexual convicts who have served their sentence as ex-sex offenders (as one does with thieves, burglars, and murderers).

The point is that those who commit sex offenses should be viewed *as others* who commit offenses. They constitute a broad range of diverse individuals guilty of a wide gamut of varying crimes. They have the same potential of transforming beyond their crimes as do others who are formerly incarcerated.

Wacquant further notes that the sociological approach to any social problem is "never to indict or exculpate, but to explain and understand (which does not imply condoning or standing by morally unperturbed)" (Wacquant, 2009, p. 215). At the onset of his wide-ranging analysis of "penalization" that goes beyond the study of sex offenses, he emphasizes that it is appropriate for some analyses to focus on punishment. I agree with Wacquant and share his approach to this subject.

My Purpose

My primary purpose in this book is to humanize and give voice to those on registries. I conducted lengthy interviews with close to two hundred individuals who are reviled and excluded from society, who thus experience a form of "civil death." While I've worked on this subject for many years, it was only while conducting these interviews that I realized how essential it is to portray the consequences of current policies on individuals. I was overwhelmed by the sheer number of people wanting to share their experiences with me.

Almost everyone I interviewed was somewhat familiar with me and my earlier work on this topic, as well as my engagement in advocacy efforts. Those I spoke to were, thus, far more comfortable opening up to me about their lives and challenges, as they viewed me as someone trustworthy. Those on registries often express understandable fears about revealing themselves to others. As someone they viewed as an ally, I learned evermore about the deep emotional and psychological impact of these policies.

From the time I first learned of our policies regarding sex crime, the research was clear that they were not driven by reason and facts but by rage and fear. My goal is not only to communicate the true impact of their cruelty, but to examine the impact of this on society and ourselves. Registries are solely a punitive tool of social control that create more harm, which then spreads this violence to families and communities. Denying so many people the opportunity to be a part of our polity and a chance to thrive while paying lip service to a carceral notion of public safety disserves the rest of us. By making monsters out of them, we reveal who the real monsters are (Horowitz, 2022).

The Recidivism Myth

The stories in this book are intended to convey the lived experience of those directly impacted by our widespread and growing—and myth-based—sex-offense legal regime. I am not presenting new or original research about the extent to which registries have failed. Decades of research, much of which is based on data from state and federal criminal justice agencies, shows that these postsentence lists and policies do not prevent new sex offenses or reduce recidivism. It's also well known and undebated at this point that almost all sex offenses, whether committed before or after registries, involve nonstranger perpetrators. Yet almost all registry provisions are aimed at protecting children from strangers. Most new sex-offense convictions involve those with no prior sex-offense history. This has been the case both before and after registries. However, the most pervasive and destructive myth involves recidivism rates.

Simply put, those with sex-offense convictions have lower recidivism rates than those having committed almost any other offense. Findings include: The Department of Justice reported tracking for three years 9,691 sex offenders released from prison in 1994; only 3.5 percent were reconvicted of a sex offense (U.S. Department of Justice, Bureau of Justice

Statistics, 2003). A Connecticut Office of Policy and Management study followed those released in 2005; 3.6 percent were charged with a new sex crime, 2.7 percent were convicted, and 1.7 percent returned to prison (Connecticut Office of Policy and Management, 2012). Additionally, sex-offense registration is often for life, yet research shows that the risk of sexual recidivism declines over time (Thornton et al., 2019), including those deemed to be at the highest risk for reoffense (Hanson et al., 2014). As one study notes, "After ten to fifteen years, most individuals with a history of sexual offenses were no more likely to commit a new sexual offense than individuals with a criminal history that did not include sexual offenses" (Hanson et al., 2018).

The Supreme Court, however, has upheld the constitutionality of registries and related postsentence restrictions due to the power of the recidivism myth. The claim that registries are not punishment but necessary civil remedies to protect public safety is based on supposedly "frightening and high" recidivism rates. Yet the Supreme Court did not use reliable research in this key ruling. In 2015, scholars Ira Ellman and Tara Ellman unearthed the source underlying this false assertion. They discovered, shockingly, that the sole evidence was an offhand comment about "frightening and high" recidivism. This was a remark made by a treatment provider quoted in an article published in the popular magazine *Psychology Today*.

The myth of "frightening and high" recidivism is pervasive in our society. It is an article of faith that those convicted of sex offenses will inevitably reoffend and are essentially subhuman time bombs on the verge of committing new sexual offenses. This is the falsehood most responsible for draconian sex-offense policies.

Terminology

In this book, I use the phrase "sex offender" almost solely in directly quoting a comment during an interview or a passage from an article or book. Rarely, I will employ the label to highlight how it functions as a slur. Most often I use formulations such as "those on registries," "registrants," or "those convicted of sex offenses" and "those with sex offense convictions." In recent years, those on registries and antiregistry organizations have made efforts to replace the term "sex offender" with humanizing, people-first language that has the possibility to diffuse and decrease some of this violence. These concerted efforts emerged in the same spirit as other justice-impacted populations, where individuals are described as more than their crimes of conviction (e.g., murderer, drug dealer, thief) or status as someone with a criminal justice history (e.g., convict, inmate, felon).

I use the terms “the registry” or “registries” or the “registry regime” to refer not only to the registry itself but to all laws and regulations that are specific to those convicted of sex offenses. These related rules most commonly include community notification and residency restrictions, but also govern domestic and international travel, proximity (e.g., laws prohibiting registrants from visiting or entering certain venues), as well as employment, education, licensing, civic engagement, volunteering, church attendance, and so on.

This book focuses on the experiences of people on sex-offense registries after jail or prison, during or after completing any terms of supervision. I use the blanket term “supervision” for the various federal or state forms of probation or parole affecting those I interviewed. For those currently under supervision, I highlight those aspects unique to being on the registry or having committed a sex offense. Those who are on registries but currently incarcerated are not included in this study.

I use the term “antiregistry movement” to indicate participation in national and state-level organizations that advocate for sex-offense-law reform. This also covers individual efforts, as well as informal, unincorporated groups that engage in lobbying and activism efforts that challenge policies and institutions that discriminate against those on registries.

It is also important to note here that in twenty states, some with sex-offense convictions are subject to “civil commitment.” Subjects are confined in what’s technically not prison but a “treatment” facility, with few legal routes for appeal or release. In the *California Law Review*, Jeslyn Miller explains some deemed at highest risk for sexual reoffense, “can be isolated until they are no longer a threat to society,” and this is constitutional because it’s classified as a civil, not criminal, sanction (Miller, 2010, p. 2094). Thus, as a “civil” and noncriminal penalty, these individuals “are denied the rights . . . guaranteed in criminal proceedings, including the Fifth Amendment right against self-incrimination, the Sixth Amendment rights to jury trial and to assistance of counsel, and the requirement of proof beyond a reasonable doubt” (p. 2095).

This is a far more brutal consequence than all other sex-offense laws that follow the completion of criminal sanctions. Those civilly committed have few legal routes for appeal or release, and criminal-justice reformers are largely unaware or uninvolved in challenging policies, even though they are among the most egregious forms of criminal-legal overreach. Those in civil commitment languish invisibly in these so-called “shadow prisons” for crimes they may commit in the future, with even less power and access than others convicted of sex offenses.

Legal scholar Eric Janus notes that the sole basis for a policy that says, "We're going to lock you up before the crime," is "that these people's lives don't matter . . . that their liberties and freedoms are expendable" (Rosengren, 2022). For instance, a 2016 investigation discovered that not one person obtained release from Minnesota civil commitment in two decades, despite "the stated goal . . . to give mental health treatment to the offenders, and release those who are deemed ready for life on the outside" (Fritz & Brangham, 2016). Since that scrutiny, fifteen have been released and there have been small improvements, but "those committed are about six times more likely to die inside than to be released, making their commitment basically a life sentence" (Rosengren, 2022). While this book is limited to studying the harms of registry laws following incarceration, I acknowledge that these harms are minimal compared to those civilly confined to a lifetime of imprisonment.

Book Outline

This book is organized around the different causes and consequences of life on a sex-offense registry. Those listed are parents, children, partners, siblings, and spouses, with a vast range of overlapping professional and personal identities. I had intended to organize the interviews by the primary form of self-identification. However, while reviewing the narratives, it became clear that what was most important was how each highlighted various consequences of being on the registry. The first part of the book explores the formal impacts, including legal barriers to housing, employment, travel, and societal participation. The second part examines the informal results, including emotional and mental toll, experiences of harassment, self-isolation, and fear of others, as well as challenges related to family estrangement and making and maintaining new friends and relationships. The third part explores how these laws indirectly but profoundly ensnare and harm family members, loved ones, and friends. Throughout the book, I also describe various responses to formal and informal dehumanization. I discuss those who (often moderately) thrive, those who "get by" and try to make themselves invisible, and those who overcome some challenges but suffer deeply from others.

Part One: Formal Sanctions

In the first four chapters of this book, I focus on the formal sanctions that are the most frequent and pervasive impacts of being on a registry. In the first three chapters, I discuss how registry laws impact the ability to earn an income, secure employment, find housing, and travel freely. In chapter four, I discuss the laws and policies that deprive those on registries the right to visit or even be near certain places, such as recreational and educational facilities, as well as the impact of special supervision conditions that apply to those with sexual offenses, such as mandatory intensive treatment protocols. Specifically, the life histories presented in these chapters concern the material and easily definable impacts.

Many of those I interviewed described the experience of wanting to work and being qualified to do so, but they are unable to find work, or enough work, as a result not only of laws but also of stigmatization. The inability to support a family or yourself, particularly when there are jobs available and when one is qualified to work, exerts a huge emotional toll; many on registries must rely on others for financial support. Some can't get jobs because employers, including "felon-friendly" workplaces, simply refuse to hire those on sex registries; other individuals have been told that employers want to hire them but are afraid to do so, citing fears of liability or the fact that those on registries are publicly listed so that other employees can easily identify them. Finding housing is also a common problem for those on registries, also due to legal restrictions, as well as stigma. Here come into play the legal realities of residency restrictions in many communities, in addition to the unwillingness of many landlords to have their property listed on a registry website. Other housing issues relate to hostility from neighbors, who are, in some cases, notified when someone on a registry moves in.

Registrants also face restrictions on domestic and foreign travel. They must often follow complicated, contradictory, and unclear rules about the length of time they can be in another state before registering with law enforcement there; no others with criminal convictions are held to such a stricture after completion of probation or parole. Those on registries who wish to leave the country for work, pleasure, or family visits must follow even more burdensome and ambiguous regulations. Many with past (including nonsexual) criminal convictions are banned from traveling to certain countries. However, those on registries are the only class of citizens required to have a special identifier placed on their passports. They must also notify the government twenty-one days prior to travel. When those on registries travel abroad, they often find that the United States has notified law enforcement at their planned destination. Some are immediately turned away upon airport arrival.

Part Two: Informal Sanctions

In the second part of this book, in chapters five and six, I focus on what I call the informal sanctions of the registry. I relate the interviewees' fears of returning to prison, of being falsely accused, of new laws being passed that will force them to move or lose their jobs, of being "outed" at work or church or school. Here, I also consider those who feel their only options are to go into complete social isolation or banish themselves. Those who remove themselves from all meaningful social interactions, exile themselves from communities and relationships, or go physically abroad, do so out of shame and guilt, as well as fury at a society that has deemed them subhuman. Many stories interweave the impact of registries on those who had preexisting issues with substance abuse, mental illness, PTSD from military service or other traumatic experiences, and intellectual disabilities. Many also partly or largely attribute their having committed offenses to these problems. Others view their experiences with the criminal-legal system, including the registry, as triggers for new mental and emotional issues.

I include stories of how the registry affects the ability to form romantic relationships. Some are single because the arrest prompted a spouse or partner to leave or because the registry puts too many limitations and pressures on their relationships. Others may have been single or very young at the time of their arrest. For these individuals, finding a partner while crippled by the stigma of having a sex-offense conviction is prohibitive, to say the least. Many report that if they meet someone and disclose their status at the onset, they face immediate rejection, yet delaying disclosure can result in accusations of secrecy or manipulation. Many tell me they have given up on finding a partner and plan to live solitary lives. Their ban from dating apps and social media also limits their ability to meet potential partners. Those who divorce following a sex-offense conviction often lose all custody rights, with many ex-spouses discouraging parent-child contact. Many no longer see their children or extended family; some are even rejected by their parents.

Part Three: Families and Collateral Consequences

In chapter seven, I address the extent to which the registry impacts and punishes innocent parents, children, and partners. This situation is unique; those related to individuals with nonsexual criminal convictions don't experience the harm that can come of having someone close to them on a public registry. Anyone sharing a home with a registrant is vulnerable because public registries and community-notification polices, as well as websites and neighborhood, social media, and real estate apps, identify where registrants reside. This subjects entire families, and whoever else might be in the home, to harassment, embarrassment, and community rejection.

While having a justice-involved parent, child, or partner is always traumatic, registries add stress because of their easy accessibility. Entire families must move if a school or day care center opens near their homes; children of registrants are deprived of having both parents at school events or celebrations, and spouses are burdened when proximity laws forbid registrant partners from dropping their children at school or supervising them in parks, playgrounds, or pools, and sometimes even hospitals. Aging parents, too, are often deprived of needed care and support from registrant children due to residency and proximity laws. Family members also recounted being shunned and excised from community and family events for standing by their partners, children, or parents after a sex-offense conviction.

Responses to Dehumanization

All the interviews in this book offer insight into the different responses to the dehumanization that results from a sex-offense conviction. In my interviews, I found that everyone on registries suffers from some level of fear and underlying anxiety about what could happen, and anger and shame at what has happened. As is the case with all that may occur in a life, personality, outlook, support systems, and luck play into the way individuals respond to the reality of having a sex-offense conviction. Some abandon any hope that things may get better for them personally or professionally. Some are isolated, with few close relationships and a lack of meaningful social networks. Others view life in a wary and stoic way and characterize themselves as merely "getting by." They may have a parent or partner or friend who blunts their hopelessness, but they view the future with trepidation. There are those who express gratitude for their personal happiness and professional success but still fear that changes in laws or rules could result in a major setback at any time. One interesting discovery for me was that almost all my interviewees asserted that they are "lucky" in that they "have it better" than others on the registry. They describe fellow registrants with empathy. There is clearly a level of community and mutual support even among this highly ostracized and marginalized population.

In my conclusion, I analyze why we, as a society, should and need to care about those convicted of sex offenses, and why responding with justice, not vengeance, is the only way to stop an endless cycle of violence. Special laws for those with sex-offense convictions arose from profound misunderstandings about recidivism and the impact accountability, in an emotional context that is not based on data. The #MeToo movement emerged because of a recognition that sexual abuse is pervasive and largely tolerated, revealing the failure of these laws to address the most common forms of sexual abuse.

Further, the extending definitions of what constitutes sexual abuse or harassment, and the ease with which allegations of "predator" and "rapist" and "child molester" and "pedophile" are now used in news and social media about public and private figures, including those not facing criminal charges, highlights the need to diffuse the unending quest for vengeance. The informal branding of those we hate or political rivals as the equivalent of "sex offenders" unsurprisingly shows the ripple effect of tolerating intense hatred and dehumanization of any group. In other words, it's no surprise that when society formally and legally constructs a "sex offender" caste with limited civil and human rights, it can easily lead to branding political and personal enemies as such; especially by those who believe so vehemently in their cause that they take a "by any means necessary" approach.

I do not propose that those convicted of sex offenses do not face punishment. Rather, I urge that they receive punishment not so thoroughly unlike that meted out to others who break laws. We've created a class of people that is subject to failed, myth-based policies that are effective at public shaming but little else. We have seen how decades of general mass incarceration and lengthy sentencing policies have devastated communities and families. The harshness of those measures is finally being subjected to much-needed intense scholarly, social, and political attention; the question of sex registries should also be included in these efforts.

Those convicted of sex offenses, like all with criminal histories, face the arduousness of incarceration and postincarceration supervision, and special regulations during both. Just as anyone else with a prior offense, they are subject to swift and harsh sentencing if they are convicted of a reoffense. Ultimately, I present evidence throughout this book demonstrating the need to provide opportunities and second chances for all after they have been held accountable.

Methods

This book intersperses criminal justice, sociological, legal, and psychological research on sex offenses and resultant policies with firsthand accounts of life on the registry. Fundamentally, I present the experiences I heard from formal, in-depth, open-ended interviews with those on public registries and their family members. During our interviews, I asked subjects about five key areas:

1. How does being listed on the public sex-offense registry impact your life and the lives of your family members? This includes areas such as income, employment, housing, and education, as well as the impact of restrictions related to travel, proximity, presence, or residency.
2. Have recent movements such as #QAnon, #PizzaGate, and fears of widespread child sex-trafficking conspiracies, such as #SaveOurChildren, impacted your life? What about the #MeToo movement, "cancel culture," or the convictions in high-profile sex-crime cases such as those involving Jeffrey Epstein, Harvey Weinstein, and Larry Nassar?
3. Have you faced challenges or been excluded from resources or opportunities available for others with past justice involvement, such as education, employment, training, or service opportunities? Have any criminal-justice-reform movements or policies in your community excluded those specifically on registries? What resources or opportunities in general (not exclusively aimed at those with past justice involvement, such as income-based social benefits and housing opportunities) have you been denied because of your registry status?
4. How has the registry impacted your social life and personal relationships? These may include social activities, religious activities, volunteer opportunities, social media and social network access, or dating apps.
5. Many of those with justice involvement exit prison and are offered second chances and viewed as "redeemed." What would you say to people who view those with sex offenses as irredeemable and different from others convicted of nonsexual offenses?

I have changed the names of those interviewed to protect confidentiality in accordance with the approval granted by the Institutional Review Board at my institution. Those interviewed volunteered to participate in this project and reached out to me after seeing my call for participants in emails and postings from state and national organizations that advocate for those on sex-offense registries.

For each interview, I include publicly available information about each subject taken from state registry websites, including, when available, their race, current age, years since the offense and/or age at offense, and postincarceration years on the registry. I also provide a general offense description from their registry listing, but to protect privacy, I don't include the precise wording of charges. In some cases, I include details based on additional case or criminal history documents that were voluntarily shared with me. The number of postincarceration years on the registry includes any time on supervision (e.g., probation or parole). If the victim was under the age of consent in the state of conviction, I use the term "underage." I do this to make clear that regardless of age and the nature of the relationship, the victim is unable to legally consent.

In cases where the interviewees claim the victims are family members, I identify them as "a relative." In cases where they identify the victim as someone with whom they had a preoffense nonsexual relationship of any kind, I use the term "nonstranger" to note that the victim was not a stranger at the time of the offense. To be clear: all claims about the nature of the victim-interviewee relationship, guilt or innocence, the fairness or terms of the criminal sentence, and any other information about the nature and terms of the offenses are based on their statements and are presented as such; the purpose of the interviews was not to critique the fairness of sentencing terms or process or the details of each offense but to discern the effect of the special sanctions they faced after incarceration. Each interview presented, therefore, includes a summary of the objective information posted publicly, and their subjective narratives.

Why Do We Treat Sex Offenses as Worse Than Murder?

The book I published in 2015 argues that sex-offense laws do nothing to protect children while inflicting unnecessary pain and suffering on those caught in their web. That situation still holds.

However, since that publication, I've observed a marked increase in both rage and irrationality about this issue. There are more laws and greater surveillance of those impacted. Rising movements ideologically based on the left and the right extremes argue that we need more punishment for sex crimes, though evidence grows concerning the flawed premises of restrictions. Even more disturbingly, this heightened state of anxiety has cast a wider net as to what constitutes a sex offense. The label "sex offender" is evermore weaponized against whom we dislike or with whom we disagree. This book provides numerous examples of increased harassment faced by those on registries, as well as their advocates, making their lives more harrowing and subjecting them to greater abuse.

This climate makes it all the more challenging to critique sex-offense registries, and, thus, all the more vital to point out the direct and collateral harm they cause. During the child day care panic that emerged in the 1980s, some of those who stood up and defended those falsely accused of child sex abuse were themselves accused. Some were even formally charged and convicted.

Today, those defending those accused of sexual abuse or questioning child sex conspiracies are also often branded as sex-abuse apologists. Even efforts to propose modest model legal reforms are met with fierce opposition from legal professionals, clearly driven by fears of being targeted as someone not tough enough on sex offenders. Those advocating for rational sex-offense laws, family members of those convicted of sex offenses, or judges who fail to apply the most draconian sentences possible all face accusations of being tolerant of sexual abuse or, implicitly, being sexual abusers themselves.

During the hearings for Supreme Court Justice Ketanji Brown Jackson in early 2022, her rational and even moderate approach to sex-offense sentencing resulted in accusations by elected officials of "endangering our children" and not "protecting the most vulnerable," while those voting in her favor were branded "pro-pedophile" (Horowitz, 2022).

This reality is like witch-hunts in seventeenth-century New England, where one was viewed with suspicion simply by association. As historian John Demos writes, "Traditional lore suggested that the power to effect witchcraft was most easily transmitted from one family member, or close friend, to another; there was, in short, a literal process of 'guilt by association'" (Demos, 1976).

I hope this book will contribute to the tireless work of those seeking sane and rational sex-offense policy, undertaken by numerous activists, scholars, lawyers, and those directly impacted despite the very real personal and professional risks. I also aim to present compelling evidence of the parallels between those who commit sex offenses and all others who make terrible mistakes that cause harm to others, and how both groups are capable and deserving of redemption and opportunities after punishment. Finally, these misguided laws must change not only for the sake of the millions on registries and their families but also because they create a dangerous and terrifying climate where it is acceptable to inflict any type of harm to someone labeled a "sex offender" by the state or by enemies.

If my project is successful, the most notable contribution it can make is to shatter the myth that those convicted of sex offenses deserve banishment, public shaming, and fear-filled postsentence lives and are to be offered no second chances. I have spent a significant amount of time meeting with and speaking to those on sex-offense registries, yet after almost two decades of study, I still struggle to grasp the true reach of the web of formal and informal consequences they face. I also work closely with a program that offers educational opportunities to all those with criminal histories. In that role, I am overwhelmingly inspired by the opportunities and forgiveness our society has begun to offer those individuals convicted of serious, but nonsexual, crimes. I wonder why our society must treat so differently, the people I follow in this book.

This book aims to convey the experience of these modern-day pariahs, while proposing that a good society embraces laws and holds attitudes that allow those who harm the opportunity to repent constructively. All those who make terrible mistakes should be held accountable, but in addition to accountability, a society seeking to address and end all forms of violence must also offer the opportunity for forgiveness and reacceptance.

Registrants Matter, and So Do Victims and Accountability

Accountability Matters

In this book, I don't address questions of guilt or innocence or sentencing severity, such as length of incarceration or supervision. These are also issues that require critique, but they are not the focus of my work. While my focus is the range of sanctions that remain after serving time and completing postincarceration supervision, during my interviews, I also learned about other punishments faced by this population during incarceration and while on supervision, as well as the extreme difficulties faced by those sentenced to sex-offense lifetime supervision. In other words, my study is exclusively on the postincarceration public and specialized punishments to which those convicted of sex offenses are subject. I do not question the need for them to be held accountable or to be prosecuted in the criminal-legal system. What I address, instead, is the enhanced and extraordinary civil and criminal punishments for this group of people beyond the already extensive range of collateral consequences faced by all others with criminal histories. There is a profound and substantive difference between being held accountable and being punished in a cruel and unusual way.

Victims Matter

A common misunderstanding regarding efforts to advance rational sex-offense legislation is that it implicitly disregards the reality of the extreme pain and trauma of those who experience sexual harm. Additionally, others misperceive considering the experiences and humanity of those who have committed sexual harm as indifference toward their victims. These misunderstandings, often rooted in feminist and progressive ideologies, have partly led to the exclusion of those with sex-offense convictions from other criminal-justice reform efforts, as well as carceral responses such as the Violence Against Women Act (Goodmark, 2022).

The reasons for these misperceptions are both historical and political. First, until the 1970s, sexual victimization of women was ignored and tolerated, both by the criminal-legal system and society. Feminists forced society to recognize the extent and seriousness of violence against women and children. I share the overall feminist perspective that sexual violence is pervasive in our society and that it is not incidental that most perpetrators are male and most of those victimized are women and children.

However, recent scholarship has documented the bifurcation and complexity of feminist approaches to sexual violence and the complicity of some feminists in the expanding of violence and punitiveness within existing criminal-legal structures (Gruber, 2021; Levine & Meiners, 2020). Many feminists viewed the criminal-legal system itself as inexorably linked to a society plagued by all forms of violence and sought to build restorative and noncarceral approaches. Our current sex-offense policies, however, reflect the successes of carcerally inclined feminists who allied with law-and-order conservatives, who viewed increased sanctions and punishment as the most efficient and cost-effective cure for all social problems, including sexual violence.

I share the view of scholars, and most notably that advanced by Judith Levine and Erica Meiners in *The Feminist and the Sex Offender* (2020), that our failed policies that address sexual violence with state violence while often advanced by mainstream feminist organizations, contradict essential feminist values. I also value emerging perspectives that see restorative, rather than punitive, approaches are likely to be more helpful to some victims (Green & Bazelon, 2020). Ultimately, I believe that advancing a feminist perspective that recognizes the trauma of sexual harm and demands accountability requires one to oppose excessive, dehumanizing punishment.

CHAPTER ONE

Employment Is More Than a Job

Employment and the Meaning of Work

One of the most debilitating aspects of having a prior sex-offense conviction is the reduced ability to find employment. Working and supporting yourself and your family is among the most profound ways to participate in society. Finding employment after incarceration allows those with sex-offense convictions to reintegrate into a society where many have few preexisting ties. It is also a necessity to help address the financial devastation caused by justice involvement. It is a common-sense notion, supported by research, that employment and financial independence also create personal stability and decrease the risk of reincarceration for all those with criminal histories.

The personal toll of unwanted unemployment cannot be overstated. The stories I share in this chapter emphasize the emotional and psychological impact of being unable to secure work, despite being qualified, able, and often desperate. Having a sex-offense conviction already creates social isolation and severs community and interpersonal ties, and not being able to work worsens these effects. Research shows that unemployment itself can cause execrable psychological depression for all populations. Those on registries are already grappling with the psychological impact of stigmatization and exclusion; thus, unemployment only intensifies feelings of despair.

Clay: Credentials and Degrees Don't Matter

Clay is white and in his late forties. His crime was a sexual offense with an adult nonstranger, when he was in his midtwenties. He's been on the registry since his release from prison almost two decades ago.

Clay says the victim was his live-in girlfriend, who was in her early thirties. Clay had been honorably discharged after four years in the military. He attributes the sexual incident to postservice post-traumatic stress disorder (PTSD) that he had handled poorly and had self-medicated with alcohol. Clay took a plea deal without having to factor in the consequences of being on a registry; when he signed the agreement, the laws were different. At that point, his offense did not subject him to public registration.

After completing his sentence, Clay decided to finish his college degree and stop working at menial and dead-end jobs. He'd joined the military because of a difficult childhood and lack of resources, and no one in his family had ever earned a college degree. Clay knew he was smart and that he had talent as both a scholar and writer. Ultimately, he earned a terminal graduate degree in a demanding program and published several influential, peer-reviewed scholarly articles. He's a talented data analyst and programmer, and there are many job openings for someone with his background. Nevertheless, Clay has been unemployed since completing graduate school two years ago.

Immediately after getting his advanced degree, a large organization offered Clay a position in a research center. The job was directly related to his studies, and he was hopeful for the future. In interviewing for the position, he shared his background, including his prior sex-offense conviction. After the director and hiring manager reviewed his records, he was given the job. Clay had been offense free for almost two decades, had completed a demanding graduate program, had obtained stellar references, and had published widely in his field. He was overqualified for the position and was frank about his history and struggles. As he was preparing to move across the country for the position, word got out about his hire. One of his future colleagues did an internet search to learn more about their new colleague and discovered that Clay was on the sex-offense registry. The colleague then shared that information with others, and his future co-workers demanded a meeting with their supervisors. The director who hired Clay led an open discussion about why Clay was the best person for the position and why he was convinced that he posed no risk to the other employees.

The staff meeting regarding Clay took place as the #MeToo movement was in full swing, which had understandably heightened attention regarding workplace harassment. There was an intensive media focus on high-profile cases of employers like Harvey Weinstein, who had sexually harassed employees for years without consequence. Clay believes the timing hurt his case. The organization negotiated with the outraged employees, and there was a discussion about having a special hotline dedicated to reporting potential harassment from Clay. Such a measure seems redundant; when I examined the sexual harassment policies already in place at this organization, I noted robust preexisting requirements regarding sexual misconduct prevention and response.

Clay says he was most shocked because the research organization prided itself on its progressive approaches to social problems. He explained, "The people who worked there were into social justice, and other people who worked there had past convictions. I was surprised that they were reacting this way. I really thought I'd be welcomed." Ultimately, the company wound up rescinding the offer. According to Clay, the director was also shocked at the reaction of his staff and was sincerely apologetic.

Clay has a supportive spouse who wants him to find a job in his field. Her job allows them to survive, and he continues to struggle to find work. "She won't let me work at McDonald's or do construction," he says. "She believes in me and wants me to work in a field so I can put my degree to use." He recently completed a grueling hiring process for a similar position in a research lab at a government-funded organization. Again, the director of a research project wanted to hire him based on his demonstrated research and writing ability. He went through multiple interviews for the job, and he disclosed his registry status at each step. He explained the circumstances of his offense, the punishment he received, how he had changed, and what he had accomplished subsequently. He even went through a special security screening where he was asked to submit multiple letters of character reference, in addition to the professional recommendations he had already sent in. Ultimately, he didn't get the position. Clay is clearly frustrated. "I gave them letters from my neighbors with kids, from former employers, from professors who knew me," he says, more in resignation than in anger.

Clay knows that he'll soon have to give up and may have to go back to working at menial jobs, as he did when he returned from the military. He immediately tells everyone he meets about his registry status so that he doesn't have to deal with accusations that he's hiding his past.

Clay maintains that he tries to deal with his frustrations in productive ways and will not turn to alcohol, as he had when he returned from military service. He lives in an area where marijuana is legal; he is tempted to use it for his PTSD as others do but says he cannot take the chance in case he's offered a government job. Others he knows who are on the registry turn to substances to deal with the pain of daily life, but he says he does not because of his wife and family. Without his wife, he says, he'd probably be homeless. Clay tries to explain the pain of not being given the opportunity to work or have a second chance:

> This shows that going to college doesn't matter. They don't see my degree or my publications or my accomplishments. All that they see is the registry. My offense was twenty years ago. Time doesn't matter. It doesn't matter how long it's been; people act like I did this yesterday. If I did something else, they'd say I'd changed and deserved a second chance. But not this. There is no forgiveness or second chances when you are on the registry.

Clay's experience suggests that things are getting worse, not better, for those with sex-offense convictions, despite new laws barring discrimination against those with justice involvement. During graduate school, his background didn't prevent him from obtaining teaching-assistant positions at his institution, where he had contact with students. His professional challenges started, as he notes, around the peak of the #MeToo movement, which also signaled the start of right-wing sex panics, including #PizzaGate. Others I interviewed who have been on the registry for more than ten years, like Clay, also discussed the growing difficulty of employment in a culture of bipartisan sex panics and increasing surveillance and technology that makes it even easier to immediately discover if someone is on the registry.

After our interview, Clay reached out, excited about an offer to teach online courses at an out-of-state university. A few weeks later, he called again. He told me he notified his state registry about the position, as required with all new employment. He then contacted officials and lawyers to determine if he'd also have to register in the state of the university. No one knew, but the university police told him it wasn't required. Clay was nervous because any violations of state or federal laws are felonies, so he requested written confirmation. Registrants are responsible for following all registration laws; not knowing or getting inaccurate information is not a defense. An investigation was launched, even reaching the attorney general's office. The issue was then referred to the university's legal department, who agreed Clay didn't have to register there. However, they raised the possibility that minors could take his courses. Clay's crime didn't involve a minor; the courses were entirely online, and few college students are minors, but the university rescinded the offer days before the courses started. Clay could not contain his frustration:

> I was cleared by human resources. The department hired me because of my qualifications. They both knew about my background. I took their online teaching course and completed training for sexual harassment and student rights. I spent hours preparing the courses. I feel more rejected than ever. Everyone keeps pushing the "prison-to-college" pipeline as the answer to reentry. I guess that's for everyone else. Just not me.

Brad: If I Can't Work, I'll Be Homeless and Lose Access to My Kids

Brad, a white male in his late thirties, committed his offense over two decades ago. His offense involved sexually abusing an underage female relative, starting in his early teens. He was arrested in his twenties, a few years after the abuse ended; he has been on the registry since leaving prison about thirteen years ago.

Brad says he found stable employment as a store manager at a retail chain soon after his incarceration, while still on probation. At that time, his offense didn't show up on background checks as his convictions were misdemeanors, and his employer didn't check the registry. Until 2020, he continued to work at the chain, but in different franchises, and was regularly promoted. At each advancement, he was subject to a new background check, but it wasn't until 2018, when the firm started using an outside company that conducted expanded criminal history searches, that a regional manager discovered his registry status. After a conversation with the manager and human resources about his history and how he had changed and had no violations since serving his time, they stayed with their decision to promote him, as he'd been a reliable and successful employee for ten years. The chain where he worked served primarily adult customers, so he wasn't around children, and no colleague or client had ever voiced complaints about his behavior during that period.

In 2020, another employee found out that he was on the registry and protested his employment to a new regional manager. Brad was called into human resources and told that other employees were uncomfortable around him since learning of his registry status, and the regional manager didn't support him. Brad was fired and has since been unemployed. He is upset that he was let go because he'd never had any problems with his colleagues. "I was a good manager," he told me. "I got along with everyone, and I worked hard. But once they found out about the registry, everything changed. When I first got out jail, no one was checking the registry. But now it seems like they all do."

In his field, there is a shortage of people with his skills. He has received ten formal offers since being fired in 2018, all contingent on the background check. Each has subsequently been rescinded. He explains that the companies share the background-check reports with him. He sees that he still passes the criminal history check because his conviction was more than seven years ago, but now they also do an additional check that includes a search of the registry. Brad needs to find work soon, noting, "I hope a company will give me a chance. I was arrested fifteen years ago, and the incident was a few years before that. I went to jail, I did treatment, I got off probation with no violations. I'm a good father. If I can't work, I'll be homeless and I'll lose access to my kids." He attempted to switch careers, and a large insurance company wanted to hire him after he passed an exam, but the corporate officer ultimately rejected him.

Brad is also subject to a rash of other restrictions in the state where he resides due to the way the public registry classifies his offense. He recently moved to a new home, and the police went door to door notifying nearby residents that a "sexually violent predator" was moving in. His neighbors mostly ignore him, he says, but when he goes outside, the children in the neighborhood quickly run back inside their homes.

Brad is worried he won't be able to support his family. He is divorced, and if he can't keep up his child support, he'll lose his partial custody. He is mandated to treatment on a regular basis for life, for which he pays, and must take annual polygraphs that cost a minimum of $300 each. His ex-wife is fighting him for full custody, and he is due in court because she is now requesting that all his visitations with his kids be supervised, which she had previously never requested. He knows being on the registry will impact the decision regarding his visitation.

Soon, Brad plans to challenge his classification as a "sexually violent predator" and the diagnosis of "pedophilia" the state assigned. During treatment, he learned that because of his own age (thirteen) when he began the sexual abuse of a child, he shouldn't be classified in this way. "I was a child when it began. They call it the 'abuse cycle.' I was very different at that time. My decision-making and risk-taking has changed, and treatment changed me. Counseling was good. People don't understand how much treatment can help. They think I'll never get better. I haven't offended in twenty years. But people see me on the registry as a 'sexually violent predator,' and I can't ever escape this label."

Brad is exhausted by his inability to get a job and the possibility of seeing his kids solely in a supervised-visitation setting. He says they love him and have a great relationship, but if they must have a supervisor at all meetings, it will harm their connection. He appreciates the family members who have stood by him. The relative he abused has not done so, but he still believes that there can be future reconciliation. He has friends, and he is close to those in his treatment groups and a counselor. Though hopeful by nature, he's beginning to despair:

> I have an optimistic personality. It gets me down sometimes. I know I got myself in this situation. I know I did this. But there are times where I don't feel I deserve to be punished for the rest of my life. I paid my debt to society. Went to jail, probation, parole. I paid for what I did and what I pled to. I've been dealing with this for a long time. Even after being registered, I had good-paying jobs. Up to a couple of years ago, I felt I could still work and have a family despite this situation. That kept me going. But this much trouble finding work is stressful, and things have changed. It's gotten way worse. All the employers are so scared. We are required by law, they say, to have a "safe working environment for our employees," and they feel that hiring me will make their other employees unsafe. How will I make other employees unsafe? I'm not working in any places where kids work or are all around. Everyone is so hypersensitive. Everyone screens for "sex offenders" now. Something has changed.

Stanley: What's Going to Happen to Me?

Stanley, a Latino in his early thirties, has been on the registry for two years. His offense took place five years ago. He was arrested after having a conversation online with a police officer posing as a minor; he says he was on an adult dating website. He is married and looking for a job while on parole. He desperately wants to work to help his family. Prior to his arrest, he was employed in the criminal justice field and served in the military. He will be off parole in a few years but on the registry for life.

Stanley knows he'll never work again in his area of specialization, and he is not sure if he'll even get a job that puts his bachelor's degree to use. Though he has a supportive wife who stayed with him through his arrest and incarceration, he needs to find employment "very soon" so they can continue to meet their financial obligations. He said he tried to get jobs at a national mail-delivery service and a chain office-supply store but was denied after background checks.

The job search is grueling, and he goes on dozens of interviews a week. He says he's feeling more negative and angrier, as he's growing less certain he will ever find work. He sighs and says, "Even building-supply stores who will hire anyone rejected me. I tried to get a job at the airport doing anything, and even they wouldn't hire me. I have a college degree, and the rejections are getting to me." After his prison release, he lived in a halfway house for a period with many men convicted of violent nonsexual offenses, including murder, and they have all been employed.

During our conversation, Stanley appeared to be in a state of shock about his new reality. He is consumed with shame and feels as though he is constantly being watched and dreads going outside even to tend to his yard. Having been in the military and the criminal justice fields, Stanley was used to "getting respect," but now he feels like a "second-class citizen." "I can't even get auto insurance because of this. I'm terrified. What's going to happen to me?"

Martin: I Just Want a Job. Any Job

Martin's offense took place when he was in his early twenties. He's Latino and now in his midthirties. He was sentenced to lifetime registration and probation, and he has been on the registry for twelve years. He says he was on an adult dating site and arranged a meeting with his interlocutor, even after learning she was a minor; it turned out to be a police sting. At the time of his arrest, Martin was working as a cashier at a national office-supply chain store and going to college. He was sentenced to jail and then probation. The probation authorities wanted him to work, he said, but the manager at the office-supply store told him he was no longer welcome. He applied to dozens of jobs, including those at fast-food restaurants, but was always rejected. He says that many of the fast-food restaurants in his state hire those on probation and with criminal histories but deny anyone with a sex offense.

According to Martin, he was jobless for seven years after his arrest despite "constantly" applying for jobs. He has lived with his parents since his arrest in his early twenties. Eventually, Martin got lucky and found a job doing manual labor that lasted a few years, but he was laid off almost two years ago because of pandemic-related cutbacks. He is again in the process of "constantly" applying for jobs. He recently had an interview and got an offer, but the offer was rescinded after the background check.

Martin received a letter a few years ago from an attorney who claimed to help people get off the registry. He apparently found Martin's name on the public registry. According to Janice Bellucci, a lawyer with a full-time practice assisting registrants and a leading national advocate for sex-offense law reform, this is a common, and inappropriate, practice. The lawyer said that Martin was a good candidate for a governor's pardon. The attempt cost Martin over $10,000 but failed. Then the lawyer suggested that he apply for a "tier reduction" so that he would have fewer restrictions, but that was also costly and led to nothing.

Martin seems much younger than someone in his early thirties, partly because of his reliance on his parents and partly because his personal development seems to have been stunted since his arrest. He told me that all he wants is to be off the registry, and he does not think he deserves this never-ending punishment. “I went to jail. I finished probation. I paid my dues. I learned my lesson. I was very naive when I committed my offense. I am scared and worried and things aren’t looking good. All I want is to be off the registry and move on with my life.”

His sister was going through a divorce when Martin was arrested, and she and her children were also living with Martin and his parents. When his sister’s estranged husband found out Martin was arrested for a sex offense, he called child protective services, claiming his children could be in danger. Martin starts crying when he remembers how his young niece and nephew were interviewed by social workers about whether he’d harmed them. “I couldn’t believe it. It was all my fault. I hurt my niece and nephew and my sister because of this, and I caused so much trouble.”

His parents and family have stood by him and supported him in any way they can. He wants to move out but knows he cannot do so until he finds a steady job. Martin also fears that new neighbors will receive notification that he’s on the registry. Where he lives now, he says, “no one bothers me.” He has had no success with romantic relationships since his arrest, but says he has been in touch online with a woman who lives in another country. “She doesn’t care about the registry. She wants to come here and live with me, but she can’t get a visa.” He seems happier talking about his online girlfriend. “I told her about the registry, and she talks to me and still loves me and doesn’t care.”

Martin was shocked when he went to Mexico recently with his parents to visit his grandparents. When he got off the plane, he was met by soldiers who told him he had to fly back home immediately and could not enter the country. His mother begged and screamed at them to let him stay to see his relatives, but they refused. He was not aware of the passage of International Megan’s Law (IML) in 2016 and how it impacted the ability of those on registries to travel abroad. “That experience was horrible and embarrassing, and I felt bad because my mom was so upset. But employment is the worst. The absolute worst. I just want a job. Any job.”

After our interview, Martin updated me on his job search. He attached a letter from a company offering him a position, and the background check report that resulted in a subsequent retraction.

> Hi Emily, Hope you are doing well and being safe! I just wanted to email you about what has happened recently regarding my situation. So I got an

> interview for a company and [they] offered me an acceptance letter to which I said yes. Then they did a background check, which I did not pass because of my sex offender status. I also passed another interview for another company. [And now they are doing] a criminal background check. This is a part-time job with no benefits at all while the job responsibility is to just load freight into trailers with a forklift or by hand. It's just been very depressing passing interviews then get offers rolled back because of my status. I am no longer receiving my unemployment benefits because I have exhausted the amount I was granted and cannot extend it.

I was pleased to learn a few weeks later that Martin secured a part-time position with the latter company, even after they did the criminal background check. He wrote to tell me that he's hopeful that it will eventually become full-time and that he and his family are "very happy."

Lance: There Is No Future for Me. I Have No Way to Live

Lance was twenty-one when he was convicted of having a sexual relationship with an underage nonstranger. He says they were in a relationship, and she was just below the age of consent in his state. He was sentenced to less than a year in jail, and he completed his probation about a decade ago. He's white, in his late thirties, and he's been on the registry for fourteen years. Lance struggles with mental illness and recently moved back home with his mother due to his employment struggles. At the time of our interview, Lance expressed concern because he knew the neighbors would soon receive flyers notifying them that a "sexual predator" (his registry classification) has moved in, and he is worried he and his mother will face harassment.

It is obvious that Lance suffers from tremendous anxiety, and he says he has been diagnosed with a few mental disorders. In the state where he resides, he must register every three months for the rest of his life, and he is charged a fee each time. He is also required to update officials between his mandated quarterly registration visits if his address, employment status, or vehicle changes. Lance says the worst aspects of the registry are the random "compliance checks." If he isn't at home, the officials leave a note on the door. If he doesn't get back in touch with them within a certain amount of time, it's a violation and can result in a new felony conviction. He says he is gripped with anxiety that they'll visit and he will miss the note on the door and then be sent back to prison.

Lance attributes his current depression and fear about going outside and socializing to his inability to find work. "My mental health is getting worse, and I have no self-esteem. I really want to find a job, and I feel like I can't do anything to change my life. I got a GED and that didn't help me get any jobs. And there's no reason for me to go to college." He says his mother is happy that he's living with her now, and he worries she doesn't understand that the flyers going out at any moment to their neighbors "could be bad."

In a few days, he tells me, he will have an interview at a grocery store for a job doing fulfillment that doesn't require contact with the public. He will bring references with him, but he's cynical about his prospects. He applied for the job via a website, and they didn't ask about his criminal history. He is depressed and doesn't see a future for himself. If his mother dies, he fears he'll be homeless, and without an address, he'll go back to prison. "There is no future for me. I have no way to live. I feel hopeless."

I asked Lance to keep me updated about his grocery store interview. He emailed me a few days later that he got the job and was excited, but he was still cautious because the background check hadn't gone through. About ten days later, he emailed me again to tell me he was fired. He wrote, "They let me go . . . the day before [I] was supposed to start, [I] bought all this gear for the freezer section [I] would be in at the warehouse. Pretty bummed out about it. Thanks for wanting me to keep you updated."

Rita: Exonerated, but Still Traumatized by the Registry

For the extraordinarily rare few who are exonerated after a sex-offense (or any) conviction, the trauma of the registry can be almost as profound as the wrongful conviction itself. Rita was removed from the registry after twenty years and her record expunged when her accuser admitted he lied during his testimony about being a victim of her sexual abuse. She cries while telling me about her life on the registry and the devastation it caused, even though she's been off for over a decade.

She knows people continue to question why she pled guilty if she was innocent. Her lawyer told her it would be "a gamble" to go to trial given the claims of the accuser, and she feared losing thousands of dollars while facing a stiffer sentence. Being falsely accused of a sex offense and dealing with the criminal-legal system profoundly impacted her mental health, and she couldn't handle the stress. She pled guilty, she says, to move on with her life. This was before federal registry laws and public websites, and she didn't understand the full impact of her decision.

Rita faced employment struggles throughout her time on the registry. Prior to her arrest, she was a well-paid professional. She estimates her ordeal cost her over $50,000, including legal costs incurred while trying to get the state to remove her from the registry after her exoneration. That amount doesn't include lost income due to sporadic employment. The financial impact on her family still lingers, and the cost has hurt her plans for her retirement.

Even after the state took her off the registry, Rita, who has a graduate degree, couldn't even get a position as a cashier at a chain store because it continued to appear in outdated background checks. "It still shows up today. It's been over ten years since removal, and I'm still all over the internet." It's clear the emotional trauma of the registry still haunts her. While she was on the registry, strangers regularly targeted her house by throwing eggs. "Each egging felt so violating," she writes to me in an email after our interview. "While I was on the registry, I once had to hire and pay lawyers to fight to stay in our home because it was too close to a school. Even after being removed, I was denied an opportunity to volunteer as a mentor because they found out. I had to explain everything to get the position, and it was traumatic."

Rita still engages in advocacy for those on the registry even though she's no longer listed. The experience made her empathetic for all those on it, guilty or innocent. "I know what it's like to always look over your shoulder. Police come to your house every few months and you always feel harassed. There are very few resources out there to help someone with a sex-offense conviction." Some close to Rita are unhappy that she continues to work on behalf of those on the registry, as they view her as innocent and "not a sex offender."

The experience on the registry created profound turmoil for Rita and prevented her from achieving many of her personal and life goals. Her experience made her critical of the registry and aware of the harm it causes and the lives it destroys. Her empathy for those still subject to it is obvious, and I'm moved by her commitment to continue her advocacy. In her email after our interview she writes, "I pray for the day when children are truly cared for and those issues that truly affect them, like having plenty of food, adequate shelter, education, after-school activities, safe places to be, and mental health support for all, become more important than using the registry as political fodder."

I'm struck by how Rita is far more emotional when speaking about the harms of the registry than her innocence and the injustice of her wrongful conviction. Despite serving her sentence as agreed in her plea, the registry punished her in a way that included public shaming and humiliation for an additional fifteen years. She reminds me of Anthony Broadwater, a man wrongfully convicted of raping author Alice Sebold.

Broadwater served sixteen years in prison for the crime, but in his postexoneration interviews, he shared what it was like to face employment challenges and public humiliation on the sex-offense registry for over two decades. *The New York Times* interviewed Broadwater one day after he was formally exoneration in court:

> "It's a long day coming," Mr. Broadwater, 61, said in an interview on Tuesday, recalling the years of stigma and isolation he faced as a registered sex offender. He got married and sought work after spending 16 years in prison, but found himself cut off from opportunities because of the conviction. "On my two hands, I can count the people that allowed me to grace their homes and dinners, and I don't get past 10," he said. "That's very traumatic to me." . . . He said that he and his wife, Elizabeth, had wanted to have children, but he felt they could not, given the stigma of his conviction. (Zraick & Alter, 2021)

Another article noted that on one occasion, Broadwater "spent several days taking [college] classes in heating and air conditioning before his past caught up to him and he was ordered to stay away from campus" (Dowty, 2021). This is not to say that incarceration is not as traumatic, or more, than the registry, or that Broadwater is representative of all those exonerated who spent time on the registry. However, the experiences of shaming and banishment are notable and one of the most consistent themes among those I interviewed. There appears, in all the dialogues, far more frustration and anger about the postsentence social isolation and humiliation of the registry than about the trauma of incarceration. Two common sentiments emerged over and over. First, those who took pleas said they wished they had known the impact of the registry because they would have fought harder to stay off it or would have taken the risk of a trial. Second, many said they would have taken additional years of incarceration if it meant no registry after release.

The purpose of punishment should not be to traumatize and humiliate. Even if Rita and Broadwater had been guilty, the excessive postsentence humiliation of the registry created needless and additional harm. Many antiregistry activists rightfully focus on data showing that the registry fails to prevent new sex offenses or promote public safety. Yet there is also another effect, which is the creation of more violence and reinforcement of a culture where sexual abuse is pervasive. Early feminists recognized, long before registries, that excessive punishment creates more harm and violence. In *Rape: The First Sourcebook for Women*, it is noted, "If we begin to adopt the same flaw in treating rape in punitive terms, then we can only deal with it symptomatically as it turns up bit by bit. There will still be new rapists" (New York Radical Feminists, 1974, p. 21).

Carl: I'm Stuck

Carl is white, in his midthirties, and was convicted almost a decade ago for possession of illicit images of children. He attended elite colleges and earned a graduate degree. Prior to his arrest, he worked at various start-ups and was financially successful. Since his arrest, he's found it impossible to find and maintain employment. His wife is accomplished professionally and able to support them, but he's growing increasingly despondent about his prospects and his inability to work.

A couple of years ago, a former colleague, unaware of his past, offered him a consulting gig. He accepted, and then suddenly the friend "ghosted" him. Carl knows it's because the colleague did an internet search or learned about his arrest in some other way. It was a small business, and the friend was one of only a few employees. Carl had been hopeful because there was no background check, and it was primarily a remote position. Another friend then asked him to help set up a new business, and they worked together for a few months. The friend soon grew "paranoid" that his company would be harmed if clients ever found out he hired someone on the registry, and they parted ways.

According to Carl, the worst part about his sentence was the mandatory treatment and group therapy. He says one provider told his group that "recidivism goes up over time." Carl pushed back, but it was discouraging for him to see others with less knowledge accept the uninformed claims of the counselors.

Carl feels "stuck." He is deeply appreciative of his wife and the support she showed him after his arrest, but he worries that it may have been better for him to have left her. The experience "traumatized her," he says, and his registry status "infects every area of their lives." He knows his support for her career has contributed to her success, but he feels she is growing resentful of him and often tells him that he's not "living up to his potential."

Carl knows that he's "very lucky" because he saved enough money before his arrest to contribute to their home purchase in a less-populated area. Previously, they'd lived in an apartment complex in a dense, urban location. The relative isolation makes him less worried about harassment. Like so many I interviewed, he has installed a complex camera and alarm system to record potential vandalism.

He recently got a call from someone claiming to be a sheriff who told him he owed money for registration fees. He threatened to arrest Carl if he didn't pay. Carl could tell it was a scam, but he was deeply disturbed by the call. He grew more concerned when the person somehow found contact information for his parents and made the same threat to them. The worst part, he says, was when he called the police and they reacted to him with indifference. "I thought they'd investigate because it's illegal to impersonate a police officer. But they didn't care, and the person I spoke to dismissed me and said, 'I get spam calls too. Who cares?'"

While Carl takes responsibility for his offense, he feels the public registry is only destructive and has no deterrent effect on him or anyone else he met in treatment. The sole effects of the public listing of his offense are to render it nearly impossible to find employment in his field, despite his talent and networks, and to make him feel "vulnerable and exposed." The dismissal of his concerns by the police officer about the scam phone call made him realize that he's not considered worthy of police protection. He notes that they are in a high-income bracket and pay "tons" of taxes, yet he's not viewed as equal to other citizens.

> I'm a different person now. I know no one will protect me if I'm harassed or victimized. One woman told me she relates to me because that's how she feels walking alone at night. I know I'll never again get the benefit of the doubt. About anything. When I interact now, I focus on de-escalating. I learned that in jail. I went to jail, and I paid fines, and I completed probation. But I have a scarlet letter. It's too much.

He acknowledges he committed a crime and regrets his action, but before this, he said, he had thought highly of the justice system. It is obvious to me that he comes from means and privilege as he describes his upbringing, and he seems shocked about the unfairness and devastating impact of the public posting of his crime. "The research about these registries is clear, and they aren't effective," he says, and it's overwhelming to him that his life has been ruined due to "lies and mob justice." He had never been aware of the extent to which "truth and facts" are absent from laws and policies. "The mob," he says, is growing bolder and more influential in all areas of society, and "stupidity" is growing more pervasive. The sex-offense laws are part of this trend, says Carl, but it's a far broader issue, and he sees little hope for his own future or the future of the country.

Who Cares If a "Sex Offender" Is Suffering! That's the Point!

When I talk to Carl, it's clear that he's intelligent and thoughtful and still shocked at the turn his life has taken. He has a home and a loving wife, and he lives a comfortable life without overwhelming financial worries. The main impact of the registry on those like Carl is the experience of exile and emotional torment. He's educated and skilled and wants to work, and he's surrounded by people, including his wife, who have impressive degrees and financially rewarding and meaningful jobs. Living with personal torment may be viewed as inconsequential by many and a small price to pay for the harm caused by his offense. For Carl, a desire to work is less related to economic and material survival than the human desire to be part of the world and to have an identity outside his status as someone convicted of a sex offense.

Tim: Self-Exile

Tim was convicted of an internet-based, noncontact offense in 2000, when he was in his early twenties and in the military. He's Black and has been on the registry for fifteen years, since completing his prison sentence. After his release, he earned a college degree in information technology. He says finding work has always been challenging. In college, he worked at a restaurant and lived in a state that included work addresses on his registry listing. He said people called the restaurant and complained because they saw that someone on the registry worked there. He was harassed and eventually got a better job at a manufacturing plant. "I became a team leader, but [even there] I got called into human resources because they were receiving complaints that I was allowed to work there."

Tim says employment struggles are the hardest part of the registry. After college, he secured a job at a pharmaceutical company. Things were going well, he said, "but one day my supervisor called and just told me not to come back. I've been fired suddenly from so many jobs once people find out I'm on the registry."

He married and moved to a different state. He was hopeful things would be better there because registrants' workplace addresses were not published. In addition, he no longer had to register quarterly, at a cost of $50 each time; he now had to do so just once a year. Things were good there, he says, except he couldn't go to any school functions to support his children. "That had me bitter. My father was killed, and the person who did it is now free and doesn't have any restrictions." Tim was with his position at a major medical center for five years, but "it got too expensive to live there. So, we had to go back to our home state because we had no choice."

When they returned, his wife easily found work, but Tim struggled to do so. Renting a house was also difficult, and Tim finally found a low-paying work-from-home IT position.

> I felt like total crap. I wasn't taking care of my family. I felt guilty. And they would come over to do compliance checks all the time. They'd bring three police officers and a caseworker and it was crazy. It looked like a sting. They made a scene, and I was embarrassed for my family. It was a nightmare. They said I was a good candidate to get off the registry, but it'd cost 10,000, and it wasn't guaranteed. The cost is the biggest thing that's prevented me from trying to get off. I wish I could ask them to judge me based on who I am now, and how I've done nothing but work since I was released 15 years ago. All I do is work and take care of my kids and love my wife. That's all I do. But I don't have the money. I've had a job nonstop except when I was fired because of the registry. I have a stack of applications where I've been denied. I feel like there's nothing I can do to change things.

Tim says that even his local sheriff offered to support his application for registry removal, but he can't afford to pay a lawyer thousands of dollars just to "take a chance." He knows the prosecutor will fight his effort to get off the registry, and it's a "crapshoot."

Tim was soon able to obtain better-paying contract jobs, "but they'd always let me go because of the registry." Finally, he obtained a good-paying full-time position. "Somehow I got in, and the background check didn't get me." Yet he was "even more cautious" and "hid in the shadows" due to his fear that if he got promoted or excelled, or simply made efforts to advance his career, he'd be noticed, and "someone would put my name in Google." He ended up leaving and returning to a work-from-home position. Tim worried his supervisors were pushing hard to have him take on more responsibilities and move up, and he feared a promotion and a higher profile in the company would out him as a registrant. "This whole thing has made me into a paranoid hermit. I feel like at any minute I'll be ridiculed and harassed. It's one thing if it's just me, but it's not right to do it to my kids."

Tim speaks often of his love for his children and his wife, and his frustration at not being able to provide as good a life for them as he'd like. "I feel like I'm always at rock bottom. It makes me sad because all I want to do is give my kids the best childhood I can."

Tim joined the military immediately after finishing high school. He was in the junior Reserve Officers' Training Corps (ROTC), and tells me, "I was patriotic." While in the military, he designed a coin for his brigade that is still sold online today. "I drew it up. They saw my drawing, and I helped make it. They went with that coin." His arrest took place while he was enlisted, but he still received an honorable discharge. Tim says he believed that earning a college degree with his GI Bill benefits would be enough to overcome his conviction and the registry. "I was twenty-two, and I told myself I can become something. I thought I'd do the right thing and excel. I feel like a fool now. Why did I ever think I'd get over this?"

Tim recently decided to move abroad. He says he realized he "can't get a fair shake" in the United States. He made the decision after a short visit to another country where he met with a recruiter who said his skills would enable him to find a secure and well-paid position. He says when he went abroad to meet the recruiter, he was nervous to travel internationally. When he arrived, he was met by foreign officials who informed him that the United States alerted them about his arrival. Tim says his experience outside the United States so far "almost makes me cry."

> When I got here and they looked at my passport, I was so surprised because the officials were very respectful. I told them the truth. They didn't know why the U.S. would have alerted them about someone convicted in 2000. I told the officials it made no sense to me either. They let me in and said they couldn't believe how I was treated. I had so much respect for them to do me that way. I was just walking on the street. It felt like a million pounds was lifted off my shoulders. I felt free. I could cry to you. I love it here. I'm getting interviews and offers and trying to get a job that fits for me. The police here made me feel good.

The experience prompted his decision to move there permanently. He left the United States a few weeks ago, and when he arrived at the airport this time, he says, no officials even met him. While Tim is optimistic about his employment prospects and appreciates his new feeling of freedom, he feels "guilty" about his wife and kids. They are planning to move to be with him in a few weeks, and while "it's nice over here," he feels that his decision to move and his employment struggles are burdensome to his family. His older child is upset about the prospect of leaving the United States, and he's sad about how they must feel he's "taking away from them. I feel bad about that." He adds, "I'm not going to lie. I've had some depression here, thinking about how this move is going to be so hard for my wife and kids."

About a week after he arrived, the police came to the hotel to question him. Again, the police told him that American officials had sent them a notice. He says he again "told them everything" and explained he was currently looking for work and planning to settle there. He informed them that he was still working remotely for an American company and that his wife and children would soon join him. Tim says he was again deeply moved by their kindness and respect: "They thanked me for being honest. They told me to follow their laws, and they said they won't come again."

Tim says he's "almost paranoid" about what new registry laws the United States may eventually pass. What's most troubling to him is that he feels that he's being "punished for life." No one, he says, "will stand up for us." In the United States, he was constantly worried that he'd be sent back to jail "for any technical violation." He also feels frustrated that his registry status has done so much harm to his wife and children, by forcing them to constantly move and uproot their lives. "The average American doesn't care. No one gives a damn about us. I feel like I'm banished. What choice do I have?"

Tim is contemplative and serious, and he emphasizes that he's not opposed to punishment and that he understands the purpose and "certain aspects" of the registry. He says he has kids and understands why politicians and others want a registry. But, he stresses, "there has to be an ending. You can't let people out of prison and then make their lives a living hell. I do everything I am supposed to do because it's right. But there are no incentives for doing the right thing." On the registry, Tim is listed as a "sexually violent predator" at the highest risk for reoffense; he shakes his head and says that no one can understand what it's like to be publicly listed with those terms. "A registry with an end date is OK. But why do I have to be on it for forty years? If you told me I'd have to do forty years on the registry when I was first arrested, I don't know what I would have done."

For Tim, the registry stripped him of his ability to support his family and "be a man." For a time, he and his family lived with his mother, and Tim found it "humiliating . . . she's supposed to live with me, not me with her! I'm the young person."

> I take care of my family in a serious way. I want my daughters to see me in a serious way. I lived in bad neighborhoods, and I don't want that for them. I don't want them to see boys with sagging jeans. I want them to see a man who works, like me. My older daughter knows everything. She understands that I'm on the registry. But I'll have to tell the younger one soon.

Tim has considered engaging in antiregistry advocacy, but he finds it "upsetting" and "irritating" to read websites and blogs that post about the injustices faced by those on registries. When he learns about the challenges faced by others on registries, it makes him more aware of "how much of a punishment this really is. They've singled us out." He asked me, "What more can they possibly do?" He says his greatest fear is going back to jail for an unintentional violation.

At one point, Tim says, his brother suggested he move to his state, and Tim investigated the possibility. "I looked at their laws, and it says I can't go to the library or amusement parks, even though I was convicted in 2000!" He told his brother there was no way he could move there because he wouldn't be able to do "anything" with his daughters. Tim hears about states proposing laws that all those on registries wear ankle bracelets for life or allowing employers to pay them less than minimum wage. Again, Tim tells me that he didn't want to leave the United States but felt he had no choice. "Anything can happen. No one answers me when I call police departments."

Tim cheers up when he talks about his wife and calls her his "biggest supporter." He told her about his offense on one of their first dates, and she didn't leave. His family is the center of his life, Tim says, and he has only a few friends. He says he fears disclosing his registry status to people who will then reject him, so he doesn't make efforts to meet new people. "The registry is so taboo. People are cool if you were in a gang or killed someone, but not if you are on the registry." He feels people won't want to be his friends because they'll be "tainted" and considered "pedophiles" if they associate with him. For Tim, not having friends has fueled his sense of "social isolation." He said he had a Facebook account and it made him feel connected to the world, but one day, "because of the registry, it was gone."

I ask him how he met his wife. He was on a dating website, he said, and "looking for a fling, but I fell in love." After they wed, he saw an ad that said to contact the site if you married after meeting there. He reached out and told them they'd been married for a decade. "Then I learned that registrants can't use their website now. We have a family, and we've been married for more than ten years, but we are disqualified. I'm banned, so they aren't interested." Tim sighs. "It's just one more thing."

Effects of Employment Barriers

Unemployment rates are significantly higher for those with criminal history records (CHR), regardless of offense. A 2018 study found that those with a CHR had an unemployment rate of over 27 percent (Couloute & Kopf, 2018). More recent data on rates of joblessness as opposed to unemployment, which includes only those actively looking for work, shows it may be as high as 60 percent (Carson et al., 2021). Addressing the challenges of high unemployment for those with a CHR is a priority for policymakers, largely due to the strong correlation between employment and decreased rates of recidivism (Siwach, 2018; Uggen, 2000). Some proposals to address this problem include record expungement after a certain number of years, financial and insurance benefits for employers willing to hire those with a CHR, occupational licensing reform, and allowing those with a CHR to sue discriminatory employers for civil rights violations (Couloute & Kopf, 2018). In many states, some of these policies have already been implemented in limited ways, yet my interviews suggest that they have not had much impact for those on registries.

In the interviews in this chapter, some on the registry note the growing difficulties they face in finding employment. Research supports their perception, and studies show that technological advancements have made it increasingly simple for employers to access CHRs and registry status (Bushway & Kalra, 2021; Lageson, 2020). A report also backs up comments from those I interviewed about more invasive background screenings, with the Equal Employment Opportunity Commission observing a decade ago that employers were starting to work with "third-party background screening businesses" that include consumer reporting agencies (U.S. Equal Employment Opportunity Commission, 2012).

Those on registries are, thus, doubly marginalized. All those with a CHR experience real struggles for employment, and rates of unemployment and joblessness are high for all offense categories. We also know that, for those on registries, laws intended to help others with criminal histories offer little protection in practice. One key reason is the public nature of the registry. CHRs are often sealed after a varying number of years, but the internet makes it simple for employers to see that any applicant is on a registry. Additionally, the public nature of the registry makes it far riskier for employers because other employees and customers or clients can easily find out if someone is on the registry, leading to employee outrage and discomfort, as well as potentially embarrassing publicity and the fear of losing business. This poses another substantial barrier to employment unique to registrants.

I asked attorney Janice Bellucci about the extent to which those on registries can sue based on laws intended to prevent employment discrimination. According to Bellucci, it's not easy, and efforts generally fail, for two reasons for this. She explains, "First, although there are many laws that prohibit an employer from considering an individual's criminal history, the same laws allow an employer to consider an individual's current requirement to register. Second, many of the same laws also have an exception that negates the prohibition. Specifically, the laws allow an employer to consider an individual's criminal history to protect 'a person at risk,' which has been interpreted to refer to customers, fellow employees, and others" (Bellucci, 2022).

Finding employment is always a challenging and discouraging process. Being on a public list with a sex-offense conviction makes it far more overwhelming and, at times, impossible. To be clear, private and law enforcement registries, which existed prior to federal registry laws in 1996, also create serious challenges to employment and should not exist. At the same time, however, there are many additional consequences that are due to the currently easily accessible, public nature of the registry.

A recent study (2022) by Tovey, Winder, and Blagden analyzed the job search experiences of twelve British men with sexual offense histories. While there are more protections for job seekers with CHRs and a somewhat more robust safety net in the United Kingdom, the findings of the study are startling in the extent to which they replicate the experiences detailed in this chapter. The authors note that many jobs and other reentry programs often exclude those with sex-offense convictions, but the problems they identify go beyond these formal measures. British attitudes mirror feelings in the United States toward those with sex-offense convictions. They are viewed with more venom than all others leaving prison and "are considered largely irredeemable," due to misperceptions about the range and realities of sexual offenses. The researchers view these attitudes as driven by the media, which fixate, as do their U.S. counterparts, on horrific but extraordinarily rare sex crimes.

In the United Kingdom, as here, the issues of not being able to work and social isolation are intertwined. "The participant narratives," Tovey et al. (2022) explain, "initially echoed concern at the loss of financial autonomy, but overwhelmingly the real loss was in the social isolation that ensued [and] experienced times where they felt better off in prison [where] they had been able to exist without the same degree of stigma and exclusion" (p. 18).

Those in the U.K. study, as in my own research, understood that working was vital to emotional and mental health in ways that transcended the material. The stories I included in this chapter are from interviewees who have enough financial support from family members to stay housed and fed and are "just getting by," but their desire to work transcends meeting basic needs. Tovey, Winder, and Blagden conclude their article with the comment that work for those with past sexual offenses has greater meaning and serves "as an opportunity to reduce social isolation and is pivotal in providing a chance to invest in society and gain a sense of purpose and satisfaction" (pp. 19–20). Yet there are also deeper and darker implications.

What do we, as a society, expect to happen when we allow ourselves to effectively exile a group who cannot work or participate in social or civic life? The inability to find work, when jobs for which one qualifies are available, when one wants to partake of society and live a better material and emotional life, creates extreme hopelessness. Much of the desperation I heard from those I interviewed centered around employment insecurity. Many "joked" that they'd harm themselves if they didn't find a job soon. Even those currently employed were aware of the precariousness of their situations, and indicated they'd have no future possibility of work if fired or laid off. The men interviewed by the U.K. researchers also expressed thoughts of taking their own lives.

Throughout this book, I describe the many forms of exclusion and stigmatization faced by those on registries. While work in a neoliberal world can be exploitative and unfulfilling, the inability to work, solely because one elicits disgust, may be among the most dehumanizing of these experiences.

CHAPTER TWO

Does It Help to Make People Homeless?

Residency Restrictions and Housing Challenges

Those on sex-offense registries face significant challenges in their efforts to find housing. Some states have formal residency restrictions, which govern where those with sex-offense convictions can dwell. Residency restrictions usually require that registrants live at a certain distance, generally ranging from five hundred to two thousand feet, from such places as schools and childcare facilities. While not all states have residency restrictions, a recent study found that thirty-eight currently do (Navarro et al., 2022, p. 13). This study also found that in one-third of these states, residency laws apply to all registrants, regardless of offense; in most states, they apply only to those convicted of certain sex-offense subcategories or to those under supervision (Navarro et al., 2022).

Additionally, even in states without formal residency restrictions, many landlords are unwilling to rent to registrants. This may be partly due to discriminatory attitudes but also because the address of the property will be listed on the public sex-offense registry. In addition, landlords also risk having their properties appear on the growing number of apps and websites that feature maps with dots to warn community members where those on registries live. In places with community-notification laws, landlords may be even more unwilling to rent to registrants, as police will directly notify neighbors when they do, by postcard and sometimes via an in-person visit.

In one study, the authors reviewed the existing literature on the effectiveness of residency restrictions to reduce child sex offenses. They note that "the value of residence restrictions has yet to be established," and the studies they reviewed "do not provide evidence that residence restrictions even have the potential to substantially reduce sex crimes against children" (Savage & Windsor, 2018, p. 23). They underscore that the very premise of these laws is flawed; most offenses do not involve stranger adults searching for potential child victims in nearby parks, day care centers, or schools. In fact, in places such as these, children are supervised by adults or "capable guardianship" and, thus, further protected (p. 23). Additionally, like all registry laws, they are disconnected from reality in that almost all child sex offenses are committed by those not on registries and without prior sex-offense convictions.

From their inception, residency restrictions were not based on research or evidence. The number of states with residency laws have steadily increased since first emerging in the mid-1990s, with the greatest number enacted in 2006 (Navarro et al., 2022, p. 11). That year, a *Justice Research and Policy* study used geographical information software (GIS) to examine the housing options in a Florida county that banned registrants from residing within one thousand feet of places "where children congregate" (Zandbergen & Hart, 2006). The authors found that, in the first decade of these policies, they resulted in severely limiting housing options in urban residential areas, particularly when bus stops are coded as off-limits, thus forcing registrants into remote areas. Their analysis shows that most housing for registrants is restricted to "small, isolated clusters at the urban/rural fringe" (p. 18). They warn that the trend of broadening residency restrictions to include not only schools but the far vaguer "places where children congregate" may decrease options further. Most importantly, they note that their findings reinforce already existing research showing the laws increase isolation and homelessness while decreasing access to work, treatment, and social services, all factors that correlate with increased recidivism. The laws were, thus, implemented without any basis in research, and then continually expanded despite a decade of research documenting their ineffectiveness.

The early 2000s saw the publication of the first of numerous studies reinforcing the findings that residency restrictions failed to decrease sex offenses while creating unintended negative consequences, such as homelessness, unemployment, and social isolation. I could find no peer-reviewed research reports that provide any evidence whatsoever that forcing those with sex-offense convictions to live a certain distance from schools or "places where children congregate" results in a decrease in sex offenses or sex-offense recidivism; as Savage and Windsor (2018) note, the premise of residency restrictions is at odds with all existing research about the realities of child sex offenses. Nevertheless, we see that even as social science research about the neutral or negative impact of restrictions continued to grow, these laws continued to expand to evermore states. The Savage and Windsor (2018) paper cited above, for example, found that twenty-nine states had residency restrictions in 2018, while in 2006, when Zanbergen and Hart conducted their analyses, only sixteen states had such laws on the books. In 2007, *Criminology & Public Policy*, a leading journal in the field of criminology, published an article aptly titled, "Eliminate Residency Restrictions for Sex Offenders"; in 2014, the same journal published a plea to policymakers in the perfectly titled "Residence Restrictions Are Ineffective, Inefficient, and Inadequate: So Now What?"

Kelly Socia, the author of the 2014 article, attributes the persistence of the laws, despite the wealth of research showing their uselessness, to the unwillingness of policymakers to consider or integrate any research into public policy. He urges the creation of advisory committees where scholarly experts can help construct evidence-based policies, and he, rather optimistically, asks that policymakers to "listen to the evidence" rather than "polls and media hype" (p. 184). Given the political popularity of any measure that further excludes those with sex-offense convictions, this is a major challenge.

The haunting documentary *Untouchable* (Feige, 2016) includes scenes of Florida registrants forced to live in their cars or under bridges as a result of draconian residency laws. Lobbyist Ron Book, one of the key architects of these policies in Florida, brags about his work banishing registrants and appears to react with total indifference when told his laws are causing homelessness. The narrator in the film informs Book that research shows these laws fail to reduce sexual offenses recidivism or prevent sexual abuse. Like many policymakers, he says the research doesn't matter to him, and further, he does not believe the data. Book, like most, is driven by emotion and rage, and these emotions outweigh efforts to present research or evidence rationally.

Theo

Theo was arrested when he was eighteen, and he's been on the registry for fifteen years. He's white and in his early thirties and, thus, he's been on the registry for over half his life. He was convicted of a sexual offense with an underage acquaintance. Even though he reached out to me after seeing my post asking for registrants to share their experience, he starts by telling me that the registry doesn't impact him that much and he's "luckier and different" from most others.

Theo is married, and his wife is a homemaker who takes care of their kids full-time. His home, he says, is not in a neighborhood where they'd like to live, because residency restrictions severely limited their options by requiring that they live one thousand feet, "as the crow flies," from any school. However, they settled for it because they were newly married and it was approved by the registry office, but now he wishes they'd found something in a better location for them. Now, he says, things are expensive, and they can't afford to move. Theo seems sad about where he lives but, at the same time, he worries that they will change the laws or build a school closer to them and they'll have to move. Recently, he says, he heard a rumor that school bus stops may be added to the residency rules, and he said he has no idea how they'll find a place to live without any bus stops nearby.

His housing issues, Theo explains, are linked to his limited employment prospects. If he could get a better job, he says, they could move to a nicer place in an area with less-restrictive residency laws. "I could be making so much more money if I wasn't on a public registry. It affects everything. No firm will hire someone on a public list." He says he likes his job, where he's worked for the past five years, but there is no room for advancement. It doesn't pay enough for him to support his wife and children as he'd like, and they are on a tight budget. He used to aggressively apply for jobs, but he can no longer emotionally deal with continual rejections. He says he used to tell himself that it would be easier as he got older because he could explain to potential employers that his justice involvement was many years ago and that he has never been rearrested, but he has come to realize no one cares how long it's been. "They just see the registry. It makes me stuck. My job is OK, but there is no potential. I can do this for the next forty years and never get a raise or a promotion. There is no future there."

After we talk for about thirty minutes, he says that he wants to add that even though the registry is "no big deal," it has a significant impact on him psychologically. He says he has low self-esteem and, while his wife urges him to keep applying to jobs, he finds it extremely difficult and takes each rejection hard and personally. Theo tells me he and his family don't leave their city much, largely due to his anxiety and fears about violating registry-related travel laws. "I have delayed trauma. There is a huge mental strain from these rules and the potential consequences. It's like PTSD." He says he fixates on fears that he'll miss a registration date and get rearrested. Theo says he used to be less anxious about the registry, but now he's concerned about how his wife and children will survive if he goes back to jail.

Theo resents deeply the criminal-legal process. He says that the victim and her family fought to get him on the registry for life. He acknowledges he "did something dumb" but he's paid the price of jail and eight years' supervision. He adds that he doesn't think it's fair that he'll be on the registry forever, and he feels that his sentence was based on claims by the victim and her family that every problem she'll have will "forever" be his fault. "To be on a private registry would save me. I don't want my kids to Google me."

Theo says he's hopeful about a proposed law to make a registration error a technical violation, rather than a new felony. His anxiety would decrease if he wasn't always worried about making a mistake and being sent back to prison. At the same time, a recently introduced measure now makes it a crime to pick up his child at day care. He can do it, he says, but he must "announce" or "disclose publicly" as soon as he steps on the grounds. It's too humiliating, he says, so now only his wife takes their children to and from school. Theo gets upset talking about how he can't help his wife with carpool duties. "It's getting worse and worse."

Vince

Vince worked as a cook in the military for nearly two decades. His sexual offense involved an underage family member after his military retirement. He's Latino and has been on the registry for seventeen years, following twelve years in prison. When I video chat with Vince, he's seated in front of an enormous American flag and vivid Christian religious imagery. He tells me he's currently a manager at a national chain store, where he's worked for about a decade. "It's challenging but I'm grateful someone hired me," he says.

Prior to his arrest, Vince says he was "trying to change and stop drinking and behaving badly." He says "intensive treatment" after his conviction was helpful, but his personal growth was due mostly to his religious faith. He says he's extremely involved with and devoted to his church. "My church supported me through my entire incarceration, [and now] even pastors will give me references!" He adds that he's becoming a church leader, and "I'm even allowed to do baptisms and lead bible study and do weddings."

However, Vince says, he's become discouraged lately because of a new policy that restricts those on the registry from freely entering military bases as do all other veterans. Vince says he has a 70 percent disability classification, and his nearby base was an important part of his life. He enjoyed access to "rest and recuperation" and discounts, and particularly liked the reduced tickets to movies and events. Primarily, though, the restriction has made it difficult to do the bulk of his ministry work, which involved evangelizing to military members. "I invite them to the Lord and to bible study, and we have our church services on base." Now, he says, he cannot do this to the extent he used to, as he is only permitted to enter if he's escorted.

Vince is engaged, but he cannot live with his fiancée until they can get married and find a suitable home. He currently lives in a single-room occupancy residence, with a shared hallway shower. "No place will rent to me, because of the registry, and I don't want to move into a place with her and get kicked out. At my last place, the landlord found out about the registry and just told me to leave in one day. I don't want my fiancée to go through that." He dreams, he says, that he'll one day be able to buy a home and move out of the small room he's rented for almost a decade. He says he feels safe in his current place, but it's "like a cell. I'm in a room with a sink and a toilet."

Housing has been a major issue for Vince since leaving prison. He says he had a traumatic experience immediately after his release, in a home that offered housing and services to men on the registry. Some neighbors got angry after learning about the program and staged a protest. According to Vince, it was covered by local media, and "it was crazy." Vince says he had to leave to go to work while the protestors and local news crews were surrounding the house. "There were protestors everywhere, and they tried to block me. I tried to drive away, and they rushed me. I slowly backed up to get away, but they claimed I was trying to run them over. I got arrested and went to jail for a weekend, but then I got out, and all charges were dropped." His fiancée, Vince tells me, is someone he's known since he was twenty, and he cares deeply for her. He won't go to her home, because if he spends "frequent" time there, he's supposed to report it to the registry. "When I see her, we go out to eat or [to] the movies. I could get arrested if I spend time there, and I'm careful." He can't live there because her ex-husband doesn't want the home listed on the registry.

He can't wait, he says, to marry her and find a place for them to live together. He knew her before prison, and "we've been engaged five years." After prison, they reconnected when she commented on one of his social media posts. "She knows everything about my past," he says, but loves him anyway. "It's really a beautiful story."

> My fiancée, she was married to a military officer. He found another woman overseas and abandoned her and her daughter. They haven't lived with

anyone until me. Her daughter met me, and she was excited about having a dad. She was real excited. Happy. Her daughter wanted me to move in the next day. But her dad looked me up and found the video of me being arrested. So then, my soon-to-be stepdaughter got scared of me. But now it's been some time, and we spend birthdays and holidays and hang out, and she's happy with me. She calls me Dad now. She's happy I'm in her life. She's in college trying to get her degree. She's smart. We encourage her to finish school. We support her, and she's all we have. She's closer to me than her own dad. I encourage her to forgive her dad. Because that's what scriptures say. I teach her not to be distant. I'll be fine. I have my faith.

Nick

Nick is white and in his early thirties. He's not on a public registry but has been on a "law enforcement only" registry for a decade. His offense involved possession of illicit images of children. After his conviction, he returned to school to earn a graduate degree. As required by law, he informed the schools that accepted him of his registry status. One institution rescinded their offer, but another school was willing to admit him. There were no issues after he enrolled, and he earned his degree without incident.

Nick trained to have a career involving international relations but changed direction after realizing the registry would limit his ability to freely travel. Nick is grateful for the full-time position he secured in a related field after finishing his degree. At his agency, the human resources office knows he is on the registry, but he's not sure if his direct supervisor or anyone else at his office is aware of his status.

His family has been very supportive of him, but Nick feels guilty because he knows his parents would like to retire to Florida. They can't do that, he tells me, because he would only be able to visit them for a day or two at a time on an infrequent basis. If he visited more often or for longer, he'd be placed on the public Florida registry for life. Additionally, he is very careful about traveling to other states. As someone on a private registry in one state, he is still subject to all registry restrictions regarding domestic and international travel.

Nick would like to move to a more affordable home, but he's concerned about criminal background checks. He's lucky to have found a current residence that didn't look into those matters, but it's expensive. He has "lots of anxiety" because he and his spouse are looking for a new place they can afford, and Nick isn't sure if he'll be disqualified during the rental background check. While on supervision, he was required to disclose his registry status upfront and upon application to potential landlords, and he is traumatized from the resulting experiences of rejection.

One benefit of the private registry, for Nick, is that his spouse's family doesn't know he's on the registry. When he was first arrested, word got out in the community where his parents live and where he grew up. He said some friends of his parents stopped talking to them when they learned of his arrest. Nick says he is no longer friends with those he was close to before his arrest. He says it is partly his own fault because even the few who stuck by him trigger painful memories of the normalcy of his preregistry life. "The worst days for me," he says, "are when I have to register."

Nick found his spouse a few years ago, and the relationship provides him great solace and happiness. For his first four or five years on the registry, he was fearful of engaging with others and led a solitary existence. Nick struggles with many of the same anxieties of those publicly listed on registries. He says he panics when he sees police officers and assumes they are coming to arrest him. He avoids places where he might have to be around children, and he is frightened lest his being around minors in any setting results in a false accusation. There are no proximity restrictions where he resides, but if he's in a public park or nature reserve, he avoids using public bathrooms to prevent coinciding with children. Certain ordinary social situations cause Nick extreme discomfort. Events with those he doesn't know well worry him, particularly those with people he suspects would reject him immediately if they knew he was a registrant.

Nick is obviously nervous and has an air of resignation when he talks. He says he regrets that he cannot participate in public life or engage in political activism because of his fears of being in any spotlight. The registry, he says, is supposed to make him less likely to reoffend. But, he explains, "everything that has made me feel safer is over. Everything that has happened after my arrest has made my life more unstable and painful." He says the registry has increased his cynicism, and he is now aware of the extent of human cruelty. In turn, this doesn't help his outlook or ability to change. After his arrest, he tried to take his own life. As I've now heard from multiple people on registries, he admits that he has a fantasy that he'll save a child and it will be on the news and people will see he's not an evil child predator. He says he's considered self-immolation, like the monks who set themselves on fire to protest the Vietnam War. It's a strange fantasy, and it shocks me. A few months and dozens of interviews later, I hear the very same fantasies about saving a child and self-immolation from several others, but I'm no longer shocked.

"Law Enforcement Only" Registries Aren't the Answer

Public registries expose those listed to harassment, vigilantism, and banishment by allowing free and ready access to their personal data and criminal histories. Many I interviewed said that if the registry were "private" or "law enforcement only," as had existed in a few states prior to the mid-1990s, many of their problems would be solved. Some who were convicted decades ago said things were far better before registries were public or widely accessible on the internet, and others said technology and new background-check procedures have made things much worse just over the past few years. Clearly, there are grave and specific dangers and profound privacy violations when publicly listing the addresses and criminal history on state-run sex-offense registry websites. Additionally, that information is then easily and freely extracted by private organizations and businesses, who then use it to further publicize the identities and home addresses of registrants.

Nick's case, however, highlights how even nonpublic sex-offense registries create barriers to work, housing, and travel, as well as psychological trauma. In states that list some deemed as low risk on "private registries," their information can only be accessed via background checks. Nick's case demonstrates, however, that being off the public registry doesn't help when landlords or employers do background checks and find out he has a sex-offense conviction. There are now long-overdue laws that ban some housing and employment discrimination based on criminal history, but they tend to exclude those convicted of sexual offenses. As I argue throughout this book, it is the vengeance and irrationality underlying not only our laws but our feelings that together create the particular and endless suffering of life with a sex-offense conviction. Efforts to obtain employment and housing will still be burdensome even if registries are "private," due to the same emotions underlying policies that carve out registrants but benefit all others. Problems for those on registries are far broader than the impact of *public* banishment and shaming. This is a problem that cannot be resolved by making the registry accessible only to government agencies, employers, and landlords, as I explain in the coming sections.

Henry

Henry was convicted of a sex offense almost two decades ago. He's Black, in his early forties, and his crime is listed on the public website as "sexual assault of a child." It says he is a "moderate" risk and received a sentence of probation and lifetime registration. The victim is listed as a sixteen-year-old male; only Henry's birth date, but not his current age, is listed.

Henry is friendly and outgoing, and he starts our interview by telling me he's gay and has a steady boyfriend. He was arrested in his early twenties after a sexual encounter with someone he met on an adult dating site for those eighteen and over. Henry says he didn't realize his partner was only sixteen (the age of consent was seventeen) until the parents of the young man discovered the tryst and reported Henry to the police.

The arrest shocked Henry, who said he'd never been in trouble before. In shock, he agreed to a plea deal with no jail time but seven years of probation plus lifetime sex-offense registration. When he was arrested, Henry was a community college student. The arrest resulted in his expulsion from school, but he appealed and was eventually reinstated and graduated with a bachelor's in political science.

For the first few years of probation, Henry says he did well. The financial burden included paying for a $300 initial psychological assessment, $300 per year for polygraphs, and $25 per month for "probation fees." Many friends cut him off, and one called him a "pedophile." In general, he says, his social circle shrunk considerably. "People didn't want to be my friend [because] they didn't want be friends with a 'sex offender.'"

After three years on probation, Henry lost his job, and the registry made it hard for him to find new employment. He says he sent in hundreds of applications and, at one time, he compiled a file of two hundred rejection letters he received. Once, he tells me, "I cried in the parking lot of a Jack in the Box because I applied for a job there, and they rejected me."

Ultimately, his inability to earn an income forced Henry to move in with his parents. Things went downhill quickly from there, Henry tells me. His parents, as it turned out, lived too close to a school, and the probation supervisors ordered Henry out. Neighbors also because angry that his parents allowed Henry to move in, and all three wound up moving in with his grandmother. Probation authorities stipulated that Henry had to post signs on each entrance of her house that read, "no persons under seventeen allowed on this property." Henry felt terrible because his younger cousins could no longer visit. Not only that, Henry tells me, but probation required him to pay for the cost of printing the signs.

Henry eventually found a job, and it was "perfect." It was an accounting job in his area of expertise and paid well. Even better, he says, they hired him on the spot, without doing a background check. When Henry gave probation the address of his new job, Henry was told the office was too close to a school. Henry was now in desperate need of cash, and it had been torturous finding a place that would hire him. Henry begged probation for permission to keep the job. According to Henry, he was told that if he wished to continue, he had the option of appealing to a judge. Henry says that probation said it was fine to continue working while awaiting the judge's decision.

When Henry appeared in court, he was told he was in violation of his probation. The judge said he should have quit immediately upon learning from probation that the office was located too close to a school. Henry explained that he didn't quit because of his pending appeal, as he'd been out of work for months and, additionally, it was a term of his probation was that he be employed. Henry grows angry at this memory, saying the judge told him that he should have quit while waiting for the appeal decision. "Can you believe that? The judge said I should have quit, waited for the decision, and then gone back and ask to be rehired?" At this point, Henry had only three years left of probation. Due to his infraction, however, the judge issued the harshest ruling possible, sentencing Henry to six years in state prison. The only good thing, he says, is that "the minute I went to prison, my grandma could take those signs down."

When he was first arrested, Henry had no idea of the extent of the punishment he'd ultimately face. Prosecutors told him that if he went to trial, he faced decades in prison, but a plea would result in no jail time. He did not fully understand the consequences of probation or lifetime registration. He shakes his head. "I just pled. In the police report [the young man] admitted to telling me he was eighteen. And I had his dating profile. I was way naïve. I was stupid thinking I'd be fine." When he told the story to his treatment providers, he'd be told he was being untruthful and "minimizing" his crime. In prison, he was eventually able to get the police report supporting his claims. He says he felt vindicated when he shared it with the treatment providers who had dismissed his story.

In prison, Henry says he finally understood the true horrors of the registry and the criminal-legal system. "I met other registrants in prison. We would talk about all kinds of reentry plans. We wanted to expose the system. I began to see all of this is just undue hardship. In prison, there was no mental health care." He shakes his head at the absurdity of the situation. "I got six years in prison," he says, "for working."

Prison, he says, put a tremendous burden on his parents and he says he still feels "horrible" for making their lives so difficult. "They would drive all over the state to see me in different prisons. Sometimes they'd drive eight hours to see me. They'd do this four times a year. They paid $75 a week so I could call them from prison. And they always made sure I had $170 a month in my commissary. I hated what I did to them. I was dependent [on them] and couldn't help myself."

After his release, Henry moved to a halfway house because his parents were unable to locate any apartments that probation would approve. The halfway house, says Henry, was disgusting and "filled with bedbugs" and cost his family $600 a month. He eventually found a position at an accounting firm. He disclosed his past during his interview, and they decided to give him a chance. He says he was treated poorly at the firm. A manager would tell him he was lucky to have the job given his background and that he was only hired because "the owner did me a favor." Henry says he didn't complain.

Henry says he is lucky to have eventually found another accounting job in a large university system, where he was hired despite his background and has worked for many years. However, their offices are on a campus, so he needed approval from campus security as a condition of his hire. He was granted permission after writing them a detailed letter explaining his offense. Currently, he's also happy in an apartment he likes, where he lives with his "best friend." At the same time, he feels trapped and worried for his future. If something happens with his living situation or job, he could easily be homeless or unemployed. "I can't move because I know no complex will give me an apartment. Let's say my roommate moves, where am I gonna go? Same thing with the job. As long as I'm at the university, it'll be OK. But what if something happens?"

The registry impacts him in other ways, even though he's in a happy and healthy relationship. A coworker has invited him to dinner many times, but he doesn't accept because he is hesitant to share his story with coworkers. "It's stressful keeping secrets. I don't want to be around people with kids."

Last year, he was motivated to volunteer as a community organizer. They had a "get out the vote" event at a local sports stadium. All volunteers had to check in and show identification to security and police upon arrival. Henry was humiliated when he was forbidden entrance after they entered his identification, and it showed his registry status. "It was my first time volunteering. It was so embarrassing."

Henry is gregarious, warm, and funny. Before he was on the registry, he says he had "no clue" about "sex offenders." His case is an "easy" one, and he notes in states where the age of consent is sixteen, he wouldn't be on the registry. While he'd like to move to a state where he'd be off the registry, he says he's very close to his parents and family, and it would devastate them. "When I first started going to treatment, I told myself the others were 'real' sex offenders. I would differentiate myself. But I've learned that we all have the same barriers, and we all have the same stigma. I must extend that grace to my peers. I paid for my crime. Why am I still facing collateral consequences from something I did twenty years ago?"

Henry says he's psychologically strong, but he also has moments of fragility. He tells me that on one rainy day, a campus police officer offered him a ride from his parking spot to his office. "It was triggering. Even in that two-minute ride, I was shaking and sweating. Everything with law enforcement and the registry triggers me and causes me major anxiety." At one time, he was required to carry a special registry identification card with the name of his registry officer, and Henry is relieved that it's no longer required.

I ask him if he knows what happened to his accuser. Matter-of-factly he tells me that the individual is still part of the "gay scene" in his city, and after prison, he once saw him at a bar. But, he adds, he was too terrified to talk to him. Another time, Henry says, they matched on a dating app. "I just blocked him immediately. I never want to talk to him because I'm just too afraid."

I thank Henry for speaking to me and ask him if there is anything he'd like to add about how the registry impacts his life. For the first time, he mentions that he had a sister. His sister, Henry explains, was outraged by what happened to him and spent years writing letters to "the media, TV anchors, judges, and lawyers," pleading for them to help Henry. She ultimately grew discouraged when she realized no one would help and no one cared about what she saw as a great injustice.

> No matter how many doors she knocked on there was no remedy. It drove her to drink. She died of alcoholism. We all know it was because it was because of what happened to me. Before my arrest, my sister never ever drank. We all knew that it was because of the stress of trying to get me out of prison. It drove her crazy.

CHAPTER THREE

Restricting the Right to Travel

Travel

A possibly unsuspected consequence of being on a registry is the varied restrictions on travel. No others with criminal histories are subject to wide-ranging domestic and international travel regulations after completing criminal sentences. Yet travel restrictions for registrants are politically popular, receive little critical attention, and have been upheld as constitutional by courts. These laws create profound burdens for those on registries and their families. Family vacations often require planning around the number of days once can visit a state without having to register there or notify the police. In some cases, the destination state can place those with sexual-offense convictions on the state registry for life. Registrants cannot take jobs that require regular domestic or international travel. Those with loved ones living abroad are unable to visit relatives. Failing to adhere to local, state, and federal travel regulations can result in a new felony conviction and prison sentence. As a result, those on registries must consider travel with caution and undertake laborious research due to the ambiguity of many travel laws. Some even fear traveling from their homes at all, even for one night. The inability to travel freely intensifies the banishment and isolation caused by the registry.

Domestic Travel

The right to travel within the United States of America is a fundamental right inherent in

> citizenship and in the nature of the federal union. It existed before the creation of the United States and appears in the Articles of Confederation.

> The United States Constitution and Supreme Court recognize and protect the right to interstate travel in the U.S. jurisdiction. The travel right entails privacy, leaving citizens free to travel interstate without government interference and intrusion. (Torres & Sobel, 2013)

In *The Right to Travel: A Fundamental Right of Citizenship*, Ramon Torres and Richard Sobel (2013) argue that post-9/11 identification and screening requirements for domestic air travel undermine the constitutional rights of interstate travel and privacy. Those on registries, however, are subject to additional and far more onerous domestic travel regulations than those outlined by Torres and Sobel. Registrants must register with local police when spending more than a certain period in another state, and the number of days differs by state. In Florida, for instance, if they stay more than two days, they'll have to register and stay on the registry for life. In Alaska, one is required to register if visiting for more than one day. The laws regarding interstate travel are complicated and unclear, and understanding what is required often demands directly contacting the registry office in a planned destination. In places with residency or proximity restrictions, registrants also must carefully plan their lodging, lest they run afoul of state and local laws regarding where they may stay overnight or visit. While these travel regulations appear to be the definition of "government interference and intrusion," they have been widely implemented with little legal scrutiny or pushback from organizations concerned with civil liberties.

Criminologist Shawn Rolfe has studied the requirements facing those traveling from their home states to other states for temporary visits related to work or pleasure. Rolfe analyzed travel restrictions in every state and found a complex web of local and state laws lacking consistency and clarity. Rolfe also notes that relatives or friends may be unwilling to host those on registries when their own addresses may be shared with local law enforcement, leading to their own experiences of embarrassment.

As with most other registry consequences, Rolfe notes the economic impact of these policies, for the registrant as well as for the state governments. The cost to the registrant, he writes, "can range from being required to pay a registration fee or paying for a DNA test to unexpected lodging expenses due to not being able to stay with loved ones. States also experience increased costs because of the nonresident registration requirements and address verification checks" (Rolfe, 2019). It is not surprising that many on registries prefer not to travel at all due to the prospect of interaction with law enforcement in another state, financial costs, and the possibility of inadvertently breaking local laws.

My interviews reinforced Rolfe's findings. I found that the difficulty of interpreting the rules was a major factor in travel hesitancy. I also frequently heard that even when registrants know the strictures, dealing with a new law enforcement agency can be traumatizing. Many I interviewed reported experiencing high stress when registering even in their home precincts. An unexpected finding was that so many voluntarily, without prompting, mentioned the emotional pain of the registration process itself. I heard repeatedly that birthdays are often bittersweet because they may be associated with an appointment to perform the required registration. While I never questioned those interviewed directly about the registration process itself, without prompting, many shared with me that the cost, time, and experience of registering constitute additional punishment in psychological, emotional, and practical terms.

International Travel

For those on registries, traveling internationally is even more arduous than doing so domestically. Title I of the Adam Walsh Child Protection and Safety Act of 2006, or the Sex Offender Registration and Notification Act (SORNA), requires those on registries to notify officials twenty-one days in advance of international travel. In 2016, International Megan's Law (IML) was passed to little fanfare, even though it was the first time that any subgroup of American citizens became required to have a specialized identifier on their passports. While some countries, including Canada, will restrict entry if visitors have any criminal history, only American citizens with convictions for sexual offenses involving minors have a unique mark on their passports. According to the SORNA regulations, international travel for those with this identifier requires American officials to notify INTERPOL so that the information can be shared with police in the destination countries.

The regulations regarding travel within the United States and abroad have been upheld in court, yet it is difficult to argue, based on the experiences of those subject to them, that these are not punishments. In *International Megan's Law: Not about What Works, It's About What Sells*, the authors correctly argue that a "visible marking on an important identification document, in addition to other registration and notification requirements, arguably increase sanctions for targeted offenders" (Kamorowski et al., 2017, p. 7). The marked passport is an obvious form of stigmatization, but "sells" to politicians and the public, as well as courts, because it appears to be a policy that protects children. Kamorowski et al. (2017) note that the government can legally restrict international travel in some cases for those with ongoing or pending legal cases or those under state supervision. However, under IML, those with child sex convictions are subject to a marked passport and travel restrictions for as long they must register, regardless of how long after supervision they have lived as tax-paying, law-abiding citizens.

They further argue that IML is problematic because it applies to all those convicted of sex offenses involving minors, rather than those at high risk for engaging in international sex trafficking or sex tourism. Legal scholar Daniel Cull (2018) echoes this point, also pointing out that one remedy for this problem could be for IML to be "specifically tailored" for those posing the highest risk. These are good arguments and relate to the general problem of sex-offense laws that fail to distinguish between various offenses and assume that everyone with a sex-offense conviction is destined to reoffend.

The more significant problem with IML is that it demonstrates the willingness of political actors to continue to lob punishments at those with sex offenses, including new ones that never existed before, based on no evidence that they will be effective. Marking passports is a fundamental shift in policy; as Cull (2018) notes, in the past, passports in almost all countries have included only identifying information, not information about past behaviors or criminal history. IML demonstrates, once again, the ease with which principles of liberty, dignity, privacy, and long-cherished beliefs about civil rights are disregarded when it comes to sex offenses. Another crushing aspect of IML is that those on the registry now face interactions with law enforcement throughout the world. Since IML's implementation, those on registries have reported that consequences have included immediate deportation, the humiliation and the anxiety caused by intense police questioning before they are granted entrance, and police escorting them upon arrival off planes before other passengers.

Gary: I'll Be Done If They Change the Rules

Gary works in a high-paying job in management. He's white, in his early fifties, and he has been on the registry for more than twenty years. His conviction was for a sexual offense involving an underage non-stranger. Gary tells me he knows he's lucky, because he's been able to maintain white-collar positions since his arrest. He's happily married without children, and he owns his home, where he's lived for decades without incident. Like many I've interviewed, he starts our conversation with the caveat that his life is good, that he's one of the lucky ones, and that he is aware that other registrants have it far worse.

Gary says one issue for him is the constant fear of what will happen should he need to change jobs or move. His current employer knows his history, and while he does not consider his position ideal, the situation is far better than the pain of searching for work. He tells me that applying for jobs is a nightmare, even though he has specialized technical skills that make him a strong candidate. "When I was applying for jobs, so many firms were interested. I'd get close to getting a position, and then they'd just stop responding to me. I knew why," he tells me. He feels the same way about his house. He lives in a private community, and his neighbors know of his background. He has had a few problems, but they are manageable, and he does not want to move and face new hostility. A friend on the registry, he says, has been unemployed for years. He is afraid that if he tries to get another job, or if he's laid off, he'll be in that same position.

Gary has been off probation for over a decade, but he still informs his local registry office when he travels. It's not required, but like many, he takes this extra precaution to protect himself. His wife loves to travel and recently wanted to go to the Caribbean for vacation. Gary figured this would not be an issue, because his offense took place so long ago. When Gary and his wife landed at their destination, they were approached by officers and escorted, together, off the plane before the other passengers. They were brought into customs and denied entrance, and then forced to wait for a return flight to the United States. Gary is upset about the experience, largely because of the impact on his spouse: "My wife doesn't deserve this. We were together and booked at a vacation resort. Why was she perp-walked off a plane? Why can't we spend our money and visit a vacation destination together? My crime was twenty years ago." He says they lost "thousands of dollars" because neither the hotel nor the airline would offer them credit. "I did everything right. I told the U.S. government my travel plans. I told my local registry office. What's the purpose of doing this?"

When we started the interview, Gary focused on his good fortune and how he was "different" from the others suffering on the registry. Yet it becomes clear as we speak that he's both angry and fearful about his situation. He says his offense was "unacceptable," and he has changed because of treatment. Today, he still avoids being alone with children because he fears being falsely accused. He doesn't go outside when he sees children playing nearby. In the state where he resides, he says, he'll be on the registry for life and there is no path to removal. He's changed, he says, and contributes to society, pays taxes, and is a good husband and neighbor. "I want to tell people that I'm sorry for what I did and that it'll never happen again. But I can't. I'm not allowed to contact the victim and tell her I'm sorry."

Gary contributes to antiregistry organizations and has quietly become involved in local politics to try to make a difference. His extended family is understanding of his case and does not think he should be on the registry or that he's a "sex offender," but they do believe it's necessary for others, and he finds this frustrating.

> I try to explain to them that if they change the residency laws, I'll have to move, and I could possibly be homeless. I'll be done if they change the restrictions. People don't understand how the registry restricts my freedom. I completed probation and treatment, and I served my time. But the longer I'm on the registry, the more restrictions I face. How does that make any sense?

He says he no longer considers himself an "offender," and he hopes the person he harmed no longer feels like a victim. Gary tells me that the restrictions on travel, including to other states, are the hardest for him and his wife to deal with. He tells me that it's scary knowing that he can only travel to a few other countries at this point, and even that could end. "I'm humbled by my luck. But my chair could tip over at any moment. Sometimes I question my sanity. Sometimes I think I'm eventually just going to move to the mountains and live far away so no one bothers me. This isn't living."

James: I Pulled Myself Up by the Bootstraps, but the Registry Gives Me No Hope

James is white and in his late forties. He's been on the registry for more than twenty-five years. In his late teens, he was convicted of a sexual offense involving an underage nonstranger. He is now married with children and describes himself as a devout Christian. His work requires that he regularly travel to both domestic and international destinations. It's becoming harder to do his job, he says, as restrictions keep growing on where he can visit and for how long. James says he's experienced "redemption" but being on the registry forever doesn't allow him to move forward in his life.

James has worked for the same organization for many years, but he worries about his future, given the increasing obstacles that could keep him from engaging in the travel demanded by his job. On his most recent international work trips, he was questioned by law enforcement upon arrival. "That used to never happen. I explain my offense was over twenty-five years ago and they let me into the country. But it's scary. They now see the passport identifier, and I'm sure that's why they question me." At this point, he says, many regions where his organization operates have been placed off-limits to him entirely.

Travel is an essential part of his employment, he explains, because he must have in-person meetings with donors and others supportive of the organization. The stress of constantly researching domestic and international travel restrictions is affecting him evermore. "I can't take it much longer," he explains. "I have to time my travel so that I don't have to register in new places, and I'm paranoid because all the laws are different, and even the local registry offices tell me different things."

That experience, he says, is changing the way he looks at life. He feels things are growing worse, and he fears for his family. Recently, the school his children attend instituted a policy that keeps him from entering, and if he picks them up or drops them off, he must stay in his car. In his state, he's required to register quarterly. If any change occurs in his life, such as the acquisition of a new car, he must update the office immediately.

One way in which his family is impacted is that his children are not allowed to have sleepovers or friends in their home. They have "carefully" organized things so that other families do not have to enter or look up their address online. His kids play outside and with children at parks, but they never allow children, aside from cousins and relatives, to enter their home. He explains they worry that entering their address will bring up his registry listing. I ask him how he can arrange things so that no children from school ever come over, because that seems daunting. He agrees that it is not easy but explains that his wife puts in enormous time and effort so it's not apparent to the children. Their kids don't yet know he's on the registry, and they hope to keep them unaware for as long as possible. He doesn't want his children to face bullying or embarrassment, so James makes it clear that he and his wife are willing to take extreme measures to postpone the inevitable. They have a large and supportive extended family, so they have instituted a policy of family-only birthday parties, and their children haven't yet questioned it.

James tells me he can do manual labor and carpentry, and if he gets laid off from his management position, he will do blue-collar work or whatever is necessary to support his family. James says that the worst part of the registry is that it doesn't give people second chances.

> I pulled myself up by my bootstraps. I get things done, and I work hard. But with the registry, there is no hope. Things are getting worse and worse. I feel like a frog in water that's slowly getting hotter and hotter. It's been decades since my offense. The registry is just vengeance. Why should my kids have to bear the brunt of what I've done?

Ray: No One Cares about Facts

Ray is white, in his late fifties, and has been on the registry for more than twenty-five years. His offense involved an underage nonstranger. Ray is a college graduate and has a stable and well-paying white-collar job. He says he's not sure if his neighbors or employer know he's on the registry. If they do, he says, they've never mentioned it. He describes his life as "relatively quiet." He isn't in a romantic relationship and is childless. He enjoys volunteering and doing community service. Ray says he's happy to be alone, and having a romantic partner or an active social life isn't important to him.

Prior to his arrest, Ray was deeply involved in his church. He joined a different church after his prison release but stopped attending after the minister told him he'd found him on the registry. While he wasn't asked to leave, Ray felt uncomfortable and stopped attending. His energy is now devoted to engaging in his community and volunteering.

In recent years, being on the registry has made Ray's life more difficult. Animals are very important to him, and he has volunteered for many years at an animal rights organization. They instituted a new volunteer protocol, which required him to complete a new enrollment form. The new form required volunteers to check off a box that said they'd never been convicted of a sex offense. Ray says they didn't ask about any other offenses, just sexual ones. As a result, Ray didn't complete the form and stopped serving as a volunteer.

After his parents passed away, Ray began traveling regularly outside the United States. Initially, he had no issues, but after IML, he started to regularly interact with international police. He said that once, armed law enforcement officers escorted him off a plane, and he was interviewed for hours. According to Ray, they had apparently been informed by American authorities that he was a fugitive.

> They took me into an office and asked me some questions. It wasn't an interrogation. They seemed almost as perplexed as I was. Maybe more so. They didn't really know what to do. They asked me some questions, where I'd be, whether I'd told the American authorities. (I had.) They cleared up that I wasn't a fugitive. They escorted me to passport control and luggage pickup. I got out faster than the people in first class! Right through the passport check line.

Ray makes a point of telling me how the registry isn't that hard for him, and how he engages in some antiregistry groups primarily to help others who are far worse off than himself. He says certain aspects bother him because they are inconveniences, like being banned from using online vacation home rental agencies because of new background check policies. At the same time, he expresses anxiety about the growth in restrictions. He says that new politicians seek to make names for themselves by devising new laws to govern those on registries. This worries him, he says, because no one cares about facts regarding recidivism or the ineffectiveness of registries. Things are "OK" for him, now and he emphasizes to me the ease of his situation, but his involvement in antiregistry advocacy is also partly motivated by fears that things could become worse.

Mark: I Can't Even Volunteer

Mark is Latino, in his seventies, and he's been on the registry for almost three decades. He was convicted of a sexual offense involving an underage nonstranger while in his thirties. Mark served in Vietnam, and until IML, he returned there regularly as a volunteer with a Catholic organization. They would donate food and clothing and generally "help those harmed by Communists." Since retiring from his job more than a decade ago, he has sought to engage as much as possible in community service work and civic activism. He retired earlier than planned because people at his job learned he was on the registry. "I wanted to stay, but once my coworkers found out about me, it became a living hell."

Similarly, Mark volunteered for years at the Department of Veterans Affairs (VA) but was recently forced to stop after other volunteers learned he was on the registry. The same thing, Mark adds, happened to him at Meals on Wheels. "I'm just sharing this with you so you can see I'm not just a 'sex offender.' I volunteer and try to help people. Here and in Vietnam. But now I can't even do that. That really hurts."

The public could not access the registry when Mark was first on it. He has lived in the same home for almost fifty years but had no problems until "about ten years ago," when the registry became widely available on social media and the internet. He says that once local social media groups and an online "neighborhood watch" shared his address and registry status, things changed. He says he now regularly experiences low-level ongoing harassment, such as having his car scraped with keys and damage to his lawn. The worst part, though, is the direct hostility from others. "People would drive by and give me the finger. I even contacted the police, and they said they can't do anything unless I catch them in the act."

On one of his pre-IML trips to Vietnam, Mark met a woman, and they became engaged. Due to his registry status, it was very difficult to sponsor her move to the United States, but she was ultimately successful and now lives with him. Mark is happy to finally have her here, but it is hard when they go outside and get "dirty looks" from the neighbors.

> The thing that really gets to me is that there isn't a system in place to forgive people like me who lived a wonderful life before and after. I wanted to be actively involved in the community. I'm all for tough laws. I'm a decorated vet. I had a great job, and I helped my neighbors. I still help some of them, even today, senior citizens. But it's for naught. It gets taken away. It's not right.

A few months after our interview, Mark emailed me to tell me he successfully petitioned to be removed from his state registry: "Hello Emily. As I indicated in our interview, I had a hearing for petition to terminate sex offender registrations and am pleased to let you know it was *approved*." At least his situation has evolved positively.

Kevin: "Things Could Be Much Worse"

Kevin is white, in his late fifties, and he's been on the registry for more than two decades. His offense involved an underage nonstranger. Kevin characterizes himself as "successful" and "different" from most on the registry. He says he's "on the far end of the spectrum," and he has a wonderful job he loves. He's been in the same position in the airline industry for two decades. In his position, he must travel out of the country on a regular basis, for sometimes as much as three weeks each month.

In 2016, after IML, work became more complicated for Kevin. He knew, he explains, that he couldn't continue working internationally because of the twenty-one-day advance notice requirement. Kevin managed to shift to a position that only involved domestic travel. Kevin grows visibly upset remembering how he felt when he received his post-IML passport with a special identifier.

Kevin says that in the past year or two, things have grown worse for him personally and professionally. His employer is cutting positions requiring only domestic travel. He doubts he'll be able to continue for much longer in his current position and fears the job market. His conviction is more than two decades old and no longer comes up on his background checks, but the registry listing does.

Kevin is also worried about housing. A few years ago, a change in the residency-restriction ordinance forced him to move. It was a struggle to find a new, affordable home that wasn't in a "prohibited zone." He worries the laws may change again, and he's not sure where he'll be able to move. Even now, he panics and feels shame whenever the car clearly labeled "sex offender unit" comes by his home at random times for compliance checks.

Kevin visits those still mandated to sex-offense therapy to give them "positive feedback and hope." He tells them to present themselves "in a positive manner." "I understand why some of them look like [stereotypical] 'sex offenders.' They were on the fringes to begin with, and now they are on the registry, and they can't help it." He knows he's lucky because other states have far more restrictions, and "things could be much worse."

While Kevin is happily married and successful, he fears being forced into early retirement and facing financial stress if he's unable to find a new position. The fate of others on the registry troubles him, he says. He remembers when the reality of the registry hit him.

> The first time I went to group therapy, one guy told us that he was in a Home Depot, and he saw a mother and child in the aisle. He left his cart and ran out of the store. That made me really sad. Many others said similar things. I didn't understand it, but I felt bad. Then, a few months later, after my situation sunk in, I became the same way. And then it happened to me. If I am on an elevator in a hotel and kids get on, I get off immediately.

The fear of being around children is common among registrants. He says he is hypervigilant whenever he's near children, even in public places. If he flies and they put an unaccompanied minor next to him, he tells me that he panics and "prays for the flight to end." As our interview finishes, Kevin grows pessimistic. He says that he has "had a good run" but knows his days at his job are numbered due to his inability to fly internationally. He doubts he'll ever find work again should he be let go. "They might interview me, but once they do the background check, I'm done."

Phil: My Wife Doesn't Deserve This

Phil is Latino, in his midseventies, and has been on the registry since his release from prison thirty-five years ago. He was convicted of a sexual offense involving an adult nonstranger. While incarcerated, he says he tried to turn his life around and engage in volunteering and service. There, he taught English as a second language to other Spanish-speaking immigrants. After his release, he met his wife. He says she saw he was a "changed man" and trusted him. Today, he tells me, he continues to volunteer, helping Spanish-speaking immigrants learn the English needed for driving tests. Phil and his wife had a daughter and lived peacefully during the first years of their marriage, despite his registry status. However, once internet use and public registry access became widespread, things changed, and their community learned of his past sex-offense conviction.

For Phil, the worst part of this sudden exposure was the impact it had on his wife and daughter. His daughter was in high school when their tight-knit community learned he was on the registry. According to Phil, his daughter was subject to shunning as well as relentless bullying. She faced rejection at school, as well as from neighbors she'd known her entire life. She's now an adult, but Phil says she still resents him for her humiliation and pain. "She never really forgave me for what she went through after people found out about me. It's permanently damaged our relationship."

He says it's much worse now because his name is also posted on sites run by private companies. His business suffered due to the growing exposure, and he's now retired. Phil says he's glad that his daughter is an adult and on her own, so his offense can no longer damage her life, relationships, and career. Phil's wife has developed Parkinson's disease, and he cares for her full-time. He blames himself and the stress of the registry for her condition. "I was never rearrested. I supported my family. But the punishment never ends. It has really destroyed my wife and daughter, even though it happened before them."

He lives on a small pension and says his wife's condition is growing worse. He was hoping to take her back to their home country, but he has worries due to IML. He can handle being sent home by authorities, he says, but it would be too hard on his wife, given her physical limitations.

For Phil, the impossibility of moving forward is overwhelming:

> My daughter isn't close to me because the stigma is too much. The collateral damage to my family is much worse than for me. I knew I'd have to live with my misdeed. But why did my wife and daughter have to suffer? I don't care about the humiliation, but it's too much for them. I try not to pay attention. My offense happened over forty years ago. I've only done good since then. But the only thing people see is the website and my mug shot and "sex offender" and my address. When does it end? I'm in prison at home.

Richard: Something Changed

Richard is white and in his early seventies, and his offense involved sexual contact with an underage nonstranger. He has been on the registry for almost three decades. After his release from prison, he was able to achieve professional and financial success. He started an international business selling goods at trade shows throughout the world. Richard said his business started to suffer after he stopped traveling a few years prior to IML because the government was notifying destination countries of visits by those on registries. He decided then to stop taking the risk of being denied entry. When IML was passed in 2016, he said, it wasn't a complete surprise, given what he'd been observing in the few years before.

According to Richard, until about the mid-2000s, he wasn't consumed with paranoia and fear for his future. "Something changed. The registry was available everywhere on the internet, and I began to live a much less social existence." He owns his home, but worries he'll lose it. He no longer earns money from his business, and his home is his only asset. He used to travel domestically to visit friends in other states, but even that now gives him pause. "I could sell my house and have a bit of money," he says, "but where will I go? Who will rent to me?"

When we first started our interview, Richard was upbeat but grew despondent as we continued. He said he used to be a "social butterfly," but he now mainly remains at home. Recently, neighbors with whom he used to be friendly give him dirty looks.

He says the registry has impacted him financially and socially, but it is not the reason he's never reoffended. Even without the registry, Richard says he would never make the mistake he made as a young man. Prison was traumatizing, he says, but deserved. Parole, he says, was also difficult, but deserved. He never wants to have either experience ever again. What people don't understand, he tells me, is that if you have a sex offense and reoffend, the consequences are brutal. "I'd probably be sentenced to life in prison. That's why people with sex offenses don't reoffend. Not the registry. The registry just ruins the rest of your life."

After our conversation, he follows up with an email. He writes, "[My] social isolation [is] a direct result of being on the registry. When you're one Google search away from being 'outed' as a fiendish pariah, one is very reluctant to engage on any level with the community, let alone attempt friendships, seeing in them the potential for great disappointment and humiliation."

Louis: I Work. I Pay Taxes. But I'll Have to Register Forever

Louis is white and in his early seventies. He was convicted of his offense thirty-five years ago. He lives in a state with some of the most draconian sex-offense laws in the country.

I've never had any violations after my first offense. I've taken responsibility for what I've done. I'm remarried. I came from a good family, and my mother had nine children, and I'm the only one who has ever been to prison. I have had good family support the entire time. My wife and I have been married sixteen years.

This background has restricted my ability to work. I have been lucky financially—it's difficult to find people that will hire you. They will hire you to do stuff others don't want to do. People will hire you if you gain their trust, and they eventually will accept you.

They won't hold your past against you. Some companies would never hire me, but others would. One place wanted me, but corporate wouldn't let them hire me, even though they knew I was a great machinist. After I was there as a temp.

What I did was wrong. I should have gone to prison, and I used to try to minimize what I did, but now I don't. When I was in therapy, they told me I was in denial and I was lying, and I was totally responsible, and they wouldn't hear me. We had to write hypothetical letters to our victims, and they'd let you graduate when they thought you were remorseful and truthful enough.

They created these laws after my conviction. They are retroactive. Registration hurts me, but mostly my wife. I don't care about myself. Twice on Halloween, they come here [to do compliance checks] with news cameras, with the chief of police. Once my wife was home alone, and they showed her on TV. She's being victimized for something she has nothing to do with. The next time they came, I cracked the door and gave them my ID, and they handed me a notice.

All the cops that have come here have been nice. None of them have been disrespectful. But the TV special was disrespectful. Really? A TV camera? Expose my wife? About two months ago, a child was snatched up near my house. And six police cars came to my house at four thirty a.m. They wanted to do a house search. They left after they did a search. Part of me understands. Part of me doesn't agree with this.

When I got out of prison, my family helped me. I met my wife online when I got out. When she got past my horrible background, she saw that I'm appealing and nice in other ways. Thank goodness I found her. At first, she was hesitant, but in the end, she's here and we got married, and we never looked back. She's from South America and has European citizenship. She goes to Europe and works each year. She just retired. She owns a house there and in South America. My wife is wonderful. She makes a good living.

Her children and grandchildren live in South America. She has a very nice family. They don't know about me, and I want to tell them. But she doesn't want me to tell them. Everyone I know I tell, and they all know, and they've forgiven me because I'm totally honest with them. I think that's the way it should be. I don't think I should be advertised on the internet. People I'm close with should know. Not strangers.

I have one neighbor who quit talking to me. I got plenty of friends and family. They know my background. It was enough to give me a full life.

I just wish that some people, like my wife's family, would know because I want them to know. I wish they would know. I would rather tell them myself then have them find out. I don't think they will. When I got to South America the last time, the police pulled me aside and asked us lots of questions. My wife explained everything to them in their language. Next time, we'll carry our marriage license. We are going again soon.

All my neighbors are kind to me, and we've visited one another. Just one has rejected me.

I have to miss work and clock out when I go to register four times a year. Sometimes it takes almost two hours. It's more than ten miles. You have to do it during a six-hour span during working hours. So that's a negative. One friend of mine is in his seventies, and he's afraid he'll forget, and he'll go back to prison for forgetting.

They take your fingerprints. Sometimes they take a photo. Then they fill out paperwork about tattoos and scars. Just like you are being arrested. Then they say they'll see you again in three months. It's not fair. Maybe if I'd reoffended. I've been out for twenty years.

No arrests. Not even a traffic ticket. I work. I pay taxes. I pay my bills. I do all the right things, and I got to register for the rest of my life. I really don't think it's fair. If I was a troublemaker, that would make sense. I'm put in the same category as everybody else. I know I should have never done it. That's true. On my passport, it says I've been convicted of a sex offense with someone under twelve. And I have a stamp on my driver's license, so police know I'm a "sex offender." I haven't been in trouble since the 1980s, but I still have to go and register.

In a follow-up email, Louis tells me that soon after our interview, he attempted to travel to South America with his wife to see her family. He was turned away and forced to immediately fly home to the United States. "It has so far cost me a $1500 round-trip ticket. Last year, I was able to enter." He adds that he is sharing this information in case it can help others.

Jack: You Are Supposedly Free, but I'm Not

Jack is white and in his late fifties. His offense took place twenty years ago, and he was arrested during a sting, when he had a sexual communication with a police officer posing as a minor. He's sentenced to lifetime registration. When we start our interview, Jack is agitated. He shares that he's annoyed because the registry, which he has been on for two decades, keeps growing harsher and more restrictive.

> You are supposedly free, but I'm not. I've never considered myself free. I am always watched and tracked. I'm always scared people will look me up online. You can live and be somewhat successful, but you aren't free if you are on the registry. Even if you paid your dues. You'll never be free.

He knows he's luckier than some, partly because he's lived in the same home for nearly thirty years. He lived there before his arrest and has been able to stay there. He knows other registrants who are homeless. Jack works from home as an independent contractor. Prior to his arrest, he owned an athletic club. The registry limited his ability to continue in the fitness industry, so a friend helped him get started in his new profession. He estimates that he's spent almost $80,000 on registry-related expenses, including legal fees, polygraphs (he says he's taken thirty-five), registration fees, and treatment.

Jack recognizes, he says, that he needed help before his arrest. "I should have gotten help for my fantasies. There were no resources." He wishes that he'd had seen a therapist before his arrest who could have helped him and recognized the "warning signs" that he was engaging in risky behavior. However, he's cynical about the thousands he's spent on court-mandated treatment. "You can't get in trouble for having a fantasy. Except in treatment."

Jack confronted a neighbor recently about loud music. After the conflict, the neighbor found Jack on the registry and, in retaliation, shared this information with his other neighbors. Recently, he says, "I tried to help a woman across the street when her car alarm went off, and she screamed at me that I shouldn't come near her."

Dating is difficult because Jack isn't allowed on dating apps. He's part of a singles group at his gym, and it's a "small community"; he's terrified that he'll be outed and kicked out of his gym and the singles groups. Health and fitness are a large part of his life, and recently went to a South Asian country for a biking tour. When he arrived at the airport, he was called into security. "I heard my name when I got to the airport. Forty-five minutes later, this woman came in, and she was so nice and just wanted my itinerary. They think I'm trafficking children. The U.S. notified them, and they think I'm looking for sex slaves. I was just going there to do biking."

> I earned a second chance. We aren't the ones that are out there reoffending. They (the authorities) have to worry about others. It was a sting, and

> there were no victims. But people treat me like I had sex with a six-year-old. [Because] the registry says we are all the same. Everyone is the same, even when we've rebuilt our lives against all odds, and we can persevere. We've made it this far. A person gets a [driving under the influence] (DUI) and kills a kid or a pregnant woman, and they can do whatever they like. I am treated worse than what that person did. People don't know what the registry is. Your life is over on this thing.

Gail: I Don't Own My Body or My Life

Gail is white and in her forties. Her offense took place almost two decades ago, when she was in her twenties. She was teaching bible study, she says, and her crime involved a sexual encounter with an underage male student. She was sentenced to probation and a decade of registration after a short incarceration. Technically, her conviction involved "sodomy," which Gail says, in her state, means all sexual contact "outside of intercourse." The term itself, she says, was particularly upsetting to her devout Christian parents. At the time of her plea, the law indicated she'd be off the registry in ten years, but that has now changed, and she'll be listed for at least another decade. Gail is frustrated by this. She agreed to the terms of the plea, which explicitly required ten years of registration. It seems unfair to Gail that the state isn't upholding its end of the bargain. "Part of the negotiation and plea was that I could get off in ten years, and I agreed to those terms, and I have no voice, and I have to oblige."

Today, Gail is happily married with children, and she deeply regrets her poor decision. The registry hurts her family, and she says she wishes that they weren't casualties of her mistake. Gail shares the sense that things are growing worse for those on registries. She notes that even under supervision, she received special permission to travel abroad for work. "My judge knew I was traveling for a good cause, and I just gave them my schedule."

Gail is proud that she was granted early release from probation due to her dedication to changing her life and engaging in service. She sounds, however, discouraged about her future. Due to the classification of her crime as a hands-on offense, she's not eligible for a tier reduction that would decrease her restrictions.

The worst registry-related incident for Gail was when she and her husband were kicked out of a South American country upon arrival. They'd traveled there for a long-planned, prepaid vacation. They weren't refunded any of the money they had spent on the flight or hotel and were stuck sleeping overnight in an airport waiting for their return flight. "At that moment, I started to realize the impact the registry was going to have on the rest of my life." Gail says she and her family now fear traveling abroad. She and her husband work for a faith-based international organization, and this limits their ability to advance professionally.

Gail cries, remembering the humiliation and trauma of their trip to South America. "It was the most wretched experience. We had one bag of peanuts in the airport. I started to realize things were changing, and there were new rules. I started worrying about traveling to different states, and I asked my lawyer for guidance, but he said every state is different and it's up to me. I have a list of days I can stay in each state, and places I can go without having to check in with the police." She has asked local police about how long she can be away without reporting to them, and she said they don't give her straight answers. She suspects it's because even they aren't sure about the more recent state and federal laws. Gail is frustrated and says, "I'm basically on house arrest. I don't own my body and my life."

For Gail, the hardest part about being formally labeled a "sex offender" is that she is unable to advocate for herself. "I know," she tells me, "that I made criminal choices and immoral choices. But I've done every therapy I can do. And, no matter what I do, it doesn't matter. That's the hardest part." According to Gail, she was in an "unhealthy place" when she committed to her office, and she is a completely different person today. "I have been blessed and I got healthier."

Gail stops crying to emphasize that she's aware of how "blessed" and "lucky" she is "compared to most people." Her employer is aware of her offense and supports her. Her career today involves counseling, and she specializes in helping others who make "poor sexual decisions."

Gail struggles with deciding when and if to disclose her past because the reactions are so unpredictable. "No one else worries about finding the right time to tell new friends about long-ago mistakes from their past. It makes me feel stuck." Once, after they happened upon an online listing, a friend felt betrayed and angry that Gail hadn't previously disclosed her registry status. Outraged and feeling betrayed, the (now former) friend called Gail's workplace to complain they hired a "sex offender." Her employer was aware of her past and refused to fire her. The public registry creates constant anxiety for Gail that people will find out before she's ready to disclose to them.

Her child is getting older, forcing Gail to consider how and when to tell them about the registry. "They go to a great little school. One of the classmates has a parent who is a police officer, and they did a presentation at their school, and they loved it." That evening, her child asked her why she was in jail. Gail froze because she didn't immediately remember saying she'd ever been in jail. "Then I remembered that I'd said [at some point] that I'd met Jesus in jail, and I was relieved." Gail told them that when they are older, she'll explain why she was there.

Her child knows the police regularly come by their house, and Gail and her husband tell them that it's just "to make sure that we are safe." Once, Gail says, "they came by on Halloween to make sure we didn't have any decorations. To make sure I wasn't 'enticing kids'." Now, Gail and her husband send their child to their grandparents during Halloween to avoid embarrassment. "The police here are nice to me. One of the officers sends registrants to me who need help. I helped someone get housing."

Gail is crying again, and she says she isn't sure why she's so emotional when she generally feels that she has come to terms with her situation. She's very honest and likable but clearly tortured about the prospect of the inevitable registry conversation with her child. Gail says she tries to do good deeds and help others, and she and her husband counsel others with marital issues. "My husband has a DUI in his past. We both talk about making poor choices and do what we can to help other couples."

Her child, she tells me, is a "miracle." Gail says she knew her registry status would not have allowed her to adopt: "I have a miracle. I had fertility issues, and I couldn't adopt so I have a miracle."

Treatment and Truth

When Gail described her offense to me, she noted that she has completed treatment and takes full responsibility for her actions. She emphasizes that her involvement with the student was entirely her fault, as she was the adult and made the wrong decision. But, she says, making sure to tell me carefully and clearly that while she isn't abdicating any responsibility, in her view, she was pursued by the male teen, and her mistake was "not saying no." Gail is obviously nervous and hesitant as she explains this, similar to many interviewees who express high levels of fear and anxiety when describing their crime differently from the version in official reports. Additionally, she says, once the student reached the age of consent, he started pursuing her again. She claims to have had to get a restraining order because she wasn't permitted to talk to him and feared his pursuit would subject her to a violation. Despite evidence of his active pursuit of Gail, his family filed a civil suit against the church and received a large financial settlement. "It's not," she says, "as black and white as I'm supposed to make it when I talk about it."

It is clear from my interviews that sexual-offense treatment programs emphasize taking full responsibility for the crime of conviction without minimizing it. Many interviewees expressed frustration regarding the impossibility of describing the event with any nuance in terms of personal responsibility. For example, one person claimed his offense was triggered when he was "pursued by a sexually aggressive teen." He then visibly shuddered and loudly sighed, "You have no idea how good it feels to even be allowed to say that!" Others also told me that if they didn't acknowledge complete guilt and talk about the crime as it was detailed in official reports or pleas, they would be viewed as uncooperative or in denial, which would lead to longer terms of mandated treatment or incarceration.

Almost everyone I interviewed took plea deals, which isn't surprising given that this occurs in the vast majority of criminal cases. As a result, many said they pled to things they didn't necessarily do or that were presented in ways not reflective of the realities of their crimes. While this is common practice in all plea deals, this may cause particular harm to those with sex-offense convictions. I heard, over and over, that treatment providers insist that participants acknowledge and take full ownership of crimes as detailed in official reports.

Many viewed treatment programs as ultimately helpful to them personally and in terms of better understanding their offense. This is consistent with a survey that found 84 percent of registrants reported treatment to be "somewhat" or "very" helpful (Connecticut Sentencing Commission, 2017). Yet a large majority of those I spoke with emphasized that "graduating" from treatment often required that they describe and acknowledge things in ways that were false or exaggerated.

This constitutes another way in which those with sex-offense convictions receive extra and exceptional forms and layers of punishment, even during incarceration. Completing mandatory sex-offense treatment is clearly difficult and time-consuming and often involves coercive tactics. While many who take pleas challenge the description of their crimes in official documents, only those convicted of sex offenses must repeatedly take full and repeated responsibility, often in group settings. Many explained that to "graduate" from treatment programs requires multiple public confessions of their offenses. Most importantly, treatment, and all forms of therapy, is compromised if participants face punishment for voicing their authentic feelings and perceptions about their cases.

The genuine fear I heard from Gail and others while describing their offenses in ways they felt to be true was unnerving. This fear is indicative of how those convicted of sex offenses are subjected to unusual punishments. This is so troublesome for two reasons. First, it is common for those convicted of any crime, as well as human beings in general, to tell their stories in ways that partly explain or justify their bad decisions even when they take full responsibility. Yet those convicted of sex offenses are not granted this opportunity. Any nuance, justification, or explanation, including addiction, post-traumatic stress disorder (PTSD) after military service, childhood trauma, or their own experience of sexual abuse, is viewed as a failure to take responsibility. The requirement to admit full and complete guilt publicly in order to leave prison or supervision is more reminiscent of forced confessions under authoritarian regimes than traditional therapy or support groups.

Trevor: Before I Die, I'd Like to Visit My Partner's Home Country

Trevor is white and in his thirties. His crime, possession of illicit images of children, happened more than a decade ago. The offense, he explains, was prompted partly by not dealing with his sexuality and partly due to alcoholism, as well as an extremely stressful, demanding job. Raised in a conservative and religious family, "being gay was not an option for me." To deal with these various stressors, he'd "get drunk and look at porn."

At the time of his arrest, Trevor was working in "big law." He'd been practicing for a few years and sees his "whole life" up until then as being devoted to having a successful legal career and becoming a "partner at a big firm." "My only talent," he says, "was books and working." His life, he said, appeared perfect, and from the outside, it looked as if "everything I touched turned to gold." The job was exhausting, Trevor tells me, and he felt the only way he'd succeed was by working nonstop without breaks or vacations, because "that's how you make partner." He explains, "I even worked late Sunday nights, figuring out how to bring in new clients." He knew there were many other career paths for lawyers, but he never considered those. He drank excessively, he says, to cope with the self-imposed pressure. "I could deal with everything, as long as I had alcohol and porn," he tells me.

He'd attended an elite and hypercompetitive law school, where he excelled. While there, he had a nervous breakdown and wound up hospitalized, which "should have been a clue that my path was unsustainable." He quickly recovered and continued his academic success, pushing the incident out of his head by telling himself it was not of great import and certainly not indicative of deeper conflicts.

His life blew up after his arrest. The incident forced him to tell everyone, including his employers, what had happened. Trevor said his firm was generous by not firing him and allowed him the dignity of resigning.

The experience of disclosing to everyone in his life, he said, "was like handing them line-item veto power." Some people, he said, immediately cut him off, while others stood by him. Their reactions, he said, "ran the full spectrum. Some never talked to me again. Some dropped me but eventually came back around." Trevor still feels hurt as he thinks about the friends who abandoned him. "The other day, I drove by the house of someone who'd turned on me. It still affects me, and I wonder if he hates me."

Some at his firm wrote letters on his behalf to the judge. He believes their letters testifying to his work ethic and accomplishments helped his case, and he considers his five-year prison sentence to be fair. Trevor says many with similar charges have received significantly more time, and he views himself as lucky in this regard.

His family supported him after his arrest, and until his sentencing, they didn't accept that he was going to spend time in prison. "They thought that my fears were overblown, and because it was a first offense they believed, wrongly, that it would be a mitigating factor," he explains. "My family very generously thought my crime was a mistake. I was lucky that this was their approach." Trevor says more than a year lapsed between his arrest and his sentencing. For the first few months, he continued to drink excessively. He moved back home with his parents, and his sister covered for him when he blacked out or get sick. Eventually, he says, about six months before prison, he found Alcoholics Anonymous (AA) and sobered up.

Trevor credits AA with saving him. He says the honesty in AA was transformative, and he stopped lying to himself and others. "I realized I couldn't tell one more lie. In AA, everyone shares their wrongdoings, and no one judges anyone." He also was able to accept his sexuality. "Instead of drinking, I dealt with being gay." AA has helped Trevor build social networks that aren't centered around alcohol, also supporting his sobriety.

Trevor lost his license to practice law after his conviction. Since his release, he's found consulting work, assisting lawyers who represent clients with sex-offense convictions. He says he truly enjoys his work and finds it meaningful and rewarding. Trevor recognizes the irony that if not for his arrest, he'd probably still be working in an unsuitable corporate law job. He laughs and tells me, "I would never in a million years have pursued this path, but now I love what I do."

Today, Trevor is in a healthy and happy relationship. When he first met Dan, his partner, he shared the facts about his crime. Dan was supportive and didn't judge him. He recounts, "I told him about the offense, and he responded with a conditional statement: 'Well, that's in the past, right?'

Which I interpreted in two ways: his declaration that he did not care, since it was in the past, provided that I was indeed promising him that it was in the past. I said 'yes' in both respects, recognizing that it was my responsibility to preserve this relationship by not reoffending."

Dan grew up in South Asia and still has family there, and Trevor regrets that his registry status doesn't allow him to visit. "Before I die," Trevor says, "I'd like to see Dan's home country," and he expresses hope that, one day, the laws will change. Nevertheless, Trevor tries to live in the moment and not focus on things he can't control. Trevor remembers a turning point that happened in prison while being visited by his sister. "She told me that she never wants to see me in prison again. I could see she was scared, and I knew I had to make amends to her. But rather than blindly promise 'this will never happen again,' I told her, 'I know what to keep doing so that this never happens again,' which, for me, means staying sober and living honestly and with integrity. Because she had already seen me change in sobriety, that was good enough for her. She nodded silently and has never brought it up again."

CHAPTER FOUR

Registrants Not Allowed

> So many of us have become afraid and angry. We've become so fearful and vengeful that we've thrown away children, discarded the disabled, and sanctioned the imprisonment of the sick and the weak—not because they are a threat to public safety or beyond rehabilitation but because we think it makes us seem tough, less broken. . . . But simply punishing the broken—walking away from them or hiding them from sight—only ensures that they remain broken and we do too. There is no wholeness outside of our reciprocal humanity.—Bryan Stevenson, *Just Mercy*

"All Except for" and Animus

The preceding chapters described how the registry universally impedes the ability to work, secure housing, and travel. This chapter highlights the impact of other, often state-specific policies, such as lifetime probation, proximity restrictions, and abuses of sex-offense treatment. As noted earlier, these laws have been upheld as constitutional because they are viewed as civil regulations rather than additional, sometimes ex post facto, criminal punishment. Yet it is difficult to understand how laws restricting the ability to live freely in society do not fall into the punishment category. Increasing evidence shows that these laws are ineffective, that they are based on faulty premises, and that they function solely as punishment. Nonetheless, such measures seem to proliferate ceaselessly. One way to understand this disconnect is, as legal scholars Catherine Carpenter and Ira Ellman have argued, the basis of these laws lie in irrational prejudice or "animus."

In "All Except For: Blanket Exclusions, Animus, and the False Policies They Promote," Carpenter (2020b) highlights the many "all except for" provisions written into many criminal-justice reform laws aimed at addressing the failure of mass incarceration. For example, a law from 2014 on shoplifting, included in a broader California criminal-justice reform initiative, reduced the criminal consequences for thefts under $950. Those on the sex-offense registry are not eligible for this reduction if charged with theft. Additionally, anyone with a sex-offense conviction is excluded from parole reform initiatives such as the "Second Chance Act" and "good time credit," which all offer those who are incarcerated opportunities for early release. Carpenter also notes that some states deny other benefits, "for no reason other than animus," such as substance-abuse probation programs (in Louisiana) and expungement initiatives (in Delaware) (2020a, pp. 16–17). *Animus* is a term, when used in the legal context, that characterizes laws that exist solely due to feelings of hatred or hostility toward targeted groups.

Carpenter illustrates, in detail, how laws excluding only those on registries must be understood as rooted in animus, even if they are falsely presented to the public as reasonable safety measures. The animus inherent in these carveouts in laws aimed at helping populations harmed by mass incarceration policies extends, as Carpenter points out, even to measures intended to aid crime victims. She notes that in 2016, California passed a reform to the Victim's Compensation Fund that excludes registrants from any compensation for any harm or injuries, even when those are unrelated to their offense of conviction. Carpenter quotes a lawmaker who explicitly says that the sole purpose of the reform is to make sure those on registries are denied compensation. Carpenter writes, "An incident in Oxnard, California, supports the legislator's animus. A registrant who lost family members in [a deadly boat] fire was statutorily ineligible for recovery from the Victim's Compensation Fund only because he had been convicted of a sex offense" (p. 17). The stated basis for these exclusions is, of course, the false belief that those on registries have "frightening and high" recidivism rates. They function, Carpenter concludes, as "only further punitive measures designed to isolate and marginalize this community" (p. 46), and are most profoundly characterized by the animus that underlines them.

In "When Animus Matters and Sex Crime Underreporting Does Not: The Problematic Sex Offender Registry," Ira Ellman (2021) also considers animus as a prime motivator for the myriad of postsentence regulations imposed on those with past sex-offense convictions. He makes two key points about these laws that build on the examples offered by Carpenter.

First, Ellman highlights other cases in which courts have sustained animus claims, arguing that sex-offense registries and related postsentence policies also fall under the same "anti-animus" principles. Courts, Ellman illustrates, have ruled against laws that harm particular or targeted groups on the clear basis of animus. This is especially the case when these measures apply solely to "small and unpopular groups" without "broad public purpose," and laws must come under scrutiny all the greater "the narrower the targeted group" is and "the more sweeping the burdens" are. For these reasons, registry laws clearly justify the same "inference of animus" found in other rulings (Ellman, 2021, p. 14). Inevitably, Ellman points out, laws aimed at those "seen as evil, without regard to whether they serve any public policy, is of course the very definition of acting from animus" (Ellman, 2021, p. 16).

A second, and interrelated, issue Ellman addresses is the oft-repeated claim that sexual offense recidivism data are unreliable because of sex crime underreporting. It is well known that *all* crimes are underreported, including *most* violent and property crimes (Gramlich, 2020). It is thus consistent that self-report surveys consistently show that a significantly higher number of women and children experience sexual violence than what is represented in official arrest and conviction incident-based data. Thus, it's clear that those convicted of sexual offenses represent a miniscule percentage of perpetrators.

The very real problem of underreporting is, however, misinterpreted and weaponized to uphold draconian sex-offense laws in two common ways. One is via arguments that those convicted of sex offenses are likely to have committed many additional unreported sexual offenses. Therefore, anyone convicted of a sex offense is never punished enough, due to the unsubstantiated belief that they have surely committed additional, undetected sex crimes. Second, and far more importantly, the underreporting issue is also used to challenge the low rates of sex-offense recidivism. This argument is based on the notion that if the incidence of sex offense is underreported, so must the frequency of crimes committed by those with prior sex-offense convictions. This second issue is a fundamental one, because the pervasive myth of "frightening and high" recidivism formally functions to maintain the constitutionality of registries and, informally, justifies registrants' social and civil banishment.

For many decades, low recidivism data has been challenged on the grounds of underreporting. A highly cited 1989 meta-analysis of recidivism studies in *Psychological Bulletin* noted that "recidivism rates for sex offenders are unusually hard to establish, owing to gross underreporting of sex crimes" (Furby et al., 1989, p. 3). The authors repeat this throughout the paper, citing it as the primary reason for the potential inaccuracy of recidivism analyses because "probably less than 10 percent of rapes are reported to police" (p. 9). The source for this claim is one 1982 survey of 930 women in San Francisco (Russell, 1982). They note that given the underreporting issues, accurate recidivism data can only be calculated if "the percentage of sex offenses that are reported greatly increases ... and if they followed men for at least a decade" (Furby et al., 1989, p. 27).

A 2002 study, likewise, often referred to in the literature, echoes this view. Regarding problems with sex-offense recidivism data, it holds that "these figures are widely viewed as underestimates, because a high proportion of sexual crimes are never reported, effectively hiding these crimes from researchers" (Lisak & Miller, 2002). An Office of Justice Programs report from 2017 repeats this sentiment, noting, "recidivism rates are typically based on officially recorded information, such as an arrest, criminal conviction, or incarceration. Because these official statistics reflect only offenses that come to the attention of authorities, they are a diluted measure of reoffending. Research has clearly demonstrated that many sex offenses are never reported to authorities" (Przybylski, 2017).

Ellman demonstrates the extent to which laws and policies supportive of sex-offense registries dispute the validity of sex-offense recidivism data, with lawmakers and advocates routinely dismissing these data due to the consistent gap between the government incident information and self-reports. Recidivism rates, of course, can only be calculated based on those convicted of a sex offense and then reconvicted of a new one. Ellman demonstrates that recidivism rates for those with prior sex-offense convictions are likely *lower* than research shows. Ellman highlights the key reasons for this:

1. Victims are more likely to report sexual offenses committed by perpetrators whom they know have a prior sexual offense conviction.
2. Police are more likely to follow up on reports by victims who identify the perpetrator as someone with a prior.
3. Police are more likely to identify, and thus arrest, perpetrators with prior sexual offenses.
4. Prosecutors are more likely to file charges and win convictions in cases in which the alleged perpetrator has a prior sexual offense conviction. (Ellman, 2021, p. 16)

In many ways, claims that sex-offense recidivism rates are faulty because of "underreporting" are also, at their core, based on animus. Those convicted of nonsexual offenses aren't burdened by draconian policies and extreme stigma on the grounds that they have possibly committed many prior offenses for which they were not arrested or convicted. DUI, for instance, has among the highest recidivism rates, is well known to be vastly underreported and underdetected, and can result in the deaths of innocent victims. Yet those convicted of DUI or other offenses aren't burdened by a registry-life regime based on underreporting or high recidivism (or the lifelong trauma caused by losing a loved one to a drunk driver). These works by Carpenter and Ellman offer strong cases for how sex-offense laws are thus burdened by legal and political, as well as social scientific, animus.

A 2021 paper, "The Problem with Assumptions: Revisiting The Dark Figure of Sexual Recidivism," by legal scholars Tamara Rice Lave, J.J. Prescott, and Grady Bridges, reinforces the falsehood of high sexual recidivism. In their paper, they meticulously discredit the long-held and persistent argument that the very real problem of sex offense underreporting means that the very real low rates of sexual recidivism are unreliable. While this paper specifically challenges a 2019 paper by Nicholas Scurich and Richard S. John that again makes this claim, they emphasize two important and related points. First, the authors note that the data on low sex-offense recidivism is not based on select or "cherry-picked" studies or data, but is "the consensus of an entire field" (Lave et al., 2021, p. 280). In their debunking of the impact of underreporting on recidivism studies, they also challenge the notion that registries and related laws are the cause of the low recidivism rates. They explain both these points clearly and emphatically, writing:

> The vast majority of sexual offenses are committed by individuals who are not potential recidivists, and although some who have been convicted of such crimes do reoffend upon release, recidivism numbers are sufficiently low that it makes little public-safety sense to focus so much effort and so many resources on what is a relatively small population. This is true even if we leave to one side the fact that there is no evidence that registration, notification, and residence restrictions are effective at reducing recidivism (whether it is low or high) and even some evidence that these laws actually increase recidivism by exacerbating well-validated recidivism risk factors (Prescott, 2016; Prescott & Rockoff, 2011). (Lave et al., 2021)

Given these facts, as well as the growing scientific consensus regarding the myth of "frightening and high" recidivism, Carpenter (2022) most recently argued for judicial intervention as one way to put an end to ineffective registry laws. She makes the case that the courts have the power to do so in the form of the Irrebuttable Presumption Doctrine. She explains,

"Employed primarily in the 1970s by the United States Supreme Court, the doctrine stands for the proposition that a statute cannot confer or deny a right based on presumption that is not universally accepted as true" (Carpenter, 2022, p. 11). Her point is compelling; there is now an entire body of research that demonstrates that sexual offense recidivism is low. Data documenting low sexual offense recidivism is based on decades of criminal justice arrest and conviction data from state and federal agencies, both before and after the implementation of registries. The constitutionality of registries is based on a myth that has been thoroughly disproven, and this doctrine may offer an approach to overturning these animus and myth-based schemes. In the social and political context of nearly universal support for registries, legal scholars who propose innovative, court-based, and judicial solutions to ending registry laws are of particular significance.

Reed: Lifetime Sex-Offense Probation

Reed is white, in his early fifties, and was convicted of a sexual offense involving an underage family member. His listing, unlike most other states, doesn't indicate the year of offense, so it's impossible to see the length of time since it occurred. Reed sends me documents showing his conviction happened more than twenty years ago.

Reed has a noticeably warm and friendly affect, and he smiles throughout our video chat. In his picture on the registry website, he's also half-smiling, and he almost bounces with positive and hopeful energy. He is excited because he recently bought a home and has two tenants, and he tells me he's renting one to someone newly released from prison, "to give back!"

He says his offense involved one incident of sexual contact with his daughter, and he attributes his "bad decision" to substance abuse as well as post-traumatic stress disorder (PTSD) from his military service. His service-related injuries qualify him for 100 percent disability with lifetime healthcare benefits from the VA. This compensation level is subject to multiple layers of scrutiny and is uncommon. Reed's sentence included only a short time in jail, but he also received lifetime probation. When Reed took his plea, he didn't fully understand the particularly onerous burden of lifetime probation. His efforts to reform and change his life have been continually and repeatedly thwarted because of the endless requirements of having a sex-offense conviction while on lifetime probation.

Reed worked in architectural design after earning a degree using his postservice military benefits. After his conviction, he was unable to find work in his field, so he first worked in warehouses and other blue-collar positions after realizing "only bottom-of-the-barrel jobs hire felons." Today, the best jobs he can find are in telemarketing or phone support. He currently works from home as a telemarketer selling credit cards. The company "hires felons, and I'm very grateful." He says people hang up, yell, and curse at him, but it pays just above minimum wage, and he's eligible for bonuses. "I just follow a script when I call people," he tells me, and he seems genuinely thankful for the job.

He says he's been hired for "dozens" of jobs over the past two decades, but offers are immediately retracted after he shares his registry status. Even companies that claim they don't care about criminal history fire him as soon as he discloses. Reed always tells hiring managers immediately about his background, because they "always find out," and then it invariably becomes "a huge mess."

For years, Reed says, he worked as a paid actor. He played in weekly dinner theater productions and had spots in a few commercials for local businesses. Once, he says, he had a bit part in a feature film with "major Hollywood stars." "I met them all, and it was an amazing experience," but he didn't tell probation about his side acting gig, fearing they'd deny his request. One bonus was that productions listed cast members online, so when people looked him up, they'd see him as more than "just a felon." Unfortunately, he told me, "When probation found out I had all this information online, they made me remove everything or face jail time. This resulted in a complete erasing of years and years of creative work, networking, and opportunities." Now, he says, all people see when they search his name in his registry listing.

Reed has been on probation for more than two decades and has had several nonsexual-offense violations. Each resulted in sixty- or ninety-day jail terms, as well as new rounds of "intensive probation." Two of these violations forced him to restart the grueling, years-long sex-offense treatment program that he'd completed in the first years after his arrest. His violations, he tells me, were due to failing to fully disclose all the places he went on detailed "activity forms" required during "intensive probation," a charge of "reckless driving," and telling probation that he smoked pot on an approved trip to California, where it was legal. "It was stupid for me to smoke pot. But it was even stupider for me to tell my probation officer. For some reason, I thought he'd appreciate my honesty."

Each violation also resulted in loss of progress toward earning visitation or even communication via phone or email with his kids. "My original crime was against my daughter. What does smoking pot have to do with that?" He says this violation took place after he'd already done two rounds of treatment, and the crime was more than a decade old at this point. It was a "nightmare" to start the entire treatment process over for a third time and, once again, repeatedly confess and relive, redescribe, and reanalyze the reasons for his crime.

I ask him about his multiple violations. He tells me, "I'm not a rebellious guy. I'm a normal human. I was motivated to see my kids and earn them back. But there was no hope or encouragement. I tried to do everything right, but then I'd make a small mistake, and they'd throw the book at me." One violation was the result of an angry ex-girlfriend reporting to probation that they'd gone bowling without getting preapproval via a required "activity request." Reed says that he's met many in his groups who tell him similar stories. When you are on probation, Reed says, anyone you anger can contact your probation officer and get you in trouble.

During "intensive probation supervision" (IPS), during which Reed says he would have to write down "everything I was supposed to do, and I'd have to get my schedule approved. It would include how long everything would take, down to the minute. We call IPS 'in prison soon' because it's so hard to live by." Reed says that during these bouts, he was banned from internet use, making it nearly impossible to find and list all the addresses of each planned destination as required.

Reed says that a few years after his arrest, his ex-wife and children wanted permission to start seeing him. His ex-wife saw he'd completed treatment and was sober, and "they even wrote to the judge." It didn't matter, he said, and probation kept denying their requests, as well as his own. It took years before he got permission to see his kids one day a month, with his ex-wife supervising. Reed says that once, his ex-wife and kids requested to visit with him on Father's Day but were denied by probation. They stopped by and left a Father's Day cake outside his front door. Reed's eyes well up with tears at the memory and tells me how much it meant to him, and he repeats this story to me again during a follow-up interview.

Reed has been through an arduous, intensive sex-offense treatment protocol three times since his release from jail. He says most only complete it once, but he had to do it three times due to his probation violations. The memory of restarting treatment twice after completion makes Reed visibly upset. He says that when resentenced to treatment, it is inconsequential that one has already completed the same program. During his third treatment protocol, which took place more than a decade since the incident with his daughter, the pain of once again repeatedly and publicly confessing, explaining, and detailing the offense sent him into a "dark place." He says he almost requested to be sent "to jail forever" so he wouldn't have to go through it again. He was forced to write a third apology letter to his daughter, who was, by now, an adult and with whom he'd reconciled, that he was forbidden to share with her, and talk endlessly in group sessions about the motivations underlying his offense. In addition, he once again had to complete weekly "assignments" and share his feelings and thoughts about his original crime. He says it's never clear how long the treatment will take, which makes it "even more crazy." Each of his treatment stints ranged from three to six years. Ultimately, he managed to "graduate" from his third treatment assignation, and he reports he's relieved to be mandated now to just one weekly two-hour counseling session.

When he first started treatment, he got "punished" for "being too emotional" in groups; he said he could barely function because he was "overwhelmed with grief" after his arrest. He soon learned that the term "victim posture" was frequently used against group members when they expressed personal pain and against him when he expressed sadness about losing access to his then–young children. Reed says it took him time to understand how providers would deny compassion or empathy to those who talked honestly about their feelings. Reed said he soon learned not to say or do anything that would lead to the accusation of "victim posturing," as it would delay graduation from treatment. Those in treatment groups learn quickly to repress their true feelings, says Reed, even though they were repeatedly told it's a "safe place."

Reed remembers a friend in his group crying uncontrollably after learning he couldn't live with his wife and newborn due to his offense. It was horrible, Reed said when the counselor accused the man of "victim posturing," and still remembers the man wiping away tears and "apologizing profusely" for crying. Reed believes the mandated treatment is a failure. He tells me, "I have rarely experienced a true listening process in all the twenty years of probation counseling. The system just isn't designed that way. It's like a conveyor belt that keeps on rolling and adding more and more probationers. There isn't time for much individual work."

Reed says that one of the worst consequences of his mandated sex-offense treatment relates to sex. He says they are forbidden to have any "porn or sexually stimulating material." They also must report all sexual thoughts, including dreams, to their providers during group sessions. He says he once watched a treatment provider berate someone for an "inappropriate" dream. Reed emailed me trying to explain to me the inconsistency of the treatment protocols:

> In one group, the counselor said we were allowed the "two-second rule." This applied if we saw an attractive woman walking by. It would be

> appropriate/healthy behavior to "look" for two seconds. We were "allowed" to masturbate to thoughts of age-appropriate adults. The rules change with each counselor/group/treatment center.
>
> [In another] we were told we didn't have the "two-second rule," but it was OK to masturbate to thoughts of former wife or girlfriend. [In another], we were told we couldn't masturbate to thoughts of former loved ones. Since they were no longer in our lives, it was inappropriate. We now had to write a fantasy script, with a specific two-page instruction on how to write it properly. We would then present our writing in group, of our detailed sexually appropriate fantasy, and read it aloud. Talk about embarrassing. After weeks of correction and rewrites, we would then be granted permission to use the approved fantasy script to masturbate to. I tried this, but it felt like my entire group was in my head in my fantasy, watching my actions with my "fantasy woman." Very disturbing.
>
> Also, there was a point where me and others were placed on a "masturbation schedule" where we would pick two or three days of the week and be required to masturbate on those days. I guess this was to avoid compulsion or impulsivity. After all of these implementations, any time I was allowed sexual contact with a woman, I just felt like probation was always in the room with us, and it was difficult to feel truly intimate, aroused, and private.

During his first few years of treatment, Reed was also subject to "penile plethysmography." In this test, a device is used to measure sexual arousal in response to different images to detect whether someone is attracted is children. Reed says he's relieved that they are no longer using it. He is still required to take yearly polygraphs at a cost of $200. The stress of the test has caused him to fail at times, because the questions make him "feel like a prisoner of war." When he fails, he must pay again to retake the test until he passes.

Reed is extraordinarily friendly and talkative, and he says one of the worst parts of his life is the growing difficulty of intimate relationships. It's been "at least three years" since he's had a girlfriend or a sexual relationship. The dating rules from probation have grown increasingly strict and detailed. In the past few years, he says, probation has mandated that he disclose by the third date that he's on the registry and has a felony sex-offense conviction. Reed says it's exhausting because about "eighty percent of women walk away at that point." The few who stay leave after realizing the restrictions of his probation.

He once had a girlfriend with a minor child. His probation officer said that he could meet the child if she paid for special classes and got herself "deputized" as a kind of law enforcement proxy official. He says that even after fulfilling these requirements, probation still denied his request to be with her and her child. The stress ended the relationship. He says the years of regular group-therapy sessions where he and others had to publicly disclose all sexual feelings and behaviors has made intimacy seem clinical and "bad."

There are even rules, Reed says, covering who he can date. They can't be more than a certain number of years younger than he is ("I think it's about eight?"), and they can't have a felony conviction. He can't use dating apps or social media, and bars are off-limits. "Activity requests" are required for everything he does in "public," even when it's something not involving minors or possible romantic dates, including his weekly golf game with an adult male friend. In these requests, he says, he must answer a battery of questions about the activity, and answer "what if" scenarios relating to potential interactions with minors that could occur.

For example, he tells me, he'll read his weekly group a statement such as, "What if I'm golfing and a minor shows up. I won't talk to them and only my golfing partner will interact with them." Then members respond, and the plan is revised based on their feedback. Then probation approves or disapproves, and he must sign the document. Reed says that it can take three months to get approval for a new activity. "I used to try to get around these rules," he says, "but I don't want to go back to jail. I want to go to the movies without waiting three months, but I'm terrified of going back to jail, dealing again with probation, and starting treatment over again." Reed doesn't want another violation, but the process of asking permission is so onerous that it makes him inclined to limit activities.

When I first interviewed Reed, he focused on his happiness about his recent home purchase. A couple of days later, he sent me an email because he said he remembered something he wished he shared with me:

> In 2010, I bought a small condo. There were only about thirty units in this complex that was U-shaped, with a courtyard/community in the center. I knew the sex-offense flyer would be mailed out to everyone in my area in the next month or two, so I made sure to introduce myself to my neighbors and show I was a normal homeowner and part of their community. Everyone was friendly and open.
>
> When the flyer was mailed, the [homeowner's association] put notes on everyone's door, telling everyone not to panic or take action, but that there would be a community meeting to discuss the event of me living there. I was going to attend and called my probation officer so she could attend and support. I thought only a few people would show up inside the condo [of the association president]. No, there were so many people that we had to meet in the outside courtyard. I walked down my steps feeling like they had burned a cross for me. It was hostile, filled with fear, and one of the

> worst experiences I've had on probation. I didn't speak the entire time, as I was getting attacked verbally by several people who lumped me up with all the other stereotypes.
>
> Tears rolled down my cheeks from all the hatred. [A] female couple . . . were my immediate neighbors. When they tried to speak up on my behalf, which I will never forget, they were shut down and silenced immediately. (The next day they brought me a plate of homemade cookies, which warmed my heart. We were close neighbors afterwards.) I lived in that complex for over two years and the hateful neighbors ended up moving out, while the rest became friendly and realized I was just as normal as them and was a happy and productive member of society.

Reed talks in a soft-spoken voice, laughs easily and frequently, and expresses little anger or frustration. Yet he possesses a sadness, saying he feels increasingly isolated because of his shrinking social existence. He is artistic, and he misses being part of creative groups. Reed says he was approved by probation to participate in a local adult dance program. However, he was asked to leave after another participant discovered he was on the registry and shared that information. "It was so much fun. It was healing. It was community. It was great." Reed says when he sees people having fun and enjoying their lives, it's almost like "watching a movie" because he feels so different from them. His daughter, now almost thirty, is still referred to only as his "victim" by his treatment provider and probation.

Reed sends me multiple emails after our conversation, including a picture of him and his daughter smiling together as adults. In another, he attaches a song he wrote, sharing that he was in a military chorus and continues to compose music. In another, he tells me that he's met hundreds of men in more than two decades of treatment, but only one has ever committed a new sexual offense, and that was for having "minor images on his computer." "So put that on your stat sheet, ha ha!" He ends each email with the sign-off: "Staying *creative* on probation!"

Harry: A Different Side to the Registry

Harry was nineteen when he was arrested for engaging in sexual contact with an underage, nonrelative teen. He's white and in his early thirties. He's been on the registry since his release from prison seven years ago. He didn't understand the implications of the additional sentence of lifetime registration, and "didn't even know what the registry was." He wanted to take the case to trial, he says, but finally accepted a plea bargain after being told that not doing so could result in a much harsher sentence. According to Harry, his conviction transpired only because, "I told the truth about what happened with my girlfriend, and that's why I got in trouble. I wasn't going to lie." Harry expresses his feelings in a notably positive manner, and he tells me that he "made the best" of prison and took advantage of whatever opportunities were offered. He speaks highly of his family and says, "We are close and no one turned on me."

While on probation, Harry was forced to wear an ankle monitor. At one point, it malfunctioned, and for ten minutes, he says, the GPS lost track of his address, and he was sent to jail for thirty days. He hired a lawyer, and the violation charge was dismissed, but he spent $3,000 for attorney fees and lost his job due to his month of undeserved incarceration.

Harry is actively engaged in antiregistry activism and has filed several lawsuits challenging his registry conditions. He says he took his time in treatment seriously and got as much out of it as possible and even voluntarily attended additional treatment sessions and "aftercare" to show the court his willingness to succeed. He's teaching himself about the ways in which the registry is unconstitutional and would like, at some point, to be a loud voice for change.

Harry emphasizes that he's a "success story" and far luckier than others on the registry. He and his wife have two young children together, and his wife has full custody of a daughter from a previous relationship. Harry was granted the unusual privilege of unsupervised contact with his stepdaughter by the court, and he is proud that he can be there to fully support his wife and children. Now, if his wife is sick and needs to go to the doctor, for instance, he can stay home with all their children; he also got permission to drop his stepdaughter at school if his wife needs his help. His treatment provider came to the hearing, he says, to vouch for him and his commitment to his family. His marriage is strong, he notes, but it's hard that he can't do as much as he'd like for his family, such as attending parent-teacher conferences or school events. His sister-in-law will graduate from high school soon, and he'll be the only member of his family who can't be there to congratulate her.

"I'm a different side," he stresses, "to the registry story." He says many of his lawsuits have set precedents and helped other registrants. The registry, he says, has put up "roadblocks" for him, but Harry says that "they don't hold me down." "My counselor invites me back to talk with the group. I try to go back and tell them where I'm at." In his state, he has to register every three months, and he says, "it sucks," but "they aren't nasty to me when I have to go there." He repeats, again, "I'm a different side to the registry."

Harry is proud of his professional accomplishments, particularly because he's aware that he faces so many barriers as a registrant. "I started here as a laborer, and now I'm a plant manager. The owner knows about my past." Harry tells me that he never thought he'd have such a well-paid job with so much responsibility, noting with pride, "I don't have a college degree, and I make almost six figures." Taking care of his wife and children is the most important thing in his life, Harry says, and that's why he works so hard; he says he regularly works sixty hours weekly, but "it's worth it" to provide a good life for his family. Recently, recruiting for his firm, he hired a former police officer and shared his story with him. The ex-officer, who is from a different state, told Harry that he "wouldn't even be on the registry if [he] lived there!"

His job is something that Harry says he could never have imagined. He says, with amazement, "I was thrown into this. I had to start being around rich people. I went out to dinner after a trade show with executives from the company." Harry says he felt out of place, "like I wasn't supposed to be there," given all that he'd been through. "Look," he tells me, "I ordered a steak"—he pauses—"and it was $78."

Harry's younger brother has a unique neurological and medical condition. When Harry returned from prison, he filed a successful motion, while on probation, to be allowed unsupervised contact with his brother. His father had recently passed away, and Harry had to assist his mother with the intensive care his brother requires.

Harry acknowledges the strain of having three kids, holding down a demanding job, and helping to care for a brother with special needs. Harry gets visibly upset remembering when his brother had to get emergency surgery at a local children's hospital. When he tried to enter to visit his brother, "they flagged me and wouldn't let me in. I was really upset, and I asked to speak to a supervisor. I knew my mom needed me to help my brother. I explain I'm the only one who can calm my brother down and help him with his anxieties and outbursts. I told the supervisor my dad passed away and my brother needs surgery. I told him that my brother will lose it and beat up your staff if I'm not there. I told them my crime wasn't against any kids." Finally, Harry says, he was able to get into the hospital after telling the supervisor he would report him to the district attorney. "Most don't fight that," Harry says but adds that it was, nonetheless, a horrible and stressful encounter. A few months after this, his son got injured in an accident and was admitted to the same hospital for treatment. At first, Harry panicked because he knew his wife would have to handle things on her own. One good thing, Harry notes, stemming from the traumatic incident with his brother was that security remembered him and permitted him to visit his son.

Harry needs permission when his work requires that he travel to other states. He has to tell the registry office where he will stay and for how long. He plans his travel so that he never has to register in other states. Once, his work required him to travel to a state that demanded registration after forty-eight hours. He arranged things so he flew in and out within the designated time frame. He reported the hotel address to his registry office prior to his departure, and upon arrival, he was greeted by local police who told him that the hotel where the conference was taking place was in a zone forbidden to those on registries. "So even though I didn't have to register, the hotel was apparently in an 'exclusion zone,' and I had to find a new place to stay. I was terrified. The local police claimed that because I'd crossed state lines, it would be a federal offense if I stayed in that hotel." Harry describes the fear that gripped him during this encounter and calls the incident "a low point" in his life. Harry says he luckily found a local website that helps registrants find hotels outside zones with proximity restrictions, but it was a nightmarish experience. "I was going to a trade show for work," Harry says angrily, and says the incident highlights the craziness of his situation, noting he even had to make up stories to coworkers about why he changed hotels.

That situation was painful but also motivating for Harry, and it inspired him to want "to tell the story of the registry." The incident was also a turning point for his mother, who was taken aback at the intensity of Harry's response to the incident. Harry says he called her, crying uncontrollably, and told her might be going to jail. He let her know where he kept emergency funds for his family in case that happened. "I was terrified to go to the new hotel. When I got there, I called the local police and asked if I was in an approved location. They refused to tell me if I was safe." On the other hand, Harry says, the injustice of the trip helped him understand he needed to be more vocal and engaged in fighting the registry. Overall, he says, it "sucked," but it "inspired me and made me want me to be someone more vocal."

Harry says his greatest fear, now that he's achieved financial success, is that he'll be fired if he angers the wrong person. He's heard of registrants being fired after foes post their pictures on social media. Harry elaborates, "If I lose my job, it's not me that gets hurt, it's my kids. They shouldn't be impacted because of my past. That's what scares me the most."

He is respected in his community and has been asked to join the board of their county fair and to be a volunteer coach in a youth soccer league his company sponsors. Of course, he says, he declines, and it reminds him "that I'm successful but still not successful. My work is successful, but I can't be involved in my community, and that's what I want deep down. But the registry takes that possibility away." Another example he offers is when the fire chief suggested he become a volunteer firefighter. Harry had to turn it down, because he knew that the registry would pose too many challenges. "I had to pretend to him that I work too much and don't have time. He kept telling me that it's only a few shifts a month. But what if there's a call at a school? Or a daycare?"

Harry muses about the duality of being a well-respected member of the local business community and a registrant.

> I pay taxes, but I can't vote. I have a mark on my driver's license. When will this end? When can I take my family on a week-long vacation? Why do I have to tell the registry where I'm staying if I leave the state for my job? Living with the social stigma and the constant fear that I can lose it all. It just takes one person to ruin my life. I'm a video game nerd. If it wasn't for the registry, I'd probably be a cop. But I can't do that. I play a cop simulator game. People tell me I'd be a great cop.

Justine: The Only Ones Who Stayed with Me Were My Parents

Justine was arrested for her offense more than a decade ago, when she was in her early twenties. Her offense involved possession of illicit images of children. Initially sentenced just to supervision, she wound up serving three years in prison due to technical probation violations. She's been on the registry since her release four years ago.

> During treatment, I wanted to prove to them I'm not the person I thought I was. I did polygraphs showing I never touched or attempted to lure a child. That what I told them was true. But they still had this mentality that they thought I was guilty, but they just hadn't caught me yet. Eventually, I lost my composure and I abused alcohol to cope, and that's a violation. I got sick of being alone and I met up with people. They have to interview everyone you meet so that added another violation. So I was sent to prison for three years.
>
> Despite my circumstances, I tried to help people when I was in prison. I helped them get their GED, with computer literacy, and resumes. I met my fiancé in prison. They are applying for clemency. It's a long shot.
>
> I've realized that trying to push aside who I was led to my offense. Once I dealt with my issues, all my deviance disappeared. Now I can have healthy sexual relationships with others. I couldn't before that because I

wasn't dealing with my issues and coping in unhealthy ways that led to bad decisions.

I was a music teacher. I lost that job. I'm a college graduate. Part of the problem is companies don't want to be liable if there is a problem. Right now, I'm a full-time graduate student. I don't deal with lots of people. I lay low. I also do administrative work for a family business. I avoid putting myself in situations where I'll get rejected.

When I first went back to school, I went to a community college and I felt like things were getting normal. I started taking classes and participating in the band, and then they pulled the rug out from under me. I reported myself to the campus police, as required. After a couple of weeks, they told me that at least one person in each of my classes was seventeen, so I couldn't be on campus. They said being around minors was a violation of my parole. I was frustrated because my probation officer told me he wanted me to go to school.

The school was worried about someone blogging about me or going public. Like some article that says, "are they really allowing 'sex offenders' to be on campuses with minors?" That was really devastating to me. I wanted to be in the band. That was important to me. And, of course, things like this all of defeat the purpose of helping me reenter society.

Everyone who commits a sex offense is viewed the same. Even if you downloaded a bunch of things indiscriminately. Someone who is nineteen or twenty and goes on the registry has to still deal with the consequences twenty years later. Even though their sexual template would have been modified by sexual maturation alone.

Myths have so much power about deciding where you can live, work, or go to school. After my arrest, I got the unspoken message that people didn't want to be near me. The only ones who stayed with me were my parents. My siblings have children. I was embarrassed, and I withdrew. I didn't want to have awkward conversations with my friends. My probation officer kept accusing my parents of "enabling me" when they just defended me and tried to get them to see my humanity. But the officer saw this as me trying to manipulate my parents. I told them to stop talking to my officer because it just hurt me.

My best friend stuck with me until I went back to prison. The probation officer treated her like a criminal too. When I was arrested, they tried to find anything on me. They went through my friend's stuff also. She left and changed her phone number. I never saw her again.

I've developed social anxiety from this. I have been trying to reenter the community. I haven't tried in-person volunteering yet. I'm not sure of the rules. They might not want registrants there. I know I'm fortunate to have a good family and a safety net.

I was arrested in another state. To move here, I had to do an interstate compact. In order do that, I had to complete treatment there and pass their polygraphs. I did that, and I showed them I was honest. Then I got to here, where they had me start over. They wanted me to do all this to get here, and then I had to start over.

I was shattered when I saw a community notification postcard that put me at the highest risk level. They used the wrong test for my risk factors for me, and it inflated my score. I am supposed to be at low risk. When I saw the postcard, and it said to "watch out" for me, I lost it. I eventually had to get legal help to change it, but at that point, it was too late, and the cat was out of the bag.

Once, during a polygraph, I broke down and falsely confessed. They wanted anything to put me away because I said "it's possible" I could have come in contact with a minor. I was just saying that to try to pass the polygraph. So I ended up telling them what they wanted to hear. They say if you keep failing, they won't work with you. It's funny because this past week, we talked about false confessions in my psychology class, and I was floored because I did that.

Brett: Paying So Your Neighbors Harass You

Brett is white, in his forties, and has a management position in the oil and gas industry. He has been on the registry for more than a decade. Brett says he was arrested in a sting, after chatting online with an adult posing as a minor; he says it was an adults-only website, and he was not seeking a minor. He moves frequently for work, and when he does, he has to pay for the cost of postcards that are sent by police to his new neighbors, as well as for a newspaper ad with his personal details and advertising his new address. The cost of postcards differs, he says, depending on the population of where he moves; generally, he says, the postcards cost him around $800. The newspaper ads are usually under $200.

Brett has children, whom he believes suffer because of the registry rules. One child was recently inducted into a national honor society, and Brett requested permission to attend. The event was after school hours, and only for the inductees and their families. Brett was hopeful he'd get permission, but he was denied. He is also unable to attend their sporting events. Brett tells me his inability to be there for his children causes him terrible guilt. He isn't sure how much they know about his offense or why he can't participate fully in their lives.

Brett tells me it's difficult to explain the extent to which the registry causes him fear, anxiety, and "constant worry." He says that there are many things he must do that are simple for others, such as signing up for a new email address or getting a free phone from his employer.

If I do these things, I have to go and update my information at the registry office. If my car needs to be repaired, I have to go and register the loaner car. It takes at least an hour, and that's in addition to my required quarterly visits. The thing is that you aren't a regular citizen any longer.

The laws, he says, are just totally "crazy" and make little sense. For instance, when he was first arrested, he had to move out of the home he shared with his wife and kids because of residency rules. He had to move to "the worst motel you've ever seen, thirty minutes from our house." He drove back and forth daily and spent time as much time as he wanted at their home, but then return to sleep at the motel. What's "crazy," he says, is that his crime involved making an arrangement to travel an hour to meet the adult posing as a minor online; the distance shows that the criterion of proximity inherent in residency rules is irrelevant here. "Any rational person," he says, "would see these laws make no sense." Brett is now divorced. "My wife couldn't deal with the registry. It was easier for her to leave me than deal with the shame and the stigma. She told me that she doesn't think I should be on the registry and thinks I just made a poor decision."

While Brett tried to take advantage of his mandated group treatment, he also felt it was "a money-collection exercise." He tells me that many sessions involved taking attendance, processing payments, and then watching the show *Intervention*. The lectures and group discussions were often just a small portion of the treatment, which Brett found frustrating. He considers himself a "sex addict" and has found twelve-step recovery programs far more helpful to him than the state-mandated treatment. Brett speaks openly about how he's overcome the issues that led to his arrest and the role of recovery in his personal development:

> When I went to the recovery meeting I learned about the "bubble." It was like getting high alone. I didn't want to deal with anyone else. I got into that state with porn or [sexual] chatting with other people. All I can say is that I just felt like I was in an altered state and made a poor decision. I wasn't looking for underage person. I was really just trying to deal with my own hurts. It wasn't a healthy outlet. I'll admit that. I don't feel that I was a threat to anyone, and I still don't. I think if you met me, you'd think I'm a normal guy. I don't come across as a creepy dude driving a van, handing out candy. There are so many misconceptions. If I had my druthers, I'd like to sit down with the lawmakers. I know I made a mistake. But should I have to pay forever? There is no way this isn't punishment.

Brett is a practicing Christian, and the church is a big part of his life. It was hard, he says, when his church asked him to leave. "I wasn't allowed in the wing with the daycare, and I was always escorted anyplace in the church. Nothing happened at the church. The minister knew about me.

But I was still kicked out." He's found another church that has accepted him. Before attending services there, he reached out and told the minister about his charge. The minister, he says, was very curious about the registry. He soon learned that the minister knows someone with a sex-offense conviction, and he's hoping Brett can help that person navigate the registry.

Brett tells me his company is based outside of the United States, and his boss lives in Europe. He says he disclosed to his boss about his charge, his requirements, and the reason for his inability to travel internationally. "He was extremely sympathetic to me. He thought this was insane. He just focuses on the fact that I do a good job. He just cares that I get the work done." If Brett travels within the United States for more than a week, he is required to report this to his local registry office. "I never leave for more than seven days. I don't like to tell people where I'm going, and I'm not going to do that. I completed my penance."

Evan: The Registry Is an Excuse to Hate

Evan is white, and his offense took place ten years ago. He was sentenced to one year of probation and lifetime registration.

> My objection is that the registry is so public. I get lots of scam calls because my phone number is right there.
>
> I went to rehab after my offense. It helps me understand what I did and the harm I caused. I will never do that again. The program makes you aware of your offense and the harm caused. I don't have an addiction. I was a project engineer. I stopped working because I had a transplant. I'm on disability.
>
> After my arrest, I was going to get a job as a consultant until they found out I was on the registry. At a different company. What I did [professionally] is something very few people did. I understand the product, and I improved their yields. But they [all] lost interest [once it got out that I'm on the registry].
>
> I volunteered at a vineyard. I told the owner I was on the registry. He was fine with it until another employee found out, and that was that. It carries a very negative thing. I live with my sister. I grew up in this neighborhood. I get along with everyone. There is one neighbor that has a real problem with me being here. He's tried to make stuff up. The cops warned him to stop bothering me. I had to replace the windshield of my truck. Got hit with a rock. I'm not positive, but it was probably due to the registry.
>
> The cops come by every six months and sit there and watch my house for like thirty minutes. They go and hang out by other registrants too. People can get pretty mean.

I did volunteer work repairing tools for four years. Stuff wears out. It wasn't the owner, but some board members were concerned, I believe. They decided to [no longer] use me. Never said why.

I was married when I was arrested. Divorced now. We are still good friends. I help her when I can. And vice versa. I go [to lots of doctor appointments]. Once you get a transplant, it's constant monitoring.

I am a vet also. The VA helps me. I don't go to the base. The base can deny access if you have a felony. It's up to the gatekeeper. It's now more likely that those on the registry are denied.

I was trained to help with antipersonnel mines. Even to this day, they are still going off. Then I became a mechanic. I just have a real knack for anything mechanical or electrical. I also had my own business repairing foreign cars. Then I went back to school and learned electronics. Got a job and moved up. Went all over doing things. Even went to Helsinki.

The registry is an excuse to hate those on it. You can turn on your computer and go and look at all of us and the maps and see where we are. There are people that do this. They drive by, and there are places that try to do their own private stings. They'll set up a van with cameras and try to catch people. So you are a constant target from the public and the police.

To get a job, some of the guys I know from the rehab, one guy was working for a cable company for many years. Then the cable company was bought by a larger company. He was fired when they went through the employees just because he is on the registry. He didn't want to sue. Most places are like that; some aren't. Some places don't care. But they tend to be factories. If I wanted to work for [in my field] again I just couldn't. I couldn't get clearance. Anything with the federal government is pretty hard.

They need volunteers to plant trees because of fires. I can't do that. It says right on the application that I can't show up if I'm on the registry. Legislators want to get their names on the books.

It is unconstitutional. Continuous punishment. It doesn't stop. "Sex offenders" have the lowest recidivism rates out of all the groups. Doesn't make any sense. Other than to be mean. Because you don't like what someone did.

My neighbor told me I'm on [our neighborhood social media app]. Some lady came and took my picture and posted it. That's illegal. It's constant. I can't get on the site to get it taken down. I'm quiet. I help the neighbors.

You can't step foot on school grounds even to volunteer to help with food distribution that takes place in high school parking lots. I have a truck. I wanted to help distribute food. You have to pass a background check to help rid the coast of ice plants; it's an invasive species. Volunteers get-together to go and clean up certain beaches, but they don't want us.

(From a postinterview email):

There are groups and companies that use information provided on the public registration site to enhance their own websites. This really adds to

> the problem. [One sends] out notifications to the neighborhood around where the registrant has moved. I received an email about myself when I moved here.

Proximity Restrictions

Other formal rules for those on registries include proximity laws, which encompass rules related to certain places where registrants cannot visit or enter. The State of Missouri has measures that include being prohibited from being within five hundred feet of a childcare facility, school, public park, swimming pool, athletic complex, museum, or nature center (Missouri Revised Statutes § 566.150, 2023).

Those I interviewed, particularly those with children, suffered daily from the laws that ban their very presence from various places. I was struck by the stories of those I interviewed who lived with spouses and children under eighteen. The proximity restrictions primarily resulted in their inability to fully support their loved ones. One man told me that he can't help his wife take his children to or from school, swimming, or to playgrounds or parks, and they don't understand why. They are part of a traditional, religious community with frequent communal family events. Registry laws in his state ban him from many of them. His kids suffer because when they attend these gatherings, because it's apparent, he says, that "Dad's not there."

Tom: Everything Is Different Now

Tom is white and in his forties. He committed his offense nearly a decade ago and spent a year in prison. His crime is listed on the public registry as "sexual exploitation of a minor," but the statute code specifies that the charge was possession of illicit images of children. Tom has a graduate degree in the sciences and worked in information technology prior to his arrest. Since his arrest, he's been unemployed, he says, because the registry makes it impossible for him to work in his field. He is fortunate to have the resources to support himself from trust fund income and investments made prior to prison.

Tom speaks about his life in terms of before and after his arrest. He still lives in the small city where he was raised, near his wealthy and socially prominent family. Before his arrest, he was financially and professionally successful, had an active social life, and was usually in a romantic relationship. He had many friends from childhood and college and enjoyed spending time with them in local bars, restaurants, and clubs. His social circle, he tells me, was made up of other successful people like himself, with strong community ties and from well-connected families.

Today, Tom describes his life today as "basically isolated." He says he has lost all interest in socializing and pursuing relationships. His friends have mostly stood by him, but many have since "faded away." Tom says it was largely his own decision to push them off. He partly attributes his crime to excessive drinking, in part to avoid dealing with his own childhood traumas, so he no longer "parties" or socializes in the same ways. Like others I've interviewed, he views the one quasipositive outcome of his arrest as a form of "waking up" and finally addressing personal problems he'd long repressed. Instead of dealing with long-standing emotional issues in therapy or productive ways, Tom says he socialized and used substances in reckless ways to cope with deep personal issues. In turn, Tom believes, this contributed to bad decision-making and his crime.

The proximity restrictions in his state forbid those on the registry to approach places "children congregate." This contributes to his isolation. While the residency restrictions are clear (he must live one thousand feet from schools), the proximity rules are "ambiguous" and causes him profound anxiety. According to Tom, police give him different answers when he asks about where he's allowed to go, and he is always "on edge" that he could be arrested because he's in the wrong place. One officer told him a nearby lake area was off-limits, and another told him it wasn't, and when he tries to research the law or consult attorneys, he can't find a definitive answer. "Parole officers and police abuse their power. If they want, they can arrest me and say I'm breaking the law, and there's nothing I can do. It's always at the back of my mind. I'm constantly worried." Infractions can result in a potential five-year prison sentence. When he was first released from prison, Tom was so fearful he'd go to the wrong place and get sent back to prison that he mostly stayed home and ordered food in. Routinely, he has nightmares "that I'll get arrested because I am accidentally somewhere I am not supposed to be. Or someone finds out I'm on the registry and alleges that I was somewhere I wasn't supposed to be and reports me to police."

The presence restrictions also create barriers to forming romantic and other relationships. Tom says there was a woman with whom he was getting romantically involved, but it fizzled after she grew frustrated with his restrictions.

> She often had company social events to attend. She really wanted me to go to this holiday party, but it was at a community swimming club, but I can't be near pools. She also wanted me to go with her to museums, zoos, and

> the state fair. They are all places I can't go. This stunted any type of serious relationship we could form because most of the things she liked to do, I couldn't do with her. We still stay in touch, but I always think about what could have been. These insane laws make it impossible for me build new social or romantic relationships.

In prison, Tom says he met a few people on the registry with whom he's remained friends, and he is starting to meet others as he becomes more politically involved in advocacy for those with sex-offense convictions. He misses, however, "spontaneous and organic friendships from people I meet when I go out somewhere or in the neighborhood. I am always nice to people I meet, but I keep everyone at arm's length because I know once they find out I'm on the registry, they'll probably reject me."

The realization of the true impact of his life on the registry really hit him after he'd been home from prison for about a year. Christmas, he says, was always his favorite time of year, filled with only positive associations, and it was a meaningful holiday for his close-knit family. He was home alone when he opened his door after hearing a knock to see a large group of children singing Christmas carols. Even though Tom is permitted to be around children and it wasn't a violation of his parole conditions, he immediately began to panic and imagine his neighbors or the adult chaperones reporting him for doing something inappropriate. "I didn't freak out when they were there. I'm allowed to be around kids. I just couldn't process what was happening, and so I just made it clear I didn't want to hear them, and I closed the door as fast as possible." After they left, Tom was shaking uncontrollably and unable to calm down, and even talking about the memory is clearly painful for him. "I realized in that moment everything was different. Christmas wasn't all happy and good times. My life was totally changed. Nothing would ever be the same as before."

The shift from "before," when one felt part of a community, to "after," when one feels like an outcast, is an experience many interviewees mention. Tom wants to me understand that it's particularly acute in his case because he's "fallen so far." He realizes this sentiment is common to those in his situation, but he had been unaware of the extent to which his privilege informed his confidence, personality, and way of interacting with the world. Today, he says, he feels that he's "no longer human. Like I don't even exist. When I heard those carolers, I realized that everything from before was gone. All my positive memories of childhood, high school, and college are gone or grotesquely warped. The person I see in pictures from the past is dead."

During our interview, Tom insists he's never experienced harassment, and he tells me repeatedly how he's "lucky" and "better off" than many others. In prison, Tom met people on the registry in far worse situations, especially financially, and it's important to him that I know he understands his luck in terms of the support he continues to receive from his family and friends.

After our first video chat, we speak a few more times, and he sends me emails elaborating on his thoughts. He's close to his sister and feels guilty because his conviction has hurt her as well. Once, an ex-friend reported to his sister's neighbors that Tom, who occasionally visited his sister for dinner, was on the registry and a danger to children. His sister felt the need to move after the revelation. Tom says that he has many fears for his future, despite his financial comfort. He worries, for instance, what will happen if he ever requires full-time nursing care when he gets older or because of an accident. The nursing homes where he lives, he says, ban those on the registry, and he's heard about bedridden men in their nineties being denied care.

Tom tells me that the pandemic was a relief to him in some ways because he no longer needed excuses to stay inside all the time. He also found wearing masks comforting because it made him feel more anonymous and less likely to be recognized. Tom assures me he is not suicidal, but he occasionally fantasizes about how it would have been easier for himself and his family if he'd just taken his life when he was first arrested. "I often think if someone could hear my entire story, maybe they would be sympathetic toward me, but who would want to take all that time to hear what I have to say? Especially because it's all so taboo and sensitive and such a painful subject."

The Ambiguity Is the Point

Proximity restrictions have profound effects on the ability of registrants, like Tom, to reenter society. Forming relationships is prohibitive when one is banned from most locations one would normally go for social excursions. In addition, proximity restrictions are often vaguely worded, and few processes are in place to notify registrants when new strictures are introduced. Currently, there is a pending Florida proposal that would allow businesses to simply declare themselves "places children congregate," and at public hearings registrants expressed grave fears about how this would make it nearly impossible to figure out where they can and cannot be.

Like most sex-offense policies, proximity restrictions are driven by emotion and premised on myths about stranger danger and inevitable recidivism. There are decades of studies documenting how policies such as the public registry and residency restrictions have failed to decrease or prevent sex offenses, yet I was unable to locate any evaluations or assessments of the effectiveness of proximity laws. A recent study is one of the first efforts to quantify the extent and number of states with geographic restrictions that include not only residency but those governing presence, loitering, and entry (Navarro et al., 2022). The authors note that their research is an effort to study the "underdiscussed" and "less notable" of all geographic restrictions that "limit spatial interactions" for some with sex-offense convictions. The authors define presence restrictions as rules banning registrants from being present at all at certain places, whereas loitering laws dictate that they can't be present at certain places for "extended period[s]." Entry laws, which they note are more recent development, are those rules that ban registrants from entering certain places. They identify nineteen states with presence restrictions, fourteen with entry laws, and eighteen with loitering restrictions. As Tom points out, residency restrictions are clearly defined, whereas the other geographic laws are not. In fact, they echo exactly what Tom observed. They note, "broad terms like 'children regularly congregate' or 'community safety zone' are criticized for being intentionally vague by scholars [and] more frequently used in loitering, presence, and entry restrictions than residency restrictions" (p. 18). Not surprisingly, they also find that geographic restrictions resemble other provisions related to the registry in that they are only extended and broadened, and almost never repealed or rolled back.

Even more notably, Tom expressed that the lack of clarity on the proximity-restriction statutes enhance his anxiety that he will unintentionally violate them. His nightmares about being in the wrong place at the wrong time are echoed in a very literal sense by the findings of Navarro, Knudsen, and Richardson. In fact, the authors highlighted the same confusion Tom encountered when seeking guidance about the rules. They write:

> Our communications with registry managers indicated the discretion that other municipalities had with the imposition of geographic restrictions, which can differ from the state-level geographic restriction, varying in the year enacted, the proscribed distance, the offender specified, and the prohibited venues. These discussions also revealed that while the geographic restriction exists as a statute, they are discretionarily applied on a case-by-case basis, with probation and parole officers often named the final arbiters to identify the offenders subjected to these restrictions. (p. 18)

The "discretion" applied in the case of geographic restrictions highlight the extent to which these laws function only as punishment for the sake of punishment. If, for instance, those responsible for enforcing proximity laws viewed them as legitimate tools to prevent sex offenses and keep children safe, they would be applied in transparent, uniform, and consistent ways. Registrants like Tom recognize that they are applied randomly and loosely, at the whim of law enforcement, and this is reinforced by the vague language used in the statutes themselves. The only possible reason to support laws written and enforced in such sloppy and erratic ways is due to animus, as their only function is to create more fear, anxiety, and reason to punish those on registries.

Such patently outlandish laws only make sense if we recognize the animus that underlies them. In fact, lawmakers don't have to provide evidence these laws do anything positive for society. The public will support these efforts, no matter how expensive or farcical, if it's clear they can further punish those on registries.

So, Are You the Victim Here?

In a May 2022 hearing in Brevard County, Florida, commissioners heard county residents stand up to voice their opposition to a new proximity law. The county already has residency and proximity restrictions that make daily life a challenge, including rules that those on registries must stay one thousand feet from parks, playgrounds, day cares, and schools; the proposed update allows businesses to "self-certify" that they are "places where children congregate" (eLaws.us, 2006). Those opposing the new ordinance argued that there would be no way to possibly navigate how to stay one thousand feet from businesses that decide they are "place[s] children congregate," making them vulnerable to arrest and causing further isolation without any impact on public safety.

Those on the registry had to fight for the right to even attend the meeting and voice their opposition, as the commission hearings are located less than one thousand feet from a school. The men who testified were taxpayers and active in their communities and civic lives and were on the registry for many years without reoffending. Two identified themselves as veterans; one was wearing his naval flight suit. They each stood up and testified that they were upstanding citizens and had done their time and spoke movingly about how their role as husbands, fathers, veterans, and caregivers. After the first spoke, a sneering commissioner chided their audacity to speak up. He could not contain his contempt for the men, sarcastically asking one, “So, are you the victim here?” Another testified that the restrictions make it so he cannot properly care for his disabled, wheelchair-bound partner. His partner then testified that she needs twenty-four hour constant care, and she’s constantly terrified her partner will be unable to assist her if he’s arrested for mistakenly entering an off-limits business or accompanying her to the hospital. The commissioner did not respond.

This proposed law in Florida, allowing businesses to “self-certify” they are “places children congregate,” is the natural outcome of these absurd policies. In the case of playgrounds or pools, registrants in locales with presence restrictions can at least know they are off-limits. If, say, a jewelry store “self-certifies” this way, how can registrants even know that they are banned from being there? It’s unlikely that local governments will send registrants updates whenever a business is added to the list, so the onus will be on the registrant to figure out constantly what places are off-limits.

The Price of Fighting Back

Derek Logue is among the most outspoken and provocative antiregistry activists. He’s white; in his midforties; and his offense, listed as “sexual contact with a minor,” happened more than twenty years ago. Derek is well known for his advocacy, largely because of several web pages featuring reams of registry resources and information. He also sends newsletters to those currently incarcerated, providing information about registry realities after prison. When I first interviewed Derek in 2014, he was angry about the unjustness of sex-offense laws and frustrated by the passivity and cowardice he sees in the work done by formal antiregistry organizations. He’s still angry about both issues today but is slightly calmer and more introspective.

Derek’s dedication to bold and grassroots activism is impressive, but he’s paid a heavy personal price for his confrontational tactics. Through his bluntness and recourse to expletives, Derek antagonizes those he sees responsible for constructing and expanding registries. Despite his vulnerability, Derek aggressively calls out powerful foes, including Florida lobbyist and staunch registry proponents Ron Book and his daughter Lauren. A few years ago, Derek made disparaging comments about the Books and publicly protested their proregistry agenda. Derek says these acts led to costly legal entanglements, including a restraining order and false arrest for theft. The restraining order was ultimately overturned, with a judge ruling that Derek was within his rights to advocate for sex-offense law reform, even if it’s an unpopular position. In the decision, the court noted,

"True, one side of this debate has far greater public support than the other, but that does not make the Respondent's advocacy illegitimate," and compared Derek's right to engage in antiregistry advocacy to the "free trade in ideas" of Justice Oliver Wendell Holmes (*Logue v. Book*, 2020).

The theft charges were also dismissed, but only after twenty-four days in jail and a drawn-out court case leading to his financial ruin. The case dragged on, and Derek says, "I lost everything." After his arrest, a lawyer suggested his girlfriend put up their car for collateral. "We are dirt poor! No one understands. We have no car. The lawyer said I needed $4,500. I live off $9,000 a year. The lawyer told me to borrow it. Who the hell would give that to me?" The case infuriates Derek, but he has few regrets. "Sometimes, saying mean things is necessary."

Derek, despite his bluster and anger about his arrest, is deeply committed to his work, acknowledging, "It's about helping people." He's pleased that his prison newsletter now reaches thousands of people. He mails out over twelve hundred newsletters at a time, and recipients pass them to others after reading. His self-published registry resource manual, *Life on the List*, is updated regularly and shared widely via prison networks and libraries.

While Derek is often consulted by registrants for housing, employment, and legal advice, he too struggles with these issues.

> A friend owns this house so that's the only reason we have a place to live. Even if I had money no one will rent to me. This one guy, a slumlord, told me when I applied to rent from him, "Not just no, but *hell no*." I cussed him out and told him he's a fucking slumlord and he rents to drug addicts and hookers, and I'd pay rent on time and be a good dependable renter so fuck you. I hung up on him. Housing prices hurt registrants very hard. There are no protections for us. I can't get section-eight housing because I'm a lifetime registrant. Smaller businesses that offer rental assistance also reject me.

I ask him if he thinks things are growing worse. The county commissioner who belittled registrants at the Brevard, Florida, county hearing testifying against new proximity laws, "is quite normal" and didn't surprise Derek. "Sex-offender laws are bipartisan, and it's getting worse. QAanon didn't help. It has brought myths [about government-run sex-trafficking rings] into the mainstream."

He's frustrated that few on the registry are willing to publicly challenge their oppression. He's organized several demonstrations, but generally only a few people show up. He believes the organized antiregistry nonprofits are moderate, ineffective, and fearful of engaging in the radical activism required to prompt genuine change. "They just want to do lawsuits. But we can't worry about lawsuits and lawmakers. They aren't going to help us. Why do we want to work with people who want us dead? We shouldn't worry about hurting their feelings. Nothing we are going to say will ever change their minds." Derek may be easily riled and use abrasive and colorful language at times, often pushing the bounds of free speech, but his actions and protests have always been nonviolent and peaceful.

He also blames victim-rights advocates for much of the registry regime. "People think in terms of white versus black, and good versus evil. In court, you are supposed to look at the action and not at how the action made the victims feel." He resents that victim advocates are never forced to defend their positions, yet he is summarily dismissed because he is on the registry. "The victim advocates don't want to work with us. They caused this. They think we have hundreds of victims, we're incurable, and we can't stop reoffending. They have all the power."

Last year, Derek was quoted in the media about his opposition to the term "sex offender" and why he believes it's dehumanizing. He faced ruthless mockery for this stance on right-wing websites. "The internet makes it easy to say things about people. You can call me nasty, vile things. I had to develop a thick skin. I have nothing to fear." Insults do not bother Derek, but some things get to him, such as recently learning about registrants being banned from gaming communities.

> Last night, I couldn't sleep. Someone told me they were banned from a Magic the Gathering tournament. Apparently, they now have a "zero-tolerance policy for sex offenders." So do other games like that. What if I enter and I win a tournament? Will they take my prizes back? I'd fight it. It's just depressing to have to constantly give people bad news and constantly being banned from more and more things. Now, they even out people [for being on the registry] at places like anime conventions. I'm viewed as a misogynist and racist because I'm a registrant. We are now banned even in "nerd culture!" Someone told me that he bought the Oculus [a virtual reality headset]. You need Facebook with the device, but he's banned from Facebook. He bought the device, and he can't play it? I told him to sue them for selling a defective product!

One of the most hurtful experiences for him was being asked to leave a museum. He was recognized by security and informed he needed "an escort" if he wished to stay. "I told them I was a grown man and didn't need a babysitter. So I left in disgust. I wrote a letter and complained and never got a response. I never went back." He also carries resentment about being rejected for a position at Target years earlier. "That ticked me off because the hiring person really wanted me. They even drug tested me. I still remember the wording of the corporate rejection letter."

He fantasizes about registrants getting together and "pooling their resources" to purchase a remote town, "with buildings and a water tower. Just the basics. We can start some businesses. We proved during COVID-19 going to work isn't needed. We just have to change with the times and use it to our advantage. I'm trying to think of an idea. We can make things and sell them online. So we can live in isolated places. Like where I am. There is nothing where I live now but corn and cows."

Last year, Derek was the target of "a really specific" death threat. "Someone created an entire website dedicated to me. I have no clue who did this." Someone recommended a police officer they claimed "was fair," and Derek reached out to him to file a report. The purportedly "fair" officer, Derek says, "told me that my online activism brings it upon myself. I was upset. I told the motherfucker he has no right to tell me I deserve this just because I exercise my first amendment right to free speech!"

Derek continues to return to the fallout from his wrongful arrest and unjust restraining order. While the cases were pending, he couldn't speak out about his innocence or his outrage about the false allegations. For him, being forced to stay silent is possibly the worst sanction. "I couldn't say so many things. Like the fact that I was innocent. I can now finally tell my story." Despite his mistrust of the criminal-legal system, his victory makes him reluctantly smile. "I was surprised when the courts ruled in my favor in Florida. They never rule in our favor."

William: Second-Class Student

William is in his midforties. He's Black, and his offense, involving an underage nonstranger, took place when he was in his early twenties. He's been on the registry for about two decades. When I met William, at an antiregistry panel discussion, he told me he'd been trying to earn a college degree for years. William gave an often funny, yet painful account to an audience of lawyers and advocates about his fruitless efforts to attend college after he'd served his time, completed probation, and spent two decades working in demanding and high-responsibility construction jobs.

Each time he enrolled in college, he told us, an administrator eventually called him out of class before the end of the semester to inform him he had to leave the school due to safety concerns. William said this happened at multiple institutions, including after he'd finished most of the semester. Sometimes they said it was because there was a day care center on campus or that there were students under eighteen in the class or on campus, and sometimes they wouldn't give much of a reason aside from the fact that he was on the registry.

Finally, after years of trying, he was able to enroll in a four-year institution. He pays full tuition and attends mostly evening classes after working long days in construction. His registry web page lists his home address, his work address, and the address of the college. Even though his offense took place more than twenty years ago and he's never reoffended, he is subject to special restrictions. He shared the conditions with me, which include completing special Title IX and sexual-harassment training; meeting each semester with a representative to review his schedule; agreeing to enter and exit the college via one specific location; and acknowledging his prohibition from using the pool, locker rooms, gym, and other specialized areas without special permission. Additionally, his ID card and photo are shared with an on-campus childhood center. He must sign a special document that confirms he'll adhere to these guidelines, and the public safety director receives a copy.

William receives no tuition break, even though he is forced to use only one entrance and forbidden access to the amenities freely available to other students. At one point, the school said they would allow him to pay tuition and earn a degree, but he'd have to take only online courses. Going to college has been a dream for William, and he didn't want to take classes remotely. While William is happy to have the opportunity to take classes in person and work toward a degree, he must endure humiliating ordeals and second-class treatment despite more than twenty years of following laws, supporting his family, and maintaining steady employment.

CHAPTER FIVE

Alive but Not Alive

Civil and Social Death

In "'The Sleeping Army': Necropolitics and the Collateral Consequences of Being a Sex Offender," criminologists Ethan Higgins and Shawn Rolfe (2016) examine ways that those on registries live and resist without power or status. The authors surveyed registrants about their lives and the collateral consequences of having a sex-offense conviction. They applied a "necropolitical framework" to better understand their experiences and responses to life as societal outcasts.

Higgins and Rolfe explain that necropolitics is a theoretical concept that sees highly disenfranchised and marginalized populations as living a kind of "death in life" (pp. 1–2). Their survey respondents, similar to those I interviewed, often spoke, directly and indirectly, of being in a state of being only half-free or half-alive. They write, "Social exclusion removes registered sex offenders from finding new life at all, relegating them to a constant experience of death" (p. 6). They ultimately conclude that living with a sex-offense conviction leads to the experience of living in "death worlds," where one is excluded from all civic and social institutions and forced to suffer in silence. The only way to emerge from a "death in life" existence is though actual, physical death (pp. 13–14).

The concept of necropolitics is most often applied to displaced groups such as climate refugees and innocent victims of war, famine, or corrupt governments. Yet Higgins and Rolfe demonstrate how it can also apply to those experiencing life on the registry. In both instances, the emotional and psychological impact is the same. They share the experience of living in the world as a type of collateral damage, with the horror of awareness that greater society is indifferent to your life or your death.

Necropolitics, thus, offers one way to understand the experiences of living on a registry, in that one is living and not technically behind bars but also not truly free nor viewed as fully human. One possible critique of applying this concept to registrants is that groups such as migrants escaping war and starvation are considered both innocent and victims. There is generally abstract sympathy for the "collateral damage" of those displaced by war and famine, even if society may, ultimately, do little to help. Similarly, the public also views those under political repression, for instance, as fully deserving of rights and personal autonomy and entitled to rise and challenge their oppressors.

For registrants, there is no such sympathy or understanding, even abstractly or theoretically. They are viewed as guilty and implicitly deserving of all forms of punishment, consequence, and oppression. They have brought this on themselves, and so those on registries are effectively ineligible for liberationist theories that recognize the *right* of the oppressed to revolt and challenge their status. Jean-Paul Sartre, for instance, argues that those living under colonization will inevitably revolt because "when a people has no choice but how it will die; when a people has received from its oppressors only the gift of despair, what does it have to lose?" (Memmi, 1974, p. 25). This formulation, however, assumes the virtue, goodness, and rights due to those viewed as innocent victims of political oppression and corruption. In other words, those on registries are not viewed to be entitled to advocate for their own human and civil rights, as are other mistreated or excessively punished groups. Further, suggestions that endless vengence may result in revolt and anger (or reoffense), as well as hamper efforts to successfully reenter society and change, feeds into stereotypes about their innate dangerousness.

Anthropologist Roger Lancaster has, thus, applied the "social death" concept to the specific and intensified postincarceration public shaming as a "sex offender." Lancaster writes in a *New York Times* essay that the surveillance and social banishment of the registry "have relegated a growing number of people to the logic of 'social death,' a term introduced by the sociologist Orlando Patterson, in the context of slavery, to describe permanent dishonor and exclusion from the wider moral community [and the] creation of a pariah class of unemployable, uprooted criminal outcasts" (2011b, p. 6).

"Civil death" and "social death" are related concepts, which, both implicitly and, at times, explicitly, view those with criminal convictions as undeserving of civil and legal rights. While this concept is often considered in the context of the incarcerated, particularly those with life sentences, it's also viewed in the context of the array of postincarceration collateral consequences. Indeed, in "Captive Afterlives in an Age of Mass Conviction," her ethnographic analysis of a woman convicted of a nonsexual offense searching for work, anthropologist Melissa Burch (2019) details the extent to which technology and surveillance sustain post-prison experiences of captivity and confinement. Burch characterizes employers who have access to the legal records of all applicants as the equivalent of wardens. Failing to hire applicants based on criminal histories creates a permanent form of containment and captivity when they are, as is the woman in Burch's case study, denied work based on "presumed riskiness." Burch writes, "The feeling of being held captive resonates not only with the imprisoned, but also with those who have been released." Employers and landlords, and, in the case of those on registries, everyone with an internet connection, spread, "captivity's reach to people and places with no formal connection to the criminal punishment system . . . through widespread public access to legal records" (p. 11).

In fact, Burch has started a project called "Afterlives of Conviction," where she and other social scientists utilize ethnographic methods to document the "human impact of criminal conviction," with one emphasis on the consequences of background checks (2021). Clearly, those on registries are even more profoundly and pervasively subject to this permanent form of what Burch refers to "preventative risk management," as the entire public is deputized to act as wardens, rather than only those with the power to conduct background checks.

Colin Dayan, in her book *The Law Is a White Dog: How Legal Rituals Make and Unmake Persons*, details how laws and regulations can result in "civil death." She compares how the experiences of those in slavery, those in "supermax" prisons, and those with criminal histories all experience similar losses of fundamental civil liberties and civil rights. Dayan argues that our tolerance and acceptance of excessive and brutal punishments for some leads to greater indifference to all forms of torture and repression. Punishing those we currently exclude with the equivalent of a "civil death" presents a growing danger to society. Dayan views how life is essentially taken away from those under total legal repression, noting that "in the sixth century, the Emperor Justinian declared in his Institutes: 'Slavery is death.' He knew that death takes many forms, including loss of status so extreme that life ceases to be politically relevant" (2011, p. 44).

Ryan: Did I Deserve to Lose My Kids Forever?

Some stories stick with me more than others. I spoke to one man who had an offense involving two counts of sexual contact with an underage relative. Before his offense, he'd been a great success, both professionally and personally. After his arrest, his spouse left him and ended all contact, completely cutting him out of the lives of their two then-young children. He received the harshest prison sentence possible for his offense and, aside from his parents, he was abandoned by his entire social network and extended family.

Ryan is white, in his midfifties, and has been on the registry for about five years. Ryan spoke openly about his offense, punishment, and how much he longs to see his children. "I was punished. I went to prison. But I haven't seen my kids, in any meaningful manner, for over a decade, and I've had no contact at all for the last seven years. Did I deserve to lose my kids forever? Even if I eventually see them, they will have grown up without knowing me, and I can't ever get that time back."

Prior to his conviction, Ryan had been a college and professional athlete, and a decorated military pilot with a technical graduate degree. Now he takes care of his aging parents full-time. It's hard for him to explain how he wound up in this position. "My only previous crimes were two minor traffic tickets over a thirty-five-year span. When I retired from the service, I had many friends and a family, and things were mostly good." In retrospect, Ryan says, he views his poor decision as probably associated with untreated depression, PTSD and multiple head injuries from his military service and athletic career. He has a disability rating of 80 percent from the VA. He said he began "self-medicating" with alcohol and not dealing with problems in his marriage. Ryan tells me that he knows now that he should have sought help, but at that time, he saw doing so as a sign of weakness and personal failure; he thought he could "right the ship" on his own.

The adversarial nature of the criminal-legal system was the biggest shock to Ryan. Before this, he told me, he had had total faith in the justice system and trusted law enforcement; he never imagined, "that prosecutors were capable of such misdirection and deception." He expressed deep remorse for his offense and wished that he had been able to engage in a restorative justice process. "I wanted to work it out. I didn't care about going to prison and accepting my punishment, but I wanted to save my family. I wanted to apologize and make things better, but I wasn't allowed to. Even though my crimes were relatively low-level and occurred over a year before any allegations, the state treated me like a violent rapist who just committed a savage assault. Once the state gets involved, the system just takes over." He eventually pled guilty, he says, without knowing all the collateral consequences. He had hoped his willingness to accept punishment and take accountability would save his family and help make amends for the harm he'd caused.

Ryan believes that his geopolitical location was a factor regarding the intense state involvement. At that time, he lived in a very conservative region known for its fundamentalist Christianity and aggressive law enforcement; "the pressure on my wife and relative was unrelenting." He tells me that after the charges were filed, he started receiving voicemail messages intended for his victim due to a bureaucratic mix-up. "I couldn't believe the messages that were being left on the phone. She had numerous advocates from the court, victim advocacy centers, and detectives reaching out to her, in addition to state-assigned therapists. It was clear by the words and tone of these messages that these people didn't give a damn about me, or her, or our family. It was clear that these people's only goal was to gain the maximum conviction possible." Ryan was fully cooperating with the court and pled guilty to the two allegations made against him, yet he is still perplexed about how his case, which involved no claims of assault or violence or sexual penetration and an adolescent, nonstranger victim, elicited such intense scrutiny and attention. His parents told me, "He messed up, but his offense was eighteen months before any accusations. At that time, there were no more occurrences, and he was slowly making self-improvement, but none of that seemed to matter. He told us what he did, and he told his wife. They went to therapy and were working through things. He confessed."

The worst part, he says, was at his sentencing, which was open to the public. His wife and relative read victim-impact statements, where they described, in detail, his destruction of their lives and how he had caused them brutal and permanent trauma. "The style of the statements didn't sound like anything they would write, but they were strangely familiar. I later realized, after talking to friends who attended the sentencing, that they were using similar wording as the victim in the Stanford rape case, which was a huge news story at the time." It would be the last time he would ever see them. His parents tell me that they were shocked at these claims, which portrayed their son as "a monster." They are aware that their son made a terrible mistake, but they had lived with his family and helped raise their grandchildren and, in their view, the picture the statements painted of him was nothing like what they had observed. They tell me he was awarded medals for his heroism during his military service and dedicated his life to his family. "Our son loved them, supported them financially, and took care of them. He was a good husband and father. But in those awful public statements, they weren't telling the truth about his character or what happened. We were utterly horrified at what they said."

Ryan's parents said what many told me about the victim-impact statements; they allow those harmed to vent without consequence, often with encouragement from the prosecution, while the accused must listen without the opportunity to challenge or respond. Victim-impact statements are not subject to cross-examination, as they are expressions of personal feelings and emotions, but they are designed to impact the judge's sentencing. Ryan remembers being reprimanded by a court officer for looking toward his ex-wife and relative during their statements. In the jurisdiction where he was prosecuted, the defendant cannot even look toward those making statements or even at the audience at sentencing.

It is obvious that Ryan is remorseful, but the process angers him. Ryan says he believed his then-wife was sincere when she promised to include him in their lives if he got treatment, so he quickly started pretrial therapy. Ryan actively participated in marital, group, and individual therapy sessions before any charges were filed. He was devastated and shocked, he says when his then-wife shared surreptitious recordings of sessions with the prosecutor, which promulgated the charges. Still, Ryan signed documents granting his wife nearly all their assets, full custody, and generous child support, believing her claims that she wanted him held accountable but not erased from their lives. Almost immediately after he signed, his ex-wife stopped all communication with him. He heard nothing from his family during his two years in prison nor anything in the years since. While still obliged to pay child support, he isn't permitted to initiate contact with them until his parole is over. While incarcerated, his parents visited their grandchildren, and his ex-wife forbid them to even mention Ryan's name in their presence. They never saw them again.

Another consequence for Ryan is being fully abandoned by those he'd considered lifelong friends and by his large extended family. He tried connecting with them after prison, but while a few were superficially friendly, it was obvious, he says, that they wanted nothing to do with him. Having a sex-offense conviction, Ryan says, makes him toxic to others. He stopped reaching out because he does not want to be a bother or make them feel guilty. He is aware that his very label of "sex offender" makes people uncomfortable. One friend sent him an expensive computer when he returned from prison, and they talked a few times. Ryan was unable to ever take the computer out of the box, he tells me, because he knew his friend felt guilty but didn't really want to continue communication. "I thanked him, and he never contacted me again. The computer was a gift to show both friendship while simultaneously cutting ties with me. It was a solution for 'the Ryan problem.'"

I receive an email from Ryan after our interview. "I'll be dead in less than twenty-five years, statistically speaking. After I'm gone, I'll only be remembered (if I'm remembered at all) as a pedophile, a child molester, a monster. A person that the world would be better without. How hard I've worked, the battles I've fought, the people I've helped; none of that will matter. I leave nothing behind but pain and regret."

Living in the Underworld: Unforgivable and Untouchable

Many I interviewed shared similar stories. Friends and family disappear. Another man told me that after his arrest, friends told him that they would "be there" for him, and the arrest had not changed anything. But, like Ryan, he said he could tell he was an embarrassment and a burden, and they soon drifted away.

In Ryan's case, it's possible his friends were so morally offended and disgusted by his label that they felt him unworthy of forgiveness. Another possibility: they felt that forgiving him would indicate they tolerated or even approved of sexual offending. Or perhaps they viewed his bad decision as evidence that the person they knew and loved no longer existed. Or maybe his mistake had revealed his true character, and he was never the person they thought they knew.

Even after punishment and accountability, he's apparently not someone they view as worthy of reentering their lives. Maybe they believe the myth that it is *inevitable* that he will reoffend, and it's merely a rational decision to keep their own children safe. Or perhaps it is because they believe that if they forgive him, he'll be even *more* likely to reoffend, as it will send the message that his offense was acceptable.

When I've tried to tell stories like Ryan's, I often hear from people that they really aren't concerned with the suffering of someone who has committed a sex offense. One person commented to me, half-jokingly, "These stories sound like a bunch of middle-class men whining." When I mentioned that I was distressed after talking to a grieving parent of someone on the registry who had taken their life, I was immediately asked, "Well, what was his crime?"

Sometimes, people will say that maybe people like Ryan shouldn't be on the registry or have to abide by residency restrictions, but that facing lifelong social ostracism is warranted. In debates about registries, people will frequently say outright that crimes such as murder warrant forgiveness and acceptance after punishment and accountability, but sexual crimes do not. And, whether said openly or not, this sentiment is reflected in our laws, as well as in our behaviors and attitudes.

One explanation for the inability to stand by those who commit sex offenses is that we view their decisions as deliberate and calculated and as indicators of their deepest selves. A person convicted of killing an innocent pedestrian while driving drunk or brutally beating a man for sleeping with his wife or shooting someone while seeking money for drugs in a botched robbery attempt is permitted back into society after punishment. Those who stand by them are not questioned or shunned. In a general sense, it's considered a good character to give second chances and forgive even those who make terrible mistakes. This is due to the widely accepted understanding that committing a crime may result from an irrational decision inconsistent with one's true self. Put simply, many religions and philosophies emphasize "loving the sinner, not the sin."

But it seems that in the case of sex offenses, the convicted are viewed solely and permanently by their bad decisions, and no mitigating factors are allowed. They are not seen as having reached personal low points when they make poor decisions, like others who break laws are. Rather, we view the sex offense as the product of a deliberate and highly calculated decision, rooted in the deepest recesses of a deviant core nature. People like Ryan are perceived as wholly undeserving of loyalty or support because the sexual offense subsumes the entirety of one's being.

David: Shoe Size Ten

David is white and in his early sixties. His offense took place thirty years ago and is listed on the registry as "indecency with a child by exposure." The registry ranks his risk as "moderate," and he is subject to lifetime registration; his shoe size and foot width are also noted. There are over a dozen pictures posted of his mug shot going back over twenty years, and one can see just how much older he now is. He has lost hair and fluctuated in weight. He's frowning and looks noticeably sad in each picture. When we first meet on video chat, he introduces himself and immediately asks me if I like his hair (he's bald) and reports that he's in a good mood because it's a sunny, warm day and he's often down when it's gloomy or cold.

David was sentenced to five years in prison for his initial offense. He's been sent back to prison twice since then for nonsexual violations: once for a "failure to register" and once for missing a mandated treatment session after being hospitalized for suicidal thoughts. According to David, his parole officer knew he was in an inpatient psychiatric facility, but "it didn't matter. Here, parole officers can do whatever they want. I've tried to sue them multiple times as a *pro se* defendant, but I'm treated like pond scum." David was released from his third prison stint almost a decade ago and has only a few remaining years of supervision.

Prior to his sex offense, he was convicted twice for theft; he describes his crimes as passing "hot checks." But, he says, "I'm basically a good person. I'm a good neighbor. I used to help people with mental disabilities find jobs and train them and teach them how to do jobs. It was rewarding but didn't pay much. Because of the registry, I can't do that now." David says that the registry sets him up for failure because it makes day-to-day life impossible. "They just punish us over and over and over. Punish, punish, punish."

David was married and has a daughter who is now in her early twenties. He says their relationship is "off and on," and he hasn't communicated with her in two years; he suspects his ex-wife and her family have discouraged their relationship. But, he adds, "She's the apple of my eye, and she's very precious to me, and she knows I'm not mean or abusive." He lost custody after his divorce and was permitted only "supervised visitation" during her childhood, he says, because "I'm a sex offender." Social workers assumed, David believes, that he was a "bad dad" because of his past. Though his daughter was born a decade after his offense, they told him they had concerns he was "grooming" her. "I was so angry when they told me that. Just such stupidity. I lost my daughter because of their assumptions. I'm very bitter."

During his third stint in prison, David started taking college classes. He's proud that he was able to earn a degree while incarcerated and with a 4.0 average. "I was in my fifties! But I decided to make the best of prison and a bad situation. I eventually even got a merit scholarship, which was awesome!" College, says David, helped him cope with the boredom and horrors of incarceration. It's clear David has spent a great deal of time considering his status on the registry and how and why he's perceived as a "monster." He tells me:

> I want people to see us as a human story, not a horror story. We are just normal people who've been convicted of a crime. Or, in my case, two or three! Our recidivism rates are low. These laws are all hysteria-based. People, even parole officers, think we are going to kidnap kids. They think our crimes will "escalate."

Finding housing was a huge challenge, and David says he's forced to live in a high-crime neighborhood. Parole denied many of the places David proposed, even when they met all the stringent five-hundred-foot residency restrictions. Additionally, he says that many nearby communities have "neighborhood-watch programs" that reject all registrants. He has no car and says that in his "rough" neighborhood, he's been repeatedly mugged but doesn't bother reporting to police because he knows they "won't care about someone on the registry." While taking walks or while riding public transportation, he says it's clear he's out of place. He tells me that local youth taunt him, calling him things like, "old-ass white dude."

David repeatedly voices the common concern of wanting to be viewed as "human." He wants people to know him for who he is and to understand that those on the registry are "good people" and "good neighbors" and just "want to get on with their lives." "Why can't we get a break? Why can't people be more open-minded? We aren't monsters. Why can't I have a normal life?"

David tells me he hopes I'll communicate to the world that registrants are more than their crimes. For example, he shares that he was recently interviewed by historians because his father witnessed the John F. Kennedy assassination. His oral history, he tells me, is now part of a segment on "childhood recollections" of the incident. He shares a picture with me of the interviewer putting on his microphone to prepare for the interview, and jokes, "This is my *60 Minutes* look!"

During our interview, David says he lives on social security and works from home "on the computer" for minimum wage as part of a government initiative to employ senior citizens. A few weeks after we speak, he emails me to tell me he was fired on his birthday. The program decided to assign him to work at a food pantry, but he was denied by parole after they determined the site was too close to a school.

He's now looking for work. His employment counselor told him not to disclose to potential employers that he has a sex-offense conviction. This, he says, highlights the horrors of his situation, because not disclosing your registry status to a potential employer is, in itself, a violation. David says he feels this type of contradictory guidance is a "set-up" to send him back to prison.

David shares some of the reasons why his sex-offense parole makes relationships almost impossible. His parole officer requires that if he goes on a date, he must provide him with her name, age, and employer. Anyone with children under eighteen is off-limits. Some of his treatment counselors require a meeting with the potential partner to confirm she is fully aware of all the details of his crime. "Forget having a 'normal' relationship. It's not going to happen. Speaking from experience, this destroys the relationship. So what does this accomplish? Absolutely nothing."

Some of his parole officers and treatment providers require that he report to them if he simply converses with a woman with children, even if she is not a potential dating partner. Other requirements are not just indignities but are also costly and time-consuming. David must renew his state ID yearly, as opposed to every eight years. It costs him about $60; it's not accessible by public transport, so he has to pay for a car service, and it takes an entire workday. "I have to be reminded that, gosh, darn it, we are going to punish you in every way we can."

Holidays and birthdays further remind David of his banished status. Each year, he must complete his sex-offense registration around his birthday. This year, he says, he registered and did nothing else; he received no cards nor did anyone acknowledge his birthday in some other way. Some of David's postinterview emails to me are dark and powerfully convey his feelings of aloneness. One Saturday after our interview, he writes:

> Weekends . . . are the worst. Filled with self-doubt, isolation, emptiness, and a sheer amount of yearning . . . to belong . . . to something, to anyone. It's filled with angst and trepidation. What can I do? Go to the movies? No. Go to a baseball game? Are you kidding? Risk the public safety of others? Sarcasm. Go to a museum? Absolutely not.
>
> Are you trying to reintegrate into society? That's not allowed. We want you to he kept away from society as much as possible, and then some. We'll teach you! You should have thought of that before you committed that crime. We'll punish you ad nauseam for as long as you live. Punish punish punish.—David (shoe size 10)

In another postinterview email, he writes that it's "beautiful and unseasonably cool" outside, but he's despondent because it reminds him of his isolation. It's a perfect day to enjoy the weather, he says, "unless you're me or practically [any] sex offender. I don't have a car, can't have a relationship with a woman, can't have old (or new) friends. Can't go anywhere without parole losing their minds. What's so bad is there is not one person that asks: How was your weekend? Nobody. Nada. Zilch. This is part of the isolation that I face every day."

I'm impressed that David still seems to find joy in life. As our initial interview wrapped up, he tells me he and his roommate have a cat that "keeps me entertained." Suddenly, he grows excited and asks if I mind if he does some "shameless self-promotion." His cat, he says, is "famous" on the internet and has a YouTube channel, and he suggests I watch it after we finish. "It blows my mind. Most of the viewers are in the United States, followed by Russia. It really blows my mind! I've never had a YouTube channel, and my parole officer doesn't mind. My cat is just always doing something funny and goofy. Like two or three times a day, he does something funny." He says that his videos have gotten over a quarter of a million views. David urges me again to watch one after our interview is complete. "You'll enjoy it, even if you aren't a fan of cats." He says he hopes that no one connects his channel to the registry, because he may lose all his subscribers.

After our video chat, he emails me: "Really enjoyed our interview this afternoon. I'm glad it wasn't a cat–astrophe. Get it?" A week later, on a Saturday, he writes, "Emily, I've got Cat-turday night fever!!!!!—David (shoe size 10)."

Broken

In *Just Mercy*, lawyer Bryan Stevenson argues that our willingness to accept brutal punishments without extending compassion to those like David indulges our own personal weaknesses and insecurities. Stevenson has dedicated his life to representing those believed by most to be irredeemable. His experience working with people abandoned by society, such as juveniles sentenced to life without parole, has taught him "how easily we condemn people in this country and the injustice we create when we allow fear, anger, and distance to shape the way we treat the most vulnerable among us" (2014, p. 14). Stevenson further writes,

> We are all broken by something. We have all hurt someone and have been hurt. We all share the condition of brokenness even if our brokenness is not equivalent. . . . Our brokenness is also the source of our common humanity, the basis for our shared search for comfort, meaning, and healing. Our shared vulnerability and imperfection nurtures and sustains our capacity for compassion. We have a choice. We can embrace our humanness, which means embracing our broken natures and the compassion that remains our best hope for healing. Or we can deny our brokenness, forswear compassion, and, as a result, deny our own humanity. (2014, p. 289)

Stevenson describes the frustration of being unable to help all those who need help in the context of the injustice, cruelty, and arbitrariness of the legal system. Yet he continues to engage in this often-monotonous work because he feels that he has no choice, since he is flawed in his own way. Our ability to accept injustice is, in fact, due to our unwillingness to accept that we too are "broken" and no different, at our core, than those branded "criminals" or "sex offenders." Stevenson ultimately argues for the need to recognize our own "brokenness" and the traits we share with those we deem lesser than ourselves. Treating others as less than human, without value, or undeserving of second chances, may make us feel righteous and important in the moment, but it doesn't allow us to fully experience what Stevenson calls our "reciprocal humanity" (2014, p. 290).

An anonymous piece of prose submitted to a public hearing held by the Connecticut Sentencing Commission addressing sex-offense law reform captures the same sentiments voiced by David.

Bob, your local sex offender.

"A worm's-eye view of despair"

Being a sex offender in Connecticut is a death sentence. You can't get a job or attend college. I tried to go to several community colleges but most school presidents will not allow you to take a class. I have not had a job since 2008. Even McDonald's will not hire a sex offender, while most landscaping companies have [unauthorized immigrants] working for them.

My mother and sister pay my rent and buy my food. I have gone to all the local agencies seeking help in finding a job. Always to leave with some inspiring conversation, but never with a job. They just refer you to some other agency for a handout.

You cannot get a pardon because that board will not even look at an application from a sex offender. I sit in my apartment or take long walks to pass the days. With no hope, what else can I do? What else could anyone do?

So I sit alone in the shadows and hide from the hate. Anyway, who cares about a sex offender? (Anonymously submitted to Connecticut Sentencing Commission, 2017)

Greg: I'm Hard-Headed So I Made It

Greg has been on the registry for twenty years. He's white and in his seventies and was sentenced to lifetime registration. He was a high school teacher prior to his arrest, and he was convicted of a sexual offense involving an underage relative. Afterward, he had many jobs, from retail to meat processing. Greg says he always worked "side jobs," even while teaching, to make extra money.

Greg has muscular dystrophy and needs a wheelchair due to resulting mobility issues. He wanted to keep working, but "the registry and my wheelchair forced me to stop." Finding work was often difficult after his arrest, but Greg is proud of his "work ethic" and that he's never received unemployment benefits.

His arrest left him feeling disgraced and embarrassed, but he didn't move away because he wanted to redeem himself in his community. "I messed up in that place, so I wanted to stay in that place," he tells me. He had built his own home before his arrest, and he lived there until a few years ago. Recently, he moved back in with his mother and sister to the rural farm where he grew up.

For Greg, the registry was hardest emotionally and mentally. He was able to work and support himself, but he was consumed with guilt for his actions. Greg explains, "I can't forgive myself. I can't give myself credit for being worthy of existing. Should I even live? I was in a community that didn't shun me. That was helpful. Then a church helped me, but then my probation officer said I couldn't go there. I never tried to go back to a church." During probation, Greg says he impressed his officer because he was even more "stringent" than was required. His probation officer and treatment providers "commended me but said it was unusual. I made it harder on myself." Greg constantly worried that he'd be accused of inappropriate things, so he avoided anything that would open him up to accusations of impropriety, even if they were allowed.

After his relative reported the incident, he divorced his then-wife. "Divorce was in the cards before the offense came to light. That was the icing on the cake." He shakes his head, "It gave my wife the best excuse to leave and file." He hasn't had any serious relationships since the registry. One failed, he says, because she lived too close to a school, and he wasn't able to visit. He tells me he has some "friends with benefits," and he "texts with some ladies almost every day." In general, he says, he's never had many friends and considers himself a "hermit." He has one local friend who comes over to get eggs from his chickens, and "we visit a bit."

The registry has impacted his ability to travel because he may have to report his plans to his registry office. "I don't want to give anyone any reason to question me, so I don't do that. I would like to take a week's trip here or there. I haven't left the state for over twenty years. Once or twice, maybe, before they started making us report travel. But even though I didn't have to report back then, I did, just in case."

His health has deteriorated in the last few years, and he worried about moving in with his mother and sister when he could no longer fully care for himself alone. "My mom and sister didn't care about having their house on the registry. But that's why I waited so long to come home. I couldn't even go upstairs in my own house because of the wheelchair, and they wanted me back for several years. But I didn't want their address on the registry." Greg says that at this point in his life, it won't make much of a difference if he gets off the registry, except that his family home wouldn't be listed.

Greg tells me that politics are very important to him. He was in a small political group that advocated for his state to secede from the United States. The group welcomed him even after he disclosed his registry status to them. According to Greg, he recruited people for his group and went to local meetings and conferences. "I even came in second in a race for county chair and got a third of the votes! Some people said I shouldn't have run because of my background, but I was so happy that so many people supported me. I figured I'd step out and make a stand because I believe in the cause, and I didn't want the registry to stop me for being involved." Greg grows very animated talking about his political involvement. He says the group eventually kicked him out for insufficient loyalty. "It wasn't because of the registry. I was too independent in the group fighting for state independence. Apparently, I said that I was more loyal to independence than to the *organization* fighting independence!" He was disappointed to find that the organization turned out to be "very authoritarian."

Greg tells me that he'd sought help prior to his offense. "If I had been honest and forthright, I wouldn't have offended. I reached out for help for years. To preachers. Counselors. It was about me not being able to vocalize. I couldn't talk about my feelings. A counselor told me, 'Don't give me details about your problems' because then they'd have to be a witness, and my words would be used against me in court." Greg expresses frustration, saying it's not right if "someone who wants to get help for doing something wrong can't get help, because if they do it'll go to the authorities. So you can't get fixed without going to the criminal justice system?"

Today, Greg says he spends much of his time taking care of goats on his farm. Even in his wheelchair, he says he can care for them, but he has to "steer clear of mudholes and tire tracks and sandy areas." When he gets stuck, he has to call his sister or someone to help dislodge him. He wants me to know that caring for goats "isn't easy." He says they get worms and need their hooves trimmed. He's proud of his family farm and explains, "animal husbandry is our heritage."

I ask Greg if he has any final thoughts about the registry he would like to share. He emphasizes that he feels blessed to always have had a home and the ability to support himself. The worst part about the registry is how it "stigmatizes" those on it and makes it impossible for them to "regather" and move on with their lives. He adds, "But I been fortunate and had support. Good Lord did it for me, so I can keep going. I'm hardheaded, so I made it."

Wyatt: Off the Registry but Still Scared

Wyatt was in his early twenties when he was court-martialed in the military for a sexual relationship with an underage nonstranger. During their relationship, his victim became pregnant and gave birth. He's white and has been on the registry for almost two decades. He wants me to know that his then-girlfriend was "mature," and "everyone" he knew, including several military colleagues who supported him, agreed that "she looked old for her age." He tells me he is still friends with a few of them today. After his sentence, he says, his victim "forgave" him, and they shared child custody.

After his release, Wyatt struggled to find work but was eventually successful due to “sheer persistence.” In his first job, someone who knew of his registry reported him to police as being a possible suspect in a high-profile missing-child case. He was questioned aggressively by police, even though he wasn’t in the vicinity of the kidnapping and there was no evidence connecting him to the case in any way. They wanted his DNA, Wyatt tells me, “But I refused.” He was humiliated when the police arrived to question him at his workplace. Wyatt says it was infuriating because the only reason the police questioned him was because he was on the registry. The experience traumatized him. He soon lost his job, and he says he’s sure it was because of the kidnapping accusations and the arrival of the police at his office: “It put me at the top of the list when there were layoffs, as I was the least desirable. . . . So it was the registry that did me in.”

He managed to find other jobs, and now has a successful career as an engineer. He’s limited in his field, however, because most projects in his area, he says, “require a security clearance. I used to have a top-secret clearance, but I’ll never get it back, so opportunities are limited.” He can only pursue less stable and lower-paying contractor work where no security clearance is required.

Wyatt has been an antiregistry activist and is very knowledgeable about the relevant constitutional issues. He was eventually removed from the registry a few years ago. However, he’s been involved in disputes with private websites that repost information from state registries and those run by bail companies, that continue to post his registry listing.

Even though he’s off the public registry, the private websites cause him to still feel “deathly afraid” that others will learn of his past. Explaining why he was convicted of a sex offense “causes awkwardness,” so he avoids sharing whenever possible. When he was younger, he used to be very honest about it with everyone, but he’s learned since that reactions are unpredictable; it’s too risky.

Wyatt tells me that he’s aware of how lucky he is to have housing and a job that pays relatively well. He also knows getting off the registry isn’t easy, and he expresses solidarity with those still publicly listed. He remembers, he says, having his car vandalized while it was parked in front of his house. He has experienced verbal harassment, and recalls being called “rapist” and “pedophile.”

The experience of being listed on the registry appears to have deflated Wyatt. He tells me, “I joined the military because I considered myself a patriot.” He recognizes that his “determination and stubbornness” have helped him and is proud that he’s always paid child support and never received public benefits. He understands that others on the registry don’t necessarily have his same "will," and that other states have far worse and "torturous" registry policies.

Today, Wyatt says he has lost faith in America and would like to move abroad when his kids graduate high school. He worries, he says, that the laws will change, and he'll be back on the public registry or even reincarcerated. "I have money and equity, and I got out of prison with $350 to my name. Now I have enough saved up to leave the country and make a new life when I'm ready." He tells me again that he thinks things are going to get worse, and small legislative victories for registrants don't reassure him. Wyatt tells me that he sees how hard politicians and others "fight back" against any rational registry reforms, and he feels it's a risk for him to stay in the United States for much longer.

"I like to stay under the radar, but I've spoken before the legislature. They are nice when you talk to them, but then I hear their comments, and it's clear they don't care. They aren't going to get rid of the registry or let it go. They want policies based on useless things, and I don't buy that." The public, he says, loves the registry because "they've drunk the Kool-Aid." Registry reform, he says, will take an "unbiased" court to examine the hard evidence that the registry has failed, and he doesn't see that happening.

Wyatt insists he's one of the "lucky ones," especially because his family has stood by him throughout his ordeal. At the same time, his social life has been decimated, and he's given up on the possibility of a romantic relationship. Several women, he says, couldn't deal with the registry or the fact he had a sex-offense conviction. "I've been alone for a decade, and I've just given up on that part of life." No one, he tells me, wants to deal with someone associated with the registry, even after removal.

Patrick: It's Been Harder Than Prison

Patrick was arrested fifteen years ago for possession of illicit images of children. He's white and in his early forties. He's been on the registry for ten years, since completing five in prison. Incarceration was difficult, Patrick says, but, "I was excited about getting out and thinking things would be good. In so many ironic aspects, it's been harder than prison, getting out. I also thought things would get better after I finished probation a few years ago. But that's not the case." While his family has remained supportive, he has few friends from before his arrest.

Harassment isn't a frequent problem for Patrick in his small town, but recently he was approached by a man who warned him that "there's a red dot on my name and to be careful going out and into town. I thought maybe I should call the police. But it was subtle. This wasn't the first time something like this has happened." Patrick forces himself to leave his house and not indulge in his impulse to "stay home all the time," but "moments like that scare me. I didn't threaten back. I daydreamed about punching him, but I didn't do it." At the same time, Patrick says he has "sympathy" for those who threaten him. He tells me, "I recognize people are primed to hate sex offenders. It's a rote thing. I'm not surprised they act like this. So, I can sympathize with them, and I don't blame them."

Patrick describes himself as an introvert. He says he taught himself programming and never went to college. According to Patrick, his self-training led to a successful career as a high-level senior software engineer for government agencies. "I even had top-secret clearance," he shares, "before it all came crashing down." He attributes his crime to his reclusive nature and an "addictive" personality. He feels that he had an "addiction to porn." He told himself, he says, that looking at pictures of underage girls wasn't "sadistic" because they were "just posing"; he also says he didn't understand that viewing the images would cause him to "land in prison."

Patrick says he's had a series of "unhealthy relationships" with women and views his crime as an effort to "fill that void." He says that the "forced therapy" of his sentence enabled him to understand the reasons underlying his offense and inability to form adult partnerships. Unfortunately, he says, now that he understands these issues, it's difficult to date anyone due to a "tainted background." He's tried to meet women since leaving prison, but nothing has "panned out." He's had a few dates that he thought could lead to a relationship, "but then I have to tell them about my past, and they leave."

"In therapy, I got really good at discussing my issues. I got so comfortable with it that if someone wanted to know [about my offense], I'd make them uncomfortable. I have to remember that most people are very uncomfortable [with this issue]." Throughout his life, Patrick has struggled with anxiety and depression. Prison and being on the registry, he says, have exacerbated these problems. Today, he says his depression is triggered when he gets twice-yearly certified letters notifying him it's time to register.

> I have to remain mentally healthy, and that's the hardest thing. It's hard to hear stuff on the news, or when people approach me. I keep trying to remind myself that American society has "lost it" on how they want to respond to someone who is a sex offender. I have to remind myself that I'm a good person. I don't want being a sex offender to define me. It's hard to be out in public. I realize that I'm a human being like anyone else. One of the biggest challenges is for me to remain positive and not so depressive.

Patrick expresses the same fears many registrants have regarding being around children. He has nightmares of getting a flat tire in front of a school, and then being arrested for violating presence laws. "I'm scared of children. If I'm around them or even see them laughing on TV. I get scared and anxious. It's ironic of all creatures that I'm afraid of children. I know it's unhealthy. It's such a shame."

Since leaving prison, Patrick has developed his painting skills. He has been hired by a few local businesses to paint murals and promises to send me a link to a website posting his artwork. Patrick has also started taking small steps to engage in antiregistry advocacy. He speculates that he might be able to change things.

> I have delusions of grandeur. I could do good things and educate the public and legislators. My dream is to educate the public about the myths they are being fed. I want them to know that being a sex offender isn't special, and anyone could wind up here. [They'd understand] more if they realized they could be one. People get touchy when I say this, because they think I'm saying that they could harm a child.

After our meeting, he emails me a link to his artwork. He lets me know that he's available if I have further questions for him, but "in the meantime, feast on my art!"

Felix: I'm Going to Keep Going Forward

Felix is white. He was convicted at nineteen for the charge of burglary with "intent to violate or abuse" someone who was fourteen. He spent 15 years in prison, and he's been on the registry since his release a few years ago. Felix has a stutter and seems very nervous at the start of our interview but also anxious for someone to hear about his experience.

> I work at restaurants as a nighttime general manager. I also do warehousing. The registry impacts me but doesn't bother me too much. My brother has girlfriends, and they look my stuff up and throw it in my face. I had a circumstance where I was talking to a woman at a restaurant where I go weekly to get a milkshake. I told her about my offense after talking to her for six months. Then she looked me up and got annoyed and said that I didn't share everything with her. So things like that.
>
> I just live with my mom. This is my house. I have a house and a car. When I get home late, I am really aware of my surroundings because my information is public. I am always worried that someone might do something to me or my mom.

I have to take polygraphs yearly, and even when I tell the truth, I fail them, and then I go back the next month and pass them. I have to pay for $200 each time. Parole isn't fair. I have to spend $40 a week on mandated therapy. They say that anything that I share has to go to my parole officer. It doesn't feel like it's therapy if they tell everything to parole.

There have been many times I have trouble breathing. My mom stays with me because she has nothing. I'm over forty and over three hundred pounds and I'm running on my feet to make ends meet. I keep pushing. I try not to let others' perceptions of me become my reality. I have to stay five hundred feet from a park or a school. They are building a school pretty close to me. I don't know if I'll have to move.

I want to move to a better neighborhood soon. I hear gunshots near me. Once, I came home and I was in the kitchen eating a peanut-butter-and-jelly sandwich, and I had to duck and dodge because I heard a bullet right outside. All in all, my family is supportive and they don't hold it against me. They don't call me a child molester. I feel good with my family. My little brother has kids, and he gets that due to parole I cannot be near his kids.

I tell registry organizations [when I hear about] about job openings for "sex offenders": that hire people regardless of your charge. Lots of people are forgiven, but those labeled "sex offender" are never forgiven. I understand the nature of the offense. I understand how bad it is, but I just got a book that pretty much said, "own your past and change your future." So, all in all, I'm going to keep going forward no matter what people think of me.

Ed: How Is This Not Punitive?

Ed is white and in his late fifties. His offense involved an underage relative and took place more than fifteen years ago. He's been on the registry since his release from prison two years ago. Currently on parole, Ed is required to wear a GPS ankle bracelet at all times.

My first job when I got out was as the manager of a car wash. I worked there two weeks, but then the background check came back, and I was fired. It was a great job. Now I'm a driver. My boss told me they believe in second chances. They told me that the credit-reporting agency told them I'm on the registry. Why is a credit-reporting agency involved? They kept me on.

I'm innocent. My ex-wife made up lies about me. I was prosecuted in a county with a 98 percent conviction rate. I paid an attorney $20,000 in cash. Turned out he was under investigation, and then he got disbarred. It was a comedy of errors.

I did seventeen years. I did every single group and self-help group I could possibly do. I got credits and three years off my sentence. I was doing five groups a week. I took every course I could. Earned my way out early. I'm on parole.

I have to wear a GPS on my left ankle. Everyone knows that means I'm a "sex offender." I can't wear shorts. I have to charge this two hours a day. I have to stay plugged to the wall. I can't take a bath or swim. They say this is administrative and not punitive. How is this not punitive? I'm doing research, and I'd like to file a brief about this. The GPS does nothing to deter crime or reduce recidivism. Just helps to monitor people on parole.

I went into a program when I got out, and they gave me a rent-free home and food. I am very disciplined. I saved up. I had cash to move. I share a room in a four-bedroom house. Everyone is on parole. I been frugal. I just bought a truck. My credit score went from 0 to 740. I opened a bank account. I pay off my card every month. I'm making decent money, and I want to get a mortgage. Things are going well.

I have a sister who supports me. She's supportive, and she's stood by me the whole time. My extended family threw me under the bus. "We can't be associated with you because you are on the registry." I was a mechanic and helped them with their cars and computers, but they dropped me when I went to jail.

I lost my dad while I was in county jail. He killed himself. My mom died of breast cancer while I was in prison. The day I got out, I told my parole officer that I was innocent, and I explained my whole story. She said I still have to do treatment and admit to my crime. I said I won't lie. I pass my polygraphs. How is this not punitive?

CHAPTER SIX

Banishment and Harassment

Gratuitous Cruelty

In 2020, *USA Today* ran a story headlined, "Sex Offender Loses COVID-19 Contract at VA Hospital after USA TODAY Asks Questions" (Salman, 2020). In this muckraking article, the journalist highlights a janitorial services company, owned by a person on the registry, that received a $700,000 federal COVID-19 contract. The first sentence of the article identifies the registrant by name and notes he is "a registered child sexual predator . . . who spent more than three years in prison for sexually abusing two teenage girls under his care."

The writer lamented that federal applications only question if vendors have felony convictions from the past two years, so those with a sex-offense conviction more than a decade old, such as the company owner, weren't flagged. The VA, when asked why they contracted a company owned by someone with a past sex-offense conviction, responded that he had met their criteria. The writer notes that in the federal database, the vendor was coded as "responsible" and in good standing for "performance and integrity." Those terms in the article were placed within quotation marks, perhaps suggesting irony rather than just indicating the original wording.

However, days after the inquiry, the VA "changed course" and terminated the contract. The reporter notes that the original granting of the contract was, in part due, to policies aimed at assisting disadvantaged groups, and "his business is considered small and is owned by a veteran and American Indian."

The article purports to highlight federal government corruption and, specifically, the lack of oversight involving COVID-19 contracts. A business professor is quoted as suggesting that not having those with sex-offense convictions on the "excluded parties list" is a sign of the overall negligence of the process, and an attorney says this is a "disturbing" example "of a federal acquisition system in need of reform." According to the article, the company owner finished prison in 2010 and parole in 2012. While the COVID-19 $700,000 contract is the "largest windfall" for the company, they also received smaller contracts in past years, with a total of eight past VA awards.

The article depends wholly on the predictable public outrage toward those on registries, suggesting that corruption must be far more extensive than we can know *if someone on a registry* can access a federal contract. In this case, the corruption is enabled by federal agencies who seek to work with "small, disadvantaged companies, along with those owned by veterans—part of an effort to undo past disparities." The company owner, who served eight years in the army, "checks all the boxes." Almost as an aside, the writer notes that instead of focusing on the background of the vendor, the government may give weight to such factors as the "vendor's financial strength, past performance, and ability to meet the specifications of the contract."

If this article were not about someone with a past sex offense, it would be potentially positive that the federal government contracted with vendors based on the substantive qualities of the business, such as financial stability and ability, rather the identity of the owner. Also, if the company owner did not have a past sex offense, his status as a Native American army veteran and small business owner would also likely be viewed as positives, rather than as qualities that "checked all the boxes" and gave the government an incentive to overlook criminal history. The article specifically says other *USA Today* investigations have found vendors that "failed to deliver on their promises." Yet there is no mention of the quality of janitorial services provided by the company owned by the registrant, or whether their $700,000 "windfall" was outrageous or a standard amount for the services provided.

The article makes it clear why so many on registries report constant dread and unease even when they are prospering. Let us presume, for example, that the facts in the article are correct. Then the real story turns out to be something quite other than an exposé of government corruption and excess, as promised in the headline. Rather, it's about what registrants told me over and over in interviews: that at any moment they can be exposed and lose their jobs, homes, livelihoods, or relationships. If they are accused of any impropriety, they are assumed guilty.

In fact, another version of the story, consistent with exactly what's told in the original version, would be this: An army veteran with a past sex-offense conviction turned his life around after completing his criminal sentence. He built a successful cleaning company and secured VA contracts. A journalist with a national newspaper called the VA to ask why they'd work with someone convicted of a sex offense, and "days later," he lost his contract and his livelihood. The article included his full name, photo, and home address; identified him as a "child sexual predator" in the first sentence; and implied he had exploited his veteran status and Native American identity to secure an undeserved contract, all of which, presumably, showed him as a prime example of rampant federal corruption and lack of oversight. There is no evidence presented that suggests the company failed to deliver the contracted services or billed excessively. Yet it characterizes the $700,000 contract as a "windfall."

Jason: I Just Wanted to Be Treated the Same as Any Other Felon

The incident that landed Jason in jail took place almost fifteen years ago. A white man in his early sixties was convicted of an offense involving possession of illicit images of children.

> I lived in a halfway house for six years. I couldn't leave there until I found a job. It took me almost four years to get a job after [two years in] prison. I was a programmer before.
>
> I did some consulting work in the halfway house to keep my skills up. I never gave up and kept working to get out of there, and it took me six years. Once I had enough money to get a house, I started looking for a place to live. I'd ask if they'd lease to people with felonies. No one has done anything [to me] so far. I love my house and my neighborhood.
>
> Now I work as a data analyst at a small firm. I also fix the toilet. It's a small company. I attempted a relationship, and it ended three weeks ago. I wanted to go very slow and get to know her before disclosing to her. For two years, we went from friends to dating. I could just never get it to go further. She knew I was on the registry. She was waiting for me to tell her. She was tired of the limitations of me being on the registry. It hurt really bad. But I'm prepared and aware that on any given day, someone is going to do or say something that will mess up my life, and that's how it is.
>
> I have no social life. I have a friend I knew prior to this, and he's stood by me, and I met someone at the halfway house, and they are my friends. I have great relationships with those I work with. Nothing about me would suggest to anyone I've been in trouble with the law. I've never had kids. I'm a loner. I have avoidance personality disorder. I only do things I can do perfectly. I have a genius IQ. I earn a good salary just from what I know.
>
> The downside is that I've missed out on many things in life. If I can't get the perfect girl, I don't want anyone. I've spent my life avoiding. I figure I have less than ten years left to live. I wish I'd had kids.

When I was arrested, I didn't lie about it. Prison allowed me to realize how immature I was. Prison introduces you to many things. I had to learn to adapt. I was earmarked immediately as a "chomo" (child molester) and I had to learn to fake my way about bad situations. It matured me and saved me while it also ruined my life. I wish a friend had found out and stopped my behavior before the arrest.

I don't need to be on the registry. I have a pretty great life. I live in a nice house in a nice neighborhood. I have a great job and a nice car, and I can work there forever. Nothing to hate about my life. Only problem is the registry means that on any day, my life could be ruined in a heartbeat. People are sympathetic if you had a drug problem, but people think I'm a pervert. No one can ever come back from this.

Even if people understand this, they don't want to tell you they understand because then they will be ostracized. If someone says something about me, it's all over. A romantic interest could accuse me of hurting her or her kid. I can't even follow or remember every single registry requirement. I run the risk of going to prison for three years because I don't follow the rules correctly. I could go to register and answer a question wrong and go to prison.

I'm glad I got caught, and I'm glad it's over. Registry is lifetime for everyone, no matter what, here in my state. I'm in the tier that says I'll never reoffend, but I'm still on the registry for life. We are already felons. I just want to be treated the same as any other felon.

Chris: Harassment

Chris, like Jason, is white. He is in his late 30s and has a conviction for possession of sexual images of children. He's from a working-class background and says he had a chaotic childhood with frequent visits from child protective services. He was convicted in his midtwenties, more than a decade ago, and spent two years in prison. He's been on the registry for more than a decade.

While in prison, Chris says he was brutally beaten and partially lost his hearing. At the time of his arrest, Chris was married and his wife stood by him during his incarceration. Soon after his release, however, they got divorced. "She was wonderful while I was in prison and stood by after my arrest. But she resented what I put her through, and the damage was too great."

Chris used to work as a salesman, but after prison, he realized that background checks made that an impossibility. He then trained himself to repair cars. Chris says auto-repair shops don't care about your background, as long as you can do the work required. Chris will be on the registry for life and is currently on a term of federal probation, where he'll remain for at least two more decades. He says he was assigned a judge infamous for tough sentences for sex offenses. "I went to 'treatment' for a decade. I thought it'd end if I completed the treatment and graduated, which I did. But now they want me to go for more. I'm fighting them on that."

Chris recently remarried, and he says his life is going well. He, too, voices the claim that he's "luckier than most." I ask him if he ever experiences harassment, and at first, he says he's mostly left alone, and it doesn't "really" happen. Then he thinks for a minute, and he tells me that he lives in an apartment complex where his door camera and front door are regularly vandalized. The packages delivered to him and his wife are often stolen. Also, he says, he gets threatening "hate mail." Another embarrassing thing he mentions is a posting someone put about his status in the online reviews for his apartment complex. He insists, however, that it's not "too horrible."

Chris bemoans how one neighbor has targeted him. He'll often confront Chris in an aggressive manner, "like he wants to hit me." He tosses trash on Chris's car and lets his dog relieve itself in front of Chris's door. "I've filed three police reports. I have it all on camera. But the cops come to his apartment, and they laugh and joke around. He told them that he has kids, and he's just worried I'll harm them." Chris also notices that neighbors with children pull them close when he walks by.

His positivity about his life and new marriage has lessened. Chris seems sullen. "Listen," he tells me, "It just sucks." When he first divorced his wife, he lived with his aunt. A neighbor approached her to ask why she let a "sex offender" move in. His aunt then kicked him out, having realized all her neighbors could quickly find out about his presence. "I didn't blame her. It was a nice community. Before this, I would have been that same complaining neighbor. Who would want a 'sex offender' in their neighborhood?"

Chris says being listed on the registry makes him "feel like a child." Our video conversation, he says, is probably being viewed by his probation officer. He has software on his phone that records his every move. "Everything I do is tracked. I wanted to get my wife lingerie for her birthday, and I couldn't because my monitoring software blocked the website. A banner appeared on my screen that said 'porn.'" Being on the registry makes him ineligible to participate in a fundraising walk his wife is organizing for medical research, and he's not allowed to attend his local church.

The software tracking and GPS phone monitoring will continue until he reaches his fifties. He cannot reconcile his new life with the "successful" twenty-three-year-old he thought he was before his arrest. "They know it's not going to happen again. The offense occurred twelve years ago. I'm different now, but no one cares." Chris must get permission to attend any event with children present, and he's not allowed to go to the movies. The rules are confusing, he says, and once went to see a film with his wife, unaware the theater was off-limits. Multiple probation officers showed up. It humiliated him profoundly.

His wife is understanding and loves him, he says, but she hasn't told all her friends about his registry status. A few have found out and confronted her, assuming she didn't know. The problem with the registry, for Chris, is that it's with him "forever." Whatever he does with his life, someone can always point the finger and call him a "sex offender," thereby obliterating any other aspect of his existence. "I've moved on and paid the price. But I have to think about my crime every minute of every day."

Steven: Moving to Stay Alive

Steven promises to "stay in control" and not cry during our interview, "but I'm a very emotional person." He is white and was convicted almost three decades ago when he was in his midtwenties. He's been on the registry for more than twenty years. His victim was an underage nonstranger, and at that time, Steven worked as a pizza deliveryman. He tells me he knows of my research about the registry but hasn't read my work because "I've lived it!"

Steven says he is deeply appreciative of those who study and criticize the registry. He is grateful for the opportunity to participate in this project and share his perspective. He has learned more about those challenging the registry, and he has recently attended a meeting of a local antiregistry group. "It's overwhelming to meet people that not only see the problems with this but want to help. At this meeting, there were some lawyers there who help people like me, and I was shocked. The general consensus in society is that you don't help 'sex offenders.' It was really mind-blowing for me to be there."

Steven was sentenced to five years' probation but remained on supervision for an additional year because he did not pass the required polygraphs. "I am extremely honest, and I'd tell the polygrapher everything. I had a sex addiction, and I was struggling with that." He consistently failed when he shared his true feelings about sex with the polygrapher. Finally, he laughs, "I got off probation because I fell asleep during the polygraph, and it came up 'inconclusive.'"

Today, Steven works as a mechanic. He's done this for two decades and for dozens of employers. His skills are in demand, he says, but he's "rejected constantly" whenever he changes jobs. "Places always want to hire me, but they can't because of the registry, so I'm always moving around."

A few years ago, Steven realized the laws where he lived were becoming "impossible" and increasingly complex and ultimately moved to a different state where he felt the restrictions were easier to navigate and comprehend. "I was either going to kill myself or be put in prison because I couldn't deal with them. Even my lawyer couldn't interpret them." One example of the "crazy laws," he says, was when he lived in a "sober house" with several others. The registry required that all cars at any home where he resided be listed. "I lived with fifteen guys and with many coming and going, and I had to register every single car of everyone who lived there, even though I basically just rented an apartment in the house and wasn't involved with most of them."

A few years ago, Steven was arrested for "failing to register" in front of a home he had recently purchased. He argued that he had gone to the registry office to list a new car during the month in which he had to register. He "got confused and forgot" about the need to make an additional visit to complete his birthday registration. According to Steven, "there is no legal defense to forgetting" and failure to register is, essentially, "an indefensible crime."

The arrest was extremely stressful and led to a year of legal issues. He received an additional felony conviction for the charge, a year of probation, and spent almost $20,000 in legal fees. He was "lucky" because he's known people sentenced to years in prison for the same infraction. Steven could afford a lawyer and secure letters of support, which helped his case. After completing probation for the new offense, "I realized I needed to think about moving to a place with less complicated and crazy laws. When I got arrested for forgetting, I started looking at the laws more closely. I realized I needed to take them more seriously." He noticed his roommate had a new truck and panicked because he's required to register new vehicles within three days. "I realized I hadn't done that, then I realized that I was in danger of getting another felony and going back to prison for making another mistake, a human error. There are endless rules. That's when I decided I had no choice but to pack up right then and move to another state."

Steven owned a home, was employed, and had a family where he resided. Yet the "failure to register" felony conviction convinced him he would wind up incarcerated if he didn't move. "I had to leave my life. My mother. My friends. Everything I knew. But I was afraid of going back to prison." He moved during the pandemic and found a state where it appeared that the rules were more straightforward. "I had nowhere to live, and when I got here, no one would rent to me. Even slumlords wouldn't rent to me. Even in the ghetto, I couldn't find a place. I'd gotten rid of all my possessions. I found a motel filled with people addicted to crack." It was a terrible time, Steven says, but he met people in his recovery meetings and started building a community where someone helped him find work. "I left everything to save my life and my freedom. Then I got a break and got an apartment."

Steven wants me to know that he has many thoughts about the registry and how it has destroyed his life. He raises his voice because the issue agitates him so.

"Here's what it does: it tells society that I am so incorrigible and that I'm so deviant that if I'm not under constant surveillance, something terrible will happen. But it's not even based on what could happen but what will happen! This is telling my psyche over and over that I will, no matter what, go out and hurt children sexually! This is what the registry keeps telling me and it puts it on the internet and tells this to everyone I know and everyone I do not know. This fills me with dread."

Steven expresses, with great intensity, that he's fully aware that his life may become unraveled due to new and more restrictive laws. "I just want to live in the world. I want to do whatever everyone else is doing, without living in fear that at any moment I could lose all my rights." He gives me examples of how he deals with frequent upheavals, such as being kicked out of a gym.

For Steven, the registry has eliminated the possibility of serious romantic involvement. He says he's had a few short-term relationships, but "the stress of the registry always kills them." Once, in his former state, he moved in with a boyfriend and registered the address. The police notified all the neighbors, by phone calls and flyers, that a registrant had moved nearby. The landlord demanded he leave the apartment, and the relationship ended. "Being on the registry is an insane label and stigma. Why would anyone want to date me?"

Steven admits he wants a relationship, but he also finds the idea "terrifying." "I don't want to put anyone else through this suffering and torment." The idea of someone on the registry having children, he says, "enrages" him. "Why would they do that? Can you imagine the humiliation of that child? Having a parent on the registry? Didn't they read *The Scarlet Letter* in high school like I did?"

It's a daily struggle, Steven says, to "live in my reality," to "just stay alive and not kill myself because of the ostracization and destruction these laws have caused me." His family, too, is affected. His mother lives in a senior community and fears having him stay overnight, lest her residence wind up on the registry. Steven has been involved in some antiregistry activism, but is hesitant to venture further. The work is "traumatizing and reminds me of what happened." But he is aware that fighting back by engaging in advocacy might be "the best thing I can do therapeutically."

Steven feels constantly "judged," and it takes a toll on his mental health; even in his twelve-step programs, he has experienced ostracism when he shares his story and opens up about being on the registry.

> All these years I've tried to pretend I'm a human being. I try to pretend I'm worthy of a life. Worthy of respect. I think I have good character. Yet part of me believes I'm despicable and it's inevitable I'll reoffend. When I was a kid, I remember seeing the Buddhist guy self-immolate. It impacted me so much. I didn't understand why. It stuck in me forever. I literally thought a couple of years ago, when things kept getting worse for me, that maybe I'll do that.

Liam: To Understand the Sheer Complexity of the Rules, You Need a PhD

When I talk to Liam, he's annoyed. He's been on the registry for almost twenty years, yet still forgets certain registry rules. He's white, in his sixties, and was convicted of sexual contact with an underage nonbiological relative. Liam says he has received technical violations sheerly out of ignorance. Once he forgot a registration date. He says he was lucky that the registry office believed him that it was an oversight. He mentions a concern that others on the registry have: the rules are so complicated that they worry lest the routine forgetfulness that comes with aging result in violations. "To understand the sheer complexity of the rules," he says, "you need a PhD."

Liam explains he's cranky today because he's dealing with a registry-related banking issue. He has a high net worth and tells me he's been a customer at his bank for five decades. Very recently, he was told he's no longer welcome there as a customer and was given no explanation. They told him he has sixty days to transfer all his funds and accounts, as well as his safety deposit boxes, to a new institution. It's frustrating because he can't get answers, but he suspects it has to do with a new credit-reporting feature that indicates registry status. He cannot prove this because the bank won't give him an explanation, but a credit reporting agency recently emailed him with a warning that he may know a "sex offender." Liam starts laughing and tells me that the automatic alert essentially warned him not to do business with himself. "I flipped out at that one!" He cheers up and tells me he's managing. He has found a new bank. "Listen," he tells me, "I don't mope around. People don't fuck with me generally; I'm meeting with their wealth advisor tomorrow. I'm finished playing with banks. I'm happy." He shares another email he received from an internet-safety company that warns him, "Some of your personal information matched that of a registered sex offender." The email tells him that he can report this possible identity error to the safety company, but, if he is aware of this, "there is nothing to worry about."

Due to his financial resources, Liam has been able to insulate himself. He lives quietly on a vast and remote farm. He says his spirituality helps him cope with the strain of the registry. "You only have right now, and everything else is bullshit in your brain. If you aren't enjoying the moment, you are missing the picture. Meditating helps." For a decade after his conviction, Liam says he suffered from crippling guilt, depression, and shame. It took him, he says, time before he could reengage with the world. He says yoga and meditation helped him better understand himself and his actions.

When Liam delved into his spiritual seeking, he started spending significant time at a local meditation center. He was devastated when someone there discovered he was on the registry. He was pulled out of a meditation session and told to leave and never return. It was hard, Liam says, because he wasn't accused of acting improperly. The center was a huge part of his life, and he credits it with his healing and personal growth, but he's also bitter about his expulsion. "They knew I was a good guy, and I'd gone there for years." It felt, he said, inconsistent with what they claimed to believe. "I know these reactions are really about all those things that they don't want to address within themselves. It's our fucked-up approach to sexuality. Like ministers who preach celibacy, and then they're caught hiring prostitutes."

Liam rarely discloses his registry status to anyone partly as a result of the incident at the meditation center. During a recent small business meeting at his home, he was embarrassed when three police cars pulled in to do a "compliance check." He hadn't yet updated his registration to indicate that he'd recently sold a car, and the officers were confrontational with him about the error. He doesn't think his colleagues figured out exactly why the police were there, but such incidents unnerve him. Despite his wealth and access to lawyers, Liam, like all registrants, is always subject to random "compliance" police visits.

After his arrest and divorce, he wasn't permitted unsupervised or overnight visits with his son. Having a "chaperone," Liam says, interfered with their relationship. The court sided with his ex-wife, who said she feared he'd sexually abuse their children if Liam was allowed to see them alone.

Liam feels his ex-wife made this claim to punish him, and not because she truly feared for his son's safety; his victim, he notes, was a female, adolescent, nonbiological relative. Now that his son is a young adult, Liam hopes a meaningful relationship will develop. "My son," Liam says, "is getting to the point where their adult brains are starting to kick in, and they are starting to cut me some slack. They're starting to think I have a brain and I'm a human being, and they can appreciate some of my nuances. Hopefully, it'll evolve."

Matthew (and Mickey): Terror at Home

Matthew is on the registry. He's white, in his late forties, and lives with his mother, Mickey, who is in her early seventies. His father passed away about a decade ago. Mother and son have lived in their home for more than twenty years and are subject to unrelenting and escalating harassment from their neighbors. I learned of Matthew after receiving a phone call from his mother. Practically crying, she begged for help. She said she'd been reaching out to lawyers and advocates for years without success. After describing to me the daily torment from her neighbors, she spoke of her fear that her son is growing unable to cope.

Matthew was convicted of sexual contact with an underage relative and served four years in prison. Days after Matthew returned home in 2008, police went door to door informing neighbors that a "Level III sex offender" was moving in. They were notified of his address and criminal history. Since that day, his mother says, the community harassed them and made every effort to drive them out of their home.

After that conversation, Matthew contacted me. We spoke at length. Matthew allowed me to view dozens of videotaped recordings of the harassment. In one, a neighbor exits her house and screamed, "Raper" over and over; in another, she screams, "They should have cut your dick off while you were in jail." In one video, another neighbor screams, "I'll kill you, Jew faggot." (Matthew has an Israeli flag in his window.) Matthew echoes his mother's fear that the harassment is increasing. He tells me in frequent emails that he will soon be harmed physically. It's not clear to me if Matthew is in true bodily danger or if the provocations are escalating. Matthew is hypervigilant and constantly worried about his safety. This severe anxiety makes life difficult for both him and his mother.

Matthew always struggled in school and in the workplace. He has a hearing disability, and in elementary school, the problem was misdiagnosed. He was placed in special education. He dropped out of high school in the ninth grade, never earning a GED, and started working immediately. His first job was in a supermarket as a wagon boy and a cashier. When he was seventeen, Matthew got into trouble and was convicted of misdemeanor burglary and criminal mischief. He went on to have what he described as numerous "horrible jobs" and never stayed in one position for long. Matthew never moved away from his parents, unlike his siblings.

Matthew's offense involved a relative, and those connected to the victim wanted Matthew to get emotional and psychological help, but they were unable to intervene once the case entered the court system. When the victim's parents discovered Matthew faced a long prison sentence, they wrote a letter to the judge, pleading that Matthew get help and not prison. Matthew says he quickly pled guilty because lawyers said a trial would require that they aggressively question his relative, and it would be lengthy and expensive. Matthew says he wanted to spare his family additional trauma. Matthew acknowledges his guilt and expresses tremendous shame and regret about his behavior. After spending nineteen months in county jail, he served four years in prison.

Since returning home, Matthew has completed parole and followed all registry laws and conditions. He receives ongoing mental health treatment and is on good terms with his siblings, including the parent of the victim. His therapist spoke to me, with Matthew's permission, and shared that Matthew is committed to treatment and that his team is aware of the situation with the neighbors. She said a colleague witnessed the harassment during a home visit.

The harassment includes minor daily incidents, such as flashing high beams from cars, spotlights, and hazard lights in their home. Less frequently, neighbors make obscene gestures or scream names at Matthew. Matthew tries as hard as possible not to react, as his therapist has counseled him, but he claims it's a growing challenge. The police will not respond to his family's complaints, even though the harassment has been recorded by surveillance cameras. In fact, he says, it was the police who initially suggested he get the cameras to document his claims.

One neighbor got an order of protection against Matthew, claiming he threatened her physically. According to Matthew, she threatened him first, and he reported the incident to the police. She then alleged *he* threatened *her*, he says, in retaliation for his complaint. Matthew faced charges of second-degree harassment in court. In the proceedings, the neighbor testified that Matthew said, "he was going to kick [her] ass"; she described his demeanor as "scary" and "mean." "He just harasses me, makes me feel uncomfortable. Every time he sees me outside, he gives me looks." Her lawyer told the court that Matthew was a "prior felon that scares her."

Evidence supported Matthew's claim that his neighbor made her accusation only after learning Matthew reported her. The judge dismissed the case and vacated the order of protection (*People v. Barone*, 2018).

A few months before these events, Matthew's house had been searched by Homeland Security agents. The local news published the story under the headline, "Homeland Security Raids Sex Offender's Home." The piece included Matthew's full name and quoted a neighbor as follows: "They should take him away. He should not be allowed to live here." Officials told reporters that "they executed the search warrant in connection with a possible case of child exploitation or pornography."

His mother was traumatized by the aggressive raid, the news crews in front of their home, and the characterization of her son as a "sexually violent offender" suspected of a crime involving children and their images. Electronics were seized. After months of investigation, no evidence was found, no charges were filed, and Matthew's mother was permitted to retrieve the confiscated computers.

Matthew and his mother want to live in peace, without constant harassment and fear. Matthew was punished for his crime and assumes full responsibility for his actions. He actively engages in his mental health treatment and appears to have done everything possible to help himself.

This case highlights how public registration and community notification harm families. Matthew and his mother say it was immediately after the police went door to door that their terror started. Essentially, the police created an opportunity for vigilantes who, in the name of social-justice activism, torment those on the registry without reprisal.

Matthew and his mother cannot afford to move. They don't want to be accepted or liked by the community where they have long lived, but they wish to be left alone. Matthew was swiftly punished with prison and parole, and he has acknowledged his guilt and continues to seek emotional and mental health support. The problem faced by Matthew, and so many others, is whether it's possible to convey to those like his neighbors that those on registries are statistically very unlikely to reoffend. The overwhelming majority are law-abiding, tax-paying citizens deserving of a second chance. Matthew's mother has committed no crime, yet her neighbors, gripped by moral panic, fail to see how their behavior is destroying her life as well.

In another altercation with a neighbor, Matthew called the police. When they asked Matthew why he thinks he has been targeted, he explained it's because he's on the registry. When Matthew saw the police report, he felt the description of his conversation with officers reflected their contempt for him. Instead of noting that Matthew credited "the registry," for his treatment, they wrote that Matthew claimed he had "ongoing problem with his neighbors ever since being convicted and serving time for a sex offense against a minor."

The hysteria surrounding sex reoffense rates make it challenging for those like Matthew to trust the police, because they, too, are part of a culture that views this population as pariahs unworthy of protection. His mother sought help from a local religious leader, who dismissed her concerns and told her it sounded like a typical case of neighbors who can't get along. A reporter familiar with their community told me it's not a good idea to seek media coverage nor attempt a community meeting or restorative-justice process to give Matthew's mother some relief. The reporter explained that because Matthew is a "sex offender," the neighbors will present themselves as the victims, and it could possibly worsen the situation.

Frank: I Was Citizen of the Year

Frank is in his early seventies. He's white and was convicted of a sexual offense involving a fourteen-year-old acquaintance in the late 1970s, when he was in his mid-twenties. He has lived four decades in the same community and has been on the registry, which didn't exist when he was convicted, for more than a quarter of a century. For the first twenty years after his conviction, he built a plumbing business and made every effort to rebuild his life and be a "good upstanding citizen." He has received commendations for his community involvement, including a "Citizen of the Year" award.

In the mid-1990s, Frank received a letter informing him that he'd have to start registering with the police and that his listing would be public. Before that time, he was active with the Chamber of Commerce and volunteered with the local parks department. Afterward, he says, "I went from being citizen of the year to publicly being listed as a 'bad guy.'"

Soon after his appearance on the registry, Frank was a victim of brutal vigilante violence. A stranger saw his listing and his name and address, entered his home, and attacked him with a hammer. Frank struggled with severe depression after the incident, and, for a time, feared leaving his home. "Part of me thought someone outside would kill me, but then I also was scared to be inside my house, because that's where I was when the guy [who] showed up with a hammer and tried to kill me." He kept his curtains drawn and bought special door locks.

Eventually, Frank made the decision to self-publish a book about his life and speak out about how the registry led to this violent, near-deadly attack. He also started engaging in antiregistry activism. "I thought I would die if it wasn't published. Every day, I never knew where the assault would come from. I became highly vigilant, and I felt like my head was on a swivel." He likens his mental state at that time to someone returning from war. Even today, he says, he'll sometimes feel anxiety when he thinks he may have accidentally left his door open.

Fred's prosperous plumbing business suffered; after he appeared on the registry, many clients disappeared. He offered his book to those who continued to hire him. "Though I never brought it up with them, I know many read the book and continued to have me come by. Few spoke of it. Some did, and they were very kind."

One of his clients was lawyer Janice Bellucci. Bellucci has shared publicly that reading Frank's story was the impetus for her decision to dedicate herself to fighting unjust sex-offense laws. Frank says that because of Janice and her tireless work advocating for those on registries, including many successful lawsuits in California, he's been able to stay in his home and do many things he enjoys "without fear." "Now we have Janice. I'm no longer scared. Everything changed when Janice bought my book. She was my voice. People listen to her."

Recently, Frank traveled outside of California and was overwhelmed by the restrictions in each state regarding how long he can stay there before registering. "It's just craziness and makes me fear living. I'm much better now, because of Janice. But I still get scared when people slow down when they drive by my house and point their fingers."

Brian: Going to Register Gives Me PTSD

Brian was convicted of his offense two decades ago, in his midtwenties. It involved sexual contact with an underage relative. He's white and has been on the registry for more than fifteen years. Brian works as a welder in a company he describes as "felon friendly." He likes his job, but he feels trapped, explaining, "If I ever want to work elsewhere, I can't."

Brian tells me that the social aspect of the registry makes his life difficult, and notes, "I watch who I talk to." He says that he's had his windows "bashed in" several times. On a number of occasions, he disclosed his status to someone he thought was a friend, but "then we have a falling out, or their friends find out, and they bash my windows." The registry makes it "impossible to be someone normal."

After his arrest, Brian was abandoned by most of his friends and family. He'd had a turbulent childhood and spent time in foster care. He says his mom was schizophrenic, and he was a victim of physical and sexual abuse. His stepmother died of an overdose, and he said, "I grew up watching people shoot heroin." After high school, he did various odd jobs. He attributes his crime to having "boundary issues."

Brian is married and has been with his wife for a decade. They don't have any children, because he doesn't want his kids to have a father on the registry. He hopes he'll somehow be removed from it one day so they can start a family. Brian's wife works at a grocery store but was forced to quit her last job after coworkers learned that Brian was on the registry. "They judged her, and they were always talking about how much they hated 'sex offenders' because of me, and she couldn't take it."

Brian tells me he has learning disabilities, and mandatory treatment was challenging for him. "I thought the treatment was fake and oppressive. It wasn't healing, and I couldn't open up or trust people. So treatment wasn't helpful. I was removed twice. I was overwhelmed. I couldn't focus on all the therapists. I had to do treatment three times before I passed. First in prison, then in the halfway house, then in outpatient."

Brian says that he's had issues with parole and registry officials. He says the reregistration process, which he does every six months, "gives me PTSD." His offense, Brian says, only required a decade of registration at the time of his conviction. Later, he says, the listing became for life. He'd like to hire a lawyer to see if he can be taken off the registry, but, "I'm not sure how to get a lawyer. It's a money thing. I'm trying to find someone to represent me pro bono." He's clearly overwhelmed by the prospect and jokes, "Maybe I can just talk to the lady who runs the registry."

I met Brian at a conference. He told me after my lecture that he'd like to engage more in advocacy and learn as much about the registry as he can. We decide to do an interview about his experience after his return home. When we video chat, he tells me how moved he was by meeting other registrants at the conference and learning about the harm caused by the registry. "Becoming an activist has helped me. Going to that conference was the best vacation I ever had. It was the best therapy. I loved it."

Brian says he has reconciled with his victim and adds, "She doesn't want me to be on the registry." His family has forgiven him but expresses cynicism about his new interest in fighting registry laws. They prefer not to hear his thoughts about it, "and why it stresses me out. They don't understand the barriers. They don't want to hear about why the registry isn't needed. They don't care. They don't want me to hear my passion about why the registry sucks. When all I'm trying to do is express myself. My dad gets offended when I talk about the registry, and I'm just trying to tell him what I've learned."

Adam: There Is Nothing Worse Than This

Adam is in his seventies. His offense, involving illicit images of children, occurred after his retirement from a career as a high-level military analyst and his move to the medical field. He was sentenced to five years on the private registry, of which he has completed two.

His presence on the registry has made it difficult to find housing, because his offense shows up during background checks, even though the public cannot see it. He is limited to undesirable, high-crime neighborhoods. "Everyone is suspicious of a new person moving in. I'm educated and I spoke and carried myself differently. Luckily, I was mostly left alone, aside from a few minor confrontations."

Adam had prospered in his new medical career but lost his job after his arrest. He was banned from working with those considered "vulnerable," and his specialization was geriatric care. He has managed to build a small independent practice with former clients who are unaware of his conviction, but his income has dropped significantly. He applied for full-time jobs and was offered interviews at every place he sent a resume but was invariably rejected after the background check. "They see I'm on the registry, and that's it. They don't care if you are a high-level or low-level offender or what you were before." Even now, he says, he excels at his work, and clients regularly tell him how much they appreciate him. "I think to myself: if they only knew. As soon as they'd learn about the registry, they would never admit to knowing my name."

Adam emphasizes the pain he feels being viewed as a pariah. He explains, "What fazed me is how [the arrest] impacted my personal life. I was ostracized because people feared they'd, in turn, be ostracized due to their association with me." He goes on: "There is nothing more personal than the friends and family members who ignore you or drop you." It's been a few years since his conviction, and he says he's accepted that he will have a solitary future. His pet brings him "some happiness," and he has resigned himself to the reality that no one will ever understand or forgive him. He keeps to himself and no longer tries to engage with others in ways that will require him to eventually share his story. Thus, he spares himself the pain of inevitable rejection.

Adam tells me that some of his geriatric clients stood by him immediately following his arrest. A group of senior citizen patients put together a petition demanding he not be fired. "They said they cared more about how I helped them than what the state said I did." While it didn't help Adam keep his job, it clearly meant a great deal to him. He also realized, he told me, that older people are more tolerant of the mistakes that people make. "As you get older, and these were all older people, they called on their own life experience, and they don't judge any longer." In fact, he says, during his short incarceration, the corrections officers laughed because he received so many elderly visitors.

Adam was arrested shortly after losing his wife to cancer. He was very close to her family, but they live outside the United States, and he's not permitted to enter their country due to his registry status. "I was very, very close to her family, and I couldn't attend her mother's funeral. I can't see my nieces and nephews grow up. That's very, very hard." Adam tries to describe the anxiety of the registry to me.

> I am a Buddhist by choice, and it's hard in this environment, and the way I am viewed in this society. Acceptance is not part of the vernacular here. That hurts. Most people on the registry are in a constant state of stress and negative flux. We never know what is going to happen to us from one moment to the next. People are getting elected on the premise that they are going to make the registry harder. It is very, very stressful.

Adam also recognizes that he's fortunate in certain ways, despite his social isolation. Unlike others on the public registry who he has met, he has never been physically attacked or harassed. He has always been treated respectfully by law enforcement. Adam expresses great empathy for others on the registry and is visibly saddened when he shares that a friend on the registry recently took his own life. The man, Adam says, was devastated after learning that he couldn't go to any activities at the school his children attended. "He was a good person and he provided for his family. The 'sex offender' label destroys lives."

Adam contends that the stigma of the registry makes people more likely to reoffend. He says that the destruction caused by the registry and "the label" give people no incentive to do good and change. "The destruction in their lives is too intense. There is nothing worse, I've found, than this."

Adam is due to be off the private registry in a few years. He says he knows that whatever happens, he will personally "be OK," and he'll possibly even get rehired full-time in his field once he's removed. However, he's heard anecdotally that even after removal, the ability to travel internationally is not a certainty, and he knows he'll never truly be "off" the registry. He worries the laws may change and he won't be removed or that his listing will remain on private websites, accessible to employers and landlords conducting background checks. Adam says it infuriates him when he thinks about how the Supreme Court argued the registry isn't punishment. "Not only is this punishment, but this is the worst type of mental punishment you can do to anyone."

Registrants Are Fair Game

Adam also repeats something I've heard from others on the registry: our society, he points out, has developed to the point where it's socially and legally unacceptable to discriminate on race, sexuality, or religion, but no such protections exist for those on registries. A post on an antiregistry website echoes this, noting that growing intolerance for discrimination toward sexual minorities has made registrants even more vulnerable. The poster notes that registrants have now "become *the* punching bag they can all still rally against and use as a distraction."

On social media and political discourse, the terms "sex offender," "pedophile," and "groomer" are used casually and interchangeably to dehumanize and smear political and personal foes. The fears and experiences of social banishment described by those on registries are easier to understand when viewed in the context of incendiary terms such as "pedophiles" people increasingly use to describe all those on registries. It's acceptable to sell merchandise that reads, "Kill Your Local Pedophile." One website offers shirts emblazoned with the phrase in toddler sizes ("Kill Your Local Pedophile Toddler Long Sleeve Shirt," 2022). Websites freely sell stickers with phrases such as, "Dead Pedophiles Don't Reoffend" (Redbubble, 2022), and advocates have reported seeing cars proudly displaying such messages.

At a "drag queen story hour" protest, a man was pictured with a "Kill Your Local Pedophile" shirt and a picture of a machine gun; attendees reported that protestors shouted "pedophile" and "groomer." Even some who question the appropriateness of "drag queen story hours" recognize the offensiveness of overt antigay or antidrag slurs (Latifi, 2022). Accusations of "pedophile" or "groomer" are not considered "hate crimes" or "hate speech," and associating enemies with these toxic terms is an easy way to gain sympathy and support. Using these terms as weapons against foes increases the impulse to disassociate from those formally labelled "sex offenders," making reform efforts even more difficult

The invisibility of those with sex-offense convictions in broader criminal-justice reform efforts leads to additional forms of marginalization. Those on registries are also inconsequential to many organizations, and thus doubly unprotected. One example: Florida excluded those with sex-offense and murder convictions from their law restoring voting rights to people with criminal convictions. Yet progressive groups such as Democratic Socialists of America and Public Citizen failed to note these exclusions when heralding this law as "voting rights history" and "the largest expansion in voting rights since the voting rights act" (Public Citizen,

2018). *The New York Times* reported the exclusion and that it means "Florida still has among the strictest laws in the country" but offered no critique or commentary from those impacted by the carveout (Robles, 2018).

Likewise, in New York State, a coalition of progressive organizations fought for a "Clean Slate Bill" that would automatically seal convictions after three years for misdemeanors and seven for felonies. All versions of the bill, in both the State Assembly (New York State Senate, 2021a) and Senate (New York State Senate, 2021b), excluded those with sex-offense convictions. The coalition of criminal-justice reform organizations initially designed catchy pamphlets emphasizing the exclusion of sex-offense convictions (Clean Slate New York, 2021). Later versions of the pamphlet removed this line (and the fact of their exclusion), perhaps in an acknowledgment that it was less offensive for the purported reformers to leave the exclusion unsaid than to highlight it.

Similarly, two leaders of major faith-based organizations ignored the exclusion of sex-offense convictions in an editorial calling for passage of the bill. In their article, they even explicitly stated that individuals are eligible as long they don't have any, "new convictions or pending charges [and] have completed probation or parole" (Walrond & Shah, 2022). They neglected to even mention the only subcategory that was explicitly carved out. Of course, one can read this in two ways: the religious leaders are making a necessary political maneuver and want to push the bill to passage in order to help, as they note, "over two million New Yorkers stuck in a perpetual cycle of punishment due to an old conviction" (2022). They understand that questioning the exclusion would not aid the passage of the bill, which was the intention of their editorial. (Ultimately, the bill failed.) On the other hand, it can also be viewed as more evidence of the invisibility and irrelevance of those on registries to reformers; there is no reason to mention them, as their exclusion is both inconsequential, politically necessary, and expected.

CHAPTER SEVEN

Families Are Collateral Damage

> Every year in the run-up to Halloween, *Patch* publishes maps showing the homes of "registered sex offenders" in various cities. Ostensibly, this information is aimed at helping parents who worry that their children might be molested while trick-or-treating. But research shows that such fears have no basis in reality, and these stories—like the warning signs and restrictions imposed by local police prior to Halloween—mainly serve to stigmatize people who have already completed their sentences, along with their spouses and children, who have committed no crimes at all. (Sullum, 2020)

Children on Registries and Children of Registrants

Our registry laws are a direct response to fears about child safety. However, the excesses of our registry regime also cause children direct harm in two important ways.

First, Human Rights Watch published an entire report nearly a decade ago about the growing problem of children on registries titled *Raised on the Registry: The Irreparable Harm of Placing Children on Sex Offense Registries in the U.S.* (Human Rights Watch, 2013). More recently, the Juvenile Law Center also published a study of the same issue, titled, *Labeled for Life: A Review of Youth Sex Offender Registration Laws* (Pickett et al., 2020). These reports are important, in that they present evidence regarding the unnecessary cruelty and of putting children and adults who committed offenses as children on registries. Like adults, those who commit sex offenses as children are responsive to treatment and accountability and have low recidivism. Like adults, being on a registry doesn't decrease the likelihood of reoffense but creates barriers to education, employment, and housing and causes additional harms associated with shaming and stigmatization.

While it's difficult to discern the precise number of children on registries or the number who are there for crimes committed as children, data shows that almost a quarter of child sexual abuse perpetrators are under eighteen (Snyder, 2000, p. 8). In their 2020 report, the Juvenile Law Center estimates that as many as two hundred thousand people on registries may be there for offenses they committed as children (Pickett et al., 2020). The authors (2020) also note that almost all states now list some children convicted of sex offenses on registries, with only eight states specifically banning this practice.

Second, a substantial number of those on registries have children, with one survey finding that 60 percent of those listed have children (Connecticut Sentencing Commission, 2017, p. 113). Others have grandchildren and other close family members who are children, and they too suffer from the stigma of being associated with a relative on the registry. One man I interviewed said his grandchild took part in a school project where the class was instructed to research their grandparents on the internet as an exercise to learn about family history, and he feared that she would suffer shaming if her teacher and classmates inadvertently learned of his past offense.

Children with parents on the registry also suffer in profound ways. In many interviews, I heard stories of how children were bullied, mocked, and humiliated when peers learned their parents were on the registry. Some children got into physical fights over the issue, while others faced social isolation and exclusion.

All children, parents, and partners of individuals with criminal histories may experience various formal and informal harms, and research documents the range of consequences faced by loved ones, who have been characterized as "hidden victims" of mass incarceration (Martin, 2017). Due to the stigma and shame associated with sex offenses, in addition to the public nature of the registry, it is likely that children of registrants face particular harms and challenges.

The formal harms of the registry impact families when, for instance, they too must reside in inconvenient or undesirable communities or move unwillingly due to residency laws, experience financial instability because of a registrant's inability to secure employment, and other deprivations caused by the registrant's presence and travel restrictions. Special

Halloween laws requiring lawn and door signs are a particularly blatant example of how entire families are punished. As described in the poem above, they also face informal harms, including the shame of having their loved one publicly listed and forms of ostracization and social exclusion.

While registries cause unnecessary suffering for all after completion of a criminal sentence, placing those who commit sex offenses as children on them and causing extreme shame and suffering to children with a listed parent, glaringly emphasizes the profound hypocrisy and bad faith underlying the registry regime. A scheme designed specifically to protect children is an obvious failure when, in practice, it subjects so many children to gratuitous pain, punishment, shame, and stigmatization.

Even Mothers Are Guilty

In 2021, a viral TikTok video received more than two million views after claiming that Brock Turner's mother "liked" the Facebook page of the antiregistry organization Women Against Registry (WAR). Brock Turner was convicted in a 2015 sexual assault case that elicited mass outrage after claims of an overly lenient six-month jail sentence due to his status as a white, male, Stanford athlete. The video targeted WAR and specifically the president Vicki Henry, a registrant's mother, subjecting her and WAR to weeks of social media harassment and personal, targeted threats. Turner's case generated such indignation that it resulted in Judge Aaron Persky's removal from the bench after an unprecedented statewide recall vote, though a subsequent investigation determined no "clear and convincing evidence of bias, abuse of authority, or other basis to conclude that Judge Persky engaged in judicial misconduct warranting discipline" (Commission on Judicial Performance, 2016).

As it turns out, at the time, Turner's sentence was within the standard range and not due to his privilege or judicial bias. As it further turns out, Turner received lifetime sex-offense registration and probation, albeit with less fanfare. In addition to the impact of his notoriety, Turner faces harsh and lifelong housing, employment, travel, and presence restrictions; expelled from Stanford when he was arrested at nineteen, his employment prospects are further dimmed due to the likelihood he'll never earn a college degree. Whatever one thinks about Turner or others convicted of sex offenses, their mothers should be free to engage in reform and advocacy. The premise of this critique is that these women have failed because of what their sons did but also because of their failure to abandon them. More broadly, in sex-offense cases, parents are often the only people who see their children as fully human and as more than just their offense. The TikTok creator clearly believes Brock Turner received leniency, but instead of advocating for, say, harsher sex-offense sentencing or sex-assault prevention, she targets the mothers of those who have already been held accountable. Even worse, more than two million people appear to agree that Turner and other registrants are so despicable and unredeemable that their mothers deserve fates similar to those of their children with sex-offense convictions.

Child Custody

Many parents on the registry report losing all access to their children, even after being discharged from prison or completing supervision and successful treatment. Assessments showing low risk for reoffense and testimony from treatment providers, employers, or others on their behalf are often dismissed by courts, who generally side with their ex-partners. There are also many cases where children are embarrassed by and angry at parents on the registry and are uninterested in building relationships with them.

One person I interviewed, Max, fought a long battle prior to his arrest with his ex-partner for shared custody of their young son. Max was a high-profile artist, and a prearrest article about his work focused on his willingness to put his rising career on hold to pursue joint custody. Soon after, he was arrested after being accused of sexual assault.

The case involved allegations of sexual assault from an underage adolescent female, which Max denied. Max believed their exchange of correspondence would exonerate him and wanted to go to trial. However, the prosecutor offered Max a plea with no jail time and lifetime registration. He accepted because, he says, he had already spent most of his savings on his custody battle and could not afford the costs he would have incurred at trial. He was told he'd face years in prison if he lost, and he knew the stress of a long trial and potential publicity would impact his ability to coparent his son, so he reluctantly took the offer. Immediately upon hearing about the charges, his ex-partner filed papers to invalidate their shared custody agreement. The basis of her claim, like that in Liam's case in the previous chapter, was that Max might sexually harm their young son, even though his offense involved a female, adolescent nonrelative. As a result, however, Max went from a fifty-fifty custody arrangement to seeing his son twice a month for a few hours. During his visits, he is required to pay to have a monitor present at all times, from a company that contracts with the court.

The unwillingness of courts to grant shared custody or unsupervised visitation to registrants is understandable to outsiders. At the same time, in my interviews, I've heard from many who have expressed tremendous pain and deep heartbreak about their lack of access as parents, and about the ease with which ex-partners weaponize their registry status. This relates to one of the most common issues faced by those on registries, which is that the punishment is endless and pervasive. Even after sentence completion, adherence to registry guidelines, and successful treatment condition, their registrant status severely weakens the likelihood of partial custody or unsupervised visitation. Losing access to their children exacerbates feelings of desperation and hopelessness.

While many complained about aspects of treatment, almost all said it also had positive impacts. This is consistent with a survey that found 84 percent of registrants reported treatment to be "somewhat" or "very" helpful (Connecticut Sentencing Commission, 2017). Most acknowledged that it offered them support and that they learned something about themselves in the process. Yet it's also a frustrating experience because even dedicated participation and successful completion of treatment doesn't open doors. While nonparticipation and noncompletion result in sanctions and even incarceration, treatment success rarely translates into positive outcomes.

Sam: People Stopped Talking to My Mom Because of My Offense

Sam's offense took place more than two decades ago, and he's been on the registry for ten years. He's white, in his late fifties, and his offense involved illicit images of children. His sentence includes lifetime registration and lifetime probation.

> My mom had a friend who accused her of being the mother of a child molester and stopped talking to her. Even some relatives fell silent with her as a result of my offense. A niece stopped talking to her. No empathy or questions, just ugliness. My mom changed how much she opens up to others in her life.
>
> I've had people ghost me. The worst example is a friend I had going back to ninth grade. They fell silent, and despite my repeated attempts by mail from prison to connect, they never again responded. That was the biggest hurt socially for me.
>
> Another thing that hurt was the cancellation of my membership and volunteering at the botanic garden. I wanted to show my interest in prosocial activities when I was back home and rebuilding my life and [that I wasn't] a safety threat. This garden became aware of my conviction somehow. I got a terse letter from an administrator, as well as a refund of my membership fees with a stay-off-our-property letter.

The nature of concern there was the fact that schools go there on field trips. The letter wasn't an abundance-of-caution letter but a get-out-of-here-stay-away letter. I didn't appreciate that. I visited there since the 1970s. I'm over that now. I can walk in nature without that kind of treatment.

I had a similar conflict with the college I attended. I signed up as a volunteer as an alum on campus to show probation my prosocial intent for a wine-and-cheese event. Someone sent word from above, and I was asked to leave. They asked me discreetly. Guns weren't drawn. They were regretful. But I was asked to leave. I was on time and ready to work and pitch in but I couldn't do that because I'm on the registry.

I'm not allowed to look at my registry listing. It's there. It bothered me when I first came home because I hid out. I wasn't sure who would know. It was a slight case of paranoia. I loved having a home and a door I could lock [after being in prison]. I was not on electronic monitoring. I was fearful of walking around and about who might approach me or say something to me.

I've never had someone come at me with the public information in public. I live my life. I found a way to explain the time I was [in prison] on my resume. I put "nontraditional worker with the U.S. Department of Justice" to explain those years. More recently, I've changed to "operations support," and that's the work I was required to do [in prison].

Fairly early on after my release from prison, I was [offered a] position at the college I'd worked with prior to my incarceration. My legal obligation was to register with the sheriff as an on-campus employee. When I went to the station, a detective told me I couldn't work there. They refused to proceed with helping me fulfill my legal obligation to register [the job]. I don't know if she ever contacted the campus. That was infuriating and saddening and very frustrating. She didn't offer any explanation as to why. It's something I could have challenged in court but chose not to at the time and still don't.

That was the biggest example of prejudice in employment. A job on a college campus for crying out loud. I don't remember if I informed my attorney. But I was pissed. There was no justification for that kind of behavior. They used their authority to screw me out of a job I would have enjoyed.

Marcus: It's Like [My Wife] Is on the Registry Too

Marcus has been on the registry for more than fifteen years. He's white and in his late sixties. His offense involves sexual contact with an underage nonstranger. He says his wife is the person most impacted by his offense, and he expresses deep gratitude that she's stayed by his side and offered her continual support. "Through all of this," he says, "she was dragged through this as if she were a criminal too." He says he is getting more involved in antiregistry activism, and he'd like to build "family support systems, because there's been no support for my wife. It's like she's on the registry too."

One way that she suffers, he says, is their inability to travel together.

> Me and my dad were air force. I lived in or visited forty-nine of the fifty states. But I haven't been to Alaska. We wanted to take a cruise to Alaska from Washington State. But we couldn't do that because they dock in Canada. I can't visit most of the Commonwealth countries. So we couldn't take the trip. The boat was in Canada for one hour. She's limited because of me.

Marcus has had problems since a day care center opened across the street. "I was grandfathered into my home. We are on the backside of the building. You don't even see the kids coming in and out. But parole made a rule that said we had to keep curtains closed all the time on our windows facing the building." His city recently made the residency laws even more restrictive, leaving few housing options for registrants. "I can live here because I'm grandfathered in. What this new law ended up doing was making a bunch of people homeless. If you want to know where people are, how does it help that they are homeless? It's illogical."

Most of his issues, he says, are because the registry is public. "I think the original intention of the registry has been warped. Background checks are OK if you want to avoid someone working with children who has a history. That's OK. It doesn't have to be public information." The public registry has exposed Marcus to scams many registrants have described to me. He once received a call from someone claiming to be from the sheriff's office. They told him he'd be arrested if he didn't purchase thousands of dollars of gift cards. Marcus says that while part of him knew it was a scam, "my programming from fifteen years of supervision was total panic. So I started moving on it. It pushed all my buttons. It was really slick." He was able to contact the registry office just before reading the gift card numbers to the caller. "The registry person told me they'd had lots of calls about it. These people were going through the registry. The public records do this. That's how they worked the scam. The registry people eventually sent out a notice to everyone on the registry about it." Marcus reported the incident to police but was told there was no possibility of finding the caller. It's the public registry, Marcus emphasizes, that exposes him and his wife to scams and other harms.

Marcus understands that he shouldn't be allowed to work with children and that employment background checks are appropriate. On the other hand, he says, he's banned from doing things that can help others and his community solely due to the registry. He volunteers, for example, with a group helping a local prison institute an education program. They were invited to tour the facility and meet with supervisors about how to implement the program. "But," he explains, "I can't go because of the registry. No one is going to run around the facility unescorted. It's just a blanket restriction. It's something positive I could do, but I'm just barred from this."

Marcus tells me that there weren't any laws or sanctions that would have prevented his offense. "I didn't think about those. These are either crimes of impulse, or you think you won't get caught. Just like any crime. There's really no way to legislate our way out of sexual abuse."

Christine: My Husband Messed Up, but the Punishment Doesn't Fit the Crime

Christine's husband is on the registry. He was arrested a decade ago for possession of illicit images of children. Christine has become an antiregistry advocate after seeing the impact of his conviction on their entire family. She stayed with her husband after his arrest and expresses deep commitment to him and keeping their family together.

Due to her job, Christine cannot engage openly in advocacy, but she does as much as she can while remaining anonymous. She tells me she knows how lucky they are, and this motivates her to help those dealing other registrants with fewer resources. The shock of her husband's arrest is still apparent when she tells me their story.

The registry is wrong, Christine tells me, because her husband can no longer do "any single thing he enjoyed," even though he's completed his sentence. The restrictions make it impossible for their family to engage in activities together, such as going to state parks. She views the restrictions as arbitrary and nonsensical. "We can't even go to any sporting events because they say children are there. But if you go to these games, there's just drinking and fighting. We can't go to a casino because they have day cares there so people who want to gamble can leave their kids. I don't get the logic of it." Her father is ill, and she worries her husband won't be allowed to attend the funeral or visit the gravesite, because the ceremony and the burial will be at a church with a preschool and day care. She fantasizes that a lawsuit based on infringement of freedom of religion could be brought against measures forbidding entrance to churches to law-abiding people who've served their time. Maybe, she says, "I'll sue and change things. I keep that in the back of my mind." She sighs. "Look, I know my husband messed up. But the punishment doesn't fit the crime."

When her husband was arrested, their home didn't meet residency requirements. Christine thought they would let her husband stay where they had lived prior to the restrictions. Their home was the requisite distance from the closest school building, but not when measured from the farthest edge of the vast property the school technically owned. Christine wanted to fight, but she feared publicity and consequently losing her job. She tried to interest the American Civil Liberties Union (ACLU) in their case she says but received no response. Her husband was forced to move out of their family home to an approved location. They lived separately for two years, with Christine staying with their younger child so he could graduate from the school he had attended his entire life.

Today they are together in the house where her husband had moved, but Christine still misses the family home they had to give up; she almost cries when she tells me, "We put our heart and soul into that house." The conviction hurt her youngest child the most, she says, because the arrest happened when he was still in high school. The disruption caused her son "to lose his high school years," and her husband was forbidden to be at his graduation, even though it was held at a sporting venue.

Christine says she's constantly worried she'll be outed as the spouse of a registrant. She worries each year on Halloween because they are required to keep the lights off and post a "no candy at this residence" notice. Each year, she hopes it will get dark earlier so the sign isn't as noticeable, and she painted her door white so the sign isn't as easy to see. It's stressful being "locked in and unable to go outside," she tells me.

Many registrants said that they feared being promoted because advancement can require a new background check. Christine is solely the spouse of a registrant, yet she shares this apprehension. She recently received a promotion and was gripped with worry that her employer would learn she lived at an address on the registry. She advanced without incident, but waiting for approval was an "incredibly stressful time" and "almost as bad" as when she awaited her husband's sentencing. He is no longer employed because of his conviction, so they depend on Christine's income. She tells me that she was planning to retire by the time we talked but cannot afford to do so.

"I know I haven't done anything wrong. But I fear this will come out, and there is a clause in my contract that says that I can't do anything that might impact relationships with clients, and I worry. I worry that just one person will make a stink, and I'll get fired." Christine is so wary of being connected to her husband that she doesn't use social media or search for registry information online.

Faith, says Christine, is very important to her. It's been a struggle to find a church where they are accepted. She's reached out to pastors to get permission for them to attend, and she's been disappointed by their lack of acceptance and understanding. They recently found a welcoming church and met with security and agreed they would avoid the children's area. She's tried to get a meeting with the pastor after being moved by a sermon he delivered about how "sinners belong in church." She hopes telling him her story will motivate him to offer those on registries help and support. But she's growing skeptical, she says, because he hasn't responded to her repeated efforts to meet. "It bothers me. I want to see if he lives what he preaches. I wonder if there is a double standard."

Before she was impacted, Christine said she never thought about the registry. Now she sees how it destroys families, and she is outraged. She tells me she doesn't understand how these laws are constitutional. "It's no big deal until it's your big deal. I never knew how awful it was for people. Until it happens to them, they don't realize it."

The experience, she says, has made her "rethink everything." She hates all technology because of the role it played in her husband's crime. Upon his arrest, she says, they confiscated all their electronics and family photos. They haven't been successful in their efforts to get the items back from the prosecutor, and she fears they've been lost. Her husband, she says, is brilliant but can't find work in his field of specialization due to his offense, which strains the family financially and also undermines the efforts her husband makes to rebuild his life and self-esteem. She feels that employers fear hiring him due to potential lawsuits and liabilities.

Christine says that despite all their challenges, she's thankful for some things, including the fact that the case didn't receive media coverage and they haven't faced harassment. On the other hand, they can't fully enjoy life. "We can't enjoy nature. We can't find a church where we are truly welcomed. We can't even walk our dogs where we'd like." These challenges add to her resolve to engage fully in advocacy and "speak out" once she's able to retire.

Since his arrest, Christine says, her husband has suffered from depression. While on probation and living separately from Christine, he was despondent after losing a job and struggling with a probation condition banning him from any contact with his son or anyone under sixteen. Overwhelmed with grief and shame, he attempted to take his own life. Christine says it "was a miracle he survived." He begged her not to call 911 because self-harm can be viewed as a probation violation, and he was terrified he'd be sent back to jail. Christine drove to multiple pharmacies to buy bandages because she feared it would raise suspicion if she bought too many at one location. There are "so many secrets" in their lives now, she says, and it often feels like she lives "a double life." After she bandaged her husband, Christine worried she'd be sent to prison for not taking him to the hospital if his wounds became infected, or worse. The system, Christine says, does more harm than good and caused her husband to lose hope.

> When my husband was at his weakest mentally, they took him away from his family and told him he was a pariah. They made him unable to work but charged him endless fees. Probation fees, polygraph fees, fees for computer monitoring software. How can they take away your ability to work, but expect you to pay all these fees? I keep thinking that if people know how awful it is, they'll understand. I keep thinking that if we educate people about these laws, we can change things.

Recent reform efforts in her state have made things better for some with criminal-justice involvement, but she says none of the changes apply to registrants. Christine is obviously accomplished and successful in her field. She is aware that many of her fears may sound irrational, and she wants me to know that her innate character is "very logical" and that she's always been "pretty upbeat and optimistic." Yet the registry and related stresses often push her to her limits:

> There have been many times that I haven't wanted to be here. People have no idea of the hell I go through. It's tough. It is a secret double life. No matter what my husband does for the rest of his life or what he did before, the only thing that will matter is what he did. It's been ten years. Sometimes I feel like I'm the living dead. Everyone around me lives. I'm just dead. Why am I even here? Why did they even release him from prison if he's really this dangerous and we can't live? I feel shame. I feel so much shame.

Amber: This Is No Way to Live

Amber Vlangas describes herself as "a veteran, crime survivor, and human rights activist." Amber's husband was arrested for a sex offense six years ago, after they'd been married for twenty years. Amber supported her husband throughout his conviction and has since become an outspoken advocate challenging sex-offense policy. Amber says she and their four children are an example of how registry laws harm entire families, including the women and children it purports to protect. She explains:

> The registry affects every part of our lives, The anxiety about having to explain and reexplain some of the restrictions our family lives under, as well as repeatedly disclose our connection to the registry can be overwhelming.

> As an adult, I have armed myself with the facts and can withstand a lot of pushback; however, being the subject of whispers and public ridicule has caused my children to be both fearful, anxious, and isolated.
>
> The most difficult part of living under the oppression of the registry is never knowing when it will come up during everyday life or how severe the outcome will be. For example, when my teenage daughter developed a serious dating relationship, I had to meet with the young man's parents to answer questions, debunk myths, and help them understand her father's probation restrictions. When the relationship ended, my daughter saw her father's conviction and registry page weaponized against her in social situations and on social media.
>
> On one occasion, my youngest child, then six, tore a piece of his clothing at the school playground and needed a change of clothes. What he needed in that moment was the reassurance of a parent, yet the registry created barriers to that support. I was an hour away at work, and though my husband was minutes away and available, the clothes were delivered by a family friend, only adding to my son's embarrassment. My son didn't understand why things had to be that way.

Amber is outspoken and confident and forcefully advocates for her husband and others on registries. While she doesn't share the same fears of Christine, who lives in perpetual panic that colleagues or neighbors will learn she is married to a registrant, she still faces significant challenges. Like many of the military veterans I interviewed, she says that her ideas about America and "American values" have changed as a result of what's happened in her life.

> I often describe it as a veil being lifted from my eyes. I grew up with a certain level of privilege. I simply didn't have to think that much about how fair or unfair the system was. I naively believed that those caught up in criminal cases put themselves there. I thought that if a person was accused of a crime, that the system was meant to seek truth and provide safety. I was very ill-prepared to experience the full force and unchecked power of the state. I also learned another hard truth that rocked me to the core—the system isn't designed to provide services *or* healing for crime survivors, nor does it focus on actual accountability, rehabilitation, or preventing crime in [the] first place. The American criminal-legal system can be described as the equivalent of setting fire to the house of the person who burned yours. In the end, we all become homeless. What we are doing is self-destructive, and we simply must do better.

I also ask Amber about what specific aspects of the registry are most unjust and unfair in her experience. She told me that she is keenly aware that the registry exposes her and her family to the possibility of vigilantism, and she's met people who have been physically harmed or had their property vandalized. Registries, she says, "rationalize violence" and puts anyone living in homes "at a registered address" in danger. "The government has created this separate class of individuals that are forced to exist largely outside of the protections of the courts and the constitution. It's frightening." Amber is actively engaged in the antiregistry movement and talks openly and publicly about her experience, yet her fears and anxiety are still apparent. She is also angry, particularly at the lifelong consequences her husband will face. "My husband will have to register for the rest of his life, no matter what he does. Our entire family lives in constant fear of my husband being ripped from our lives due to an unintentional registry violation. This causes a significant chilling effect. We find ourselves shying away from many things, particularly travel and social interactions. This is no way to live."

Jay: My Son Beat the Registry

Jay's son was on the registry. He was convicted at nineteen and passed away due to an accident in his midtwenties. Jay is involved with antiregistry advocacy and eloquently speaks of the way the registry has impacted and harmed his entire family. Jay is thoughtful and contemplative and understandably emotional when talking about his experience.

Jay shared an essay where he wrote about his response to his son's arrest. I'm struck by how Jay acknowledges that he only began to recognize the injustice of registries after he was directly impacted. Many of those I interview acknowledge this, saying they were either oblivious to, or strongly supportive of, draconian sex-offense policies. Jay has a long history of involvement in social justice movements, but he admits, "I failed to see the enormous reactionary growth of a sexual-offender registry that was ensnaring so many people who did not warrant this designation." When Jay's son was young, he'd feel fear and vulnerability when he'd hear stories of children abducted and murdered by strangers, and, in response, "I was not opposed to our government taking measures to keep our children safe."

Yet after his son's arrest, Jay learned that the registry regime, built in the name of child safety, didn't protect children or anyone else, while viciously destroying lives and families. His son, Jay says, took responsibility for his actions and participated actively in therapy. Jay notes, however, that true accountability is undermined by the disproportionality of the stigma and banishment that accompanies lifetime public branding as a "sexual predator."

As a father, Jay was overwhelmed that his son, for his entire adult life, would be labeled with the permanent outcast status shared by all those convicted of sex offenses. After his son's arrest, he and his family initially withdrew from friends and family, isolating themselves as a coping mechanism. However, Jay soon realized that engaging in antiregistry activism and educating others about the harm of registry laws, was a healthier and far more empowering tactic.

Jay told me that seeing the way the courts dehumanized his son made him feel powerless. "They treated him as a thing. I knew him from the day he was born. How could the system completely ignore his family and community?" The feeling of helplessness Jay describes is something shared by many other parents with children ensnared in the criminal-legal system. They express grief at how the process paints those they love as one-dimensional monsters, denying their humanity and defining them solely by their crimes.

Jay has continued to participate in activism since his son's passing as one effort to honor his memory. The destruction wrought by the registry reflects deep societal problems, and, for Jay, it highlights how "we disrespect life." He notes the ease with which we "judge and condemn" others and "label and condemn people as toxic." He shares with me that he was struck by the compassion the police showed him after his son passed, observing how death puts things in perspective. "Death allows people to recognize their own humanity and mortality. The police were worried we'd be traumatized when we saw our son's possessions after his accident. They were worried about us. They had compassion for us as parents who'd lost a child. But they didn't have compassion for my son when he was alive."

At their son's funeral, Jay said he was overwhelmed by the number of young people there, which he hadn't expected. Jay realized that his son, in spite of the inconceivable barriers posed by the registry, had still managed to engage with his community. For many of them, Jay told me, it was their first funeral. Jay was "blown away" by the outpouring of love and care they expressed by being there, sharing their memories of their son, and participating in the unfamiliar rituals of a burial service. In that moment, Jay realized, "My son beat the registry."

Craig: The Sins of the Father(-in-Law)

Craig was convicted of sexually abusing an underage relative three decades ago; he completed his sentence and has never reoffended. Craig and his wife are close to their children and other relatives, and Craig has reconciled with his victim. Craig's son-in-law, who is involved in local politics, has suffered professionally for having him in his family. Craig shared with me the opposing party's campaign literature that highlighted his son-in-law's relationship to "a convicted pedophile." One flyer features Craig's full name and registry photo, and local websites run paid ads warning voters that his son-in-law has an association with a "registered sex offender."

Craig is careful to make clear that he is guilty of his crime and that he has devoted his life to remedying this. "I live in fear. Some shame. It is so public. I did the crime. I did harm. I am not minimizing it." However, he is deeply disturbed about the way it impacts his wife, children, their spouses, and now even his grandchildren. His daughter is devastated when her husband is shamed because of her father's past. "Why," he asks, "should my offense be used as a political tool against him? Instead of extending compassion and privacy to my family, these items reflect the most base of responses to achieve an advantage in a political election."

The public listing of his crime, says Craig, "puts a target on me. The government continues to pound and expose me and my family. There is no safety valve outside of this system. It only grows. The registry just punishes you for life." After flyers went out in his neighborhood smearing his son-in-law and prominently displaying Craig's registry photo, Craig grew afraid. For a time, he told me, "I started pulling the blinds down and being fearful to go out at night to barbecue on our deck."

The registry also subjects his wife to pain and shame. A few years ago, he says, they went on vacation to South America, planning to spend a holiday week at a beachfront resort. When they arrived, officials told them Craig was not welcome in the country. Craig had traveled internationally for work without incident for many years, but this was immediately after the passage of IML, and Craig didn't yet understand its impact. "We slept on the airport floor and returned home early the next day. We lost all our vacation money. Worse was that it was very embarrassing and humiliating for my wife."

He and his wife counsel other families who struggle, and they share their story of overcoming the pain of Craig's offense and rebuilding their family. "We work with other couples and tell them what we went through. My pastor has even asked me to mentor individuals going through difficult situations." Craig says he's worked tirelessly to change his life and actively repent. He is proud that he once ran into his former probation officer, and "we chatted like old friends. We are still friends. He'd write a letter to help get me off the registry. Not many people are friends with their former probation officer. Most people don't believe that I'm a 'sex offender.' I'm always amazed whenever I tell my story and people tell me about their own experiences of abuse."

After his arrest, Craig and his family struggled financially. His daughter, he says, was lucky to get a college scholarship because they couldn't afford her tuition. Craig eventually started his own business, which became very successful. He is aware of his good fortune, given his registry status, and he tries to "give back" as much as possible. He knows many on the registry who cannot find work. He and his wife, he says, are actively involved in several philanthropic efforts. Craig tells me they have funded a variety of faith-based initiatives, such as rebuilding a church damaged in a windstorm to supporting drug-rehabilitation programs and orphanages in other countries. They also donate substantially to the college where their daughter received a scholarship years earlier. Craig tells me that the college even wanted to put their name on a building, but they turned down the offer.

Still, the public registry isolates Craig from his community and his past. He fears joining his college's alumni association and attending high school reunions. He'd like to participate in local service organizations, but he avoids anything that brings him attention.

After our interview, Craig emails me to share an example of how the public registry creates opportunities for extortionists aware of the vulnerabilities of those listed. He once received a call from someone claiming to be from the sheriff's office. They told him he'd registered at the wrong location and was facing a "failure to register" charge that carries a possible jail sentence. Craig says the caller informed him that to avoid the charge, he had to immediately buy $1,500 worth of prepaid cash cards and to stay on the phone while purchasing them.

He says he and his wife panicked, and he writes me, "I knew this was a scam, but my fear overrode common sense, and I caved. Being on the registry [offered] all the information they needed to run the scam and how to put fear into those they called. They were skilled and knew exactly how and when to pull the strings." In a follow-up email, he explains that he was aware that registrants were often targets of scams, and he even read about them on antiregistry websites. However, when it happened to him, panic took over, and he was unable to think clearly. The prepaid cards, he said, were a "grand tipoff" that it was a scam, "but even that could not override the fear. I was not as humiliated by the experience so much as I was angry that I had given in to my fears." Craig reported the incident to the police. He attached a copy of their report that read, "Due to the high volume of cases . . . we are unable to investigate crimes with low or no solvability factors. As such your case will not be assigned to a detective for follow up at this time."

Doug: I'll Be Registering for Fifty Years

Doug's offense took place twenty years ago. It involved an adult non-relative. He's been on the registry for eighteen years. Prior to his offense, he had a successful professional career. He lost his certification to work in his field due to the conviction and is now a full-time writer who has authored several books. He attributes his offense largely to excessive substance use, and he is very open about how his arrest also led to his long-term commitment to sobriety and the importance of AA to his recovery.

I ask Doug how the registry impacts his life, and he laughs. "What *doesn't* it affect in my life is a better question." Doug has been invited to speak about his writing at universities. Once administrators find out he's on the registry, the invitations are always rescinded. Renting a house is nearly impossible, he says, and he and his wife have been rejected by multiple owners, despite being financially qualified. They were finally able to rent from a friend. Doug thinks about moving from his city to a more rural area but worries that might make him more noticeable.

Doug is self-employed, but during the pandemic, he lost many clients. He has a graduate degree, but he couldn't find any work to compensate for his lost income, "even doing sales at a furniture store." Employers, he says, don't want to take the risk.

As a child, Doug benefited from organizations that offered food and support to low-income families. He said he'd like to volunteer and help the organizations that aided his family, but he's not allowed to. "I can't even give writing classes, where there would be lots of people and other adults in the room. I feel so much guilt. I could have made a difference."

The psychological impact of the registry is difficult for Doug, and he says that in spite of therapy, spiritual work, and recovery programs, he still has trouble dealing with the reality of the registry.

> If a neighbor doesn't say hello or isn't friendly, I worry if it's because of the registry. A local store let me do an event for my book, and I worried my presence would hurt their business or put them at risk. I still almost have a nervous breakdown when I'm around cops. I am almost incapacitated when I go to do my yearly registration.

This past year, he says, was particularly rough. Soon after dealing with the stress of his yearly registration, he learned that due to IML he wouldn't be able to accompany his wife to South America. He wanted to be there to support her during a medical procedure. "I feel so much guilt." Next, he says, he learned of a new change in the registry law that would allow many to petition for registry removal, but it excluded his offense. "It sent me into a tailspin. I felt suicidal. I'd had this dream of getting the law changed, and then it did, but it didn't apply to me." Doug also fears that the change could decrease the numbers on the registry, calling more attention to those left on it.

Doug's frustrated. He tells me that the judge in his case stated that Doug shouldn't be on the registry, but there was nothing to be done due to the laws. "How can I whine? Lots of people deserve justice more than me. I've never been assaulted or attacked. But I haven't gotten jobs. I got let go from a corporate gig, and I can't rent a house. Emotionally it's really hard. I don't want to hurt other people. I don't want to hurt my family."

Growing up, Doug says his mother was sexually assaulted by a stranger. "I used to say that rape should be a capital punishment. I was filled with revenge. It's not like I don't understand [why people want a registry]. Sometimes I want to fight. A lawyer recently told me the only way I'll ever get off the registry is if I get a pardon. Maybe I'll try that."

For Doug, lifetime registration feels similar to death row or a life sentence in prison. "I gotta do this forever. Forever. I was in my early thirties when I pled guilty. I'll be maybe eighty when I die. The idea of registering for fifty years. It's overwhelming. It's forever."

Prioritizing Child Sexual Abuse

In a 2013 article in *The Atlantic*, writer Mia Fontaine pronounces:

> Here are some statistics that should be familiar to us all, but aren't, either because they're too mind-boggling to be absorbed easily, or because they're not publicized enough. One in three-to-four girls, and one in five-to-seven boys are sexually abused before they turn 18, an overwhelming incidence of which happens within the family. These statistics are well known among industry professionals, who are often quick to add, "and this is a notoriously underreported crime." (Fontaine, 2013, p. 1)

This piece, published just prior to the #MeToo wave, in a mainstream and respected publication, highlights the contradictions inherent in our collective understanding of sex offenses. If these widely cited statistics are even close to correct, and as many as one-third of girls experience childhood sexual abuse, that also must mean as many as one-third of (mostly) men are perpetrators of sexual abuse. If this is so, the one million (or so) currently on registries are a miniscule portion of this population.

The author also writes that these statistics implicitly mean that, "close to a *third* of the population has experienced psychic and/or physical trauma during the years they're developing neurologically and emotionally" (Fontaine, 2013). She emphasizes that this problem is far broader in scope than recognized and calls for sexual abuse to be addressed loudly and directly; in her view, the issue is overlooked by policymakers. It impacts more people, she argues, than all the social problems addressed in a recent speech she cites by then-president Obama. These statistics are repeated frequently both by feminists and advocates for women and children, and those who make claims of that there is a vast epidemic of child sex trafficking and that a cabal of Democrats and elites are involved in global child sex rings. Yet data analyses present a far different picture.

First, the majority (about 75 percent) of child maltreatment cases involve neglect, followed by physical abuse (about 18 percent), while sexual abuse ranks a distant third at 8.6 percent of cases (Hinds & Giardino, 2020, p. 2). The most recent data also shows about 0.2 percent of child maltreatment victims as sex trafficked (U.S. Department of Health & Human Services, 2022, p. 47). Clearly, neglect and physical abuse are far more prevalent problems facing children than sexual abuse, but Fontaine doesn't urge the country to tackle those issues. The data also show that child sexual abuse and physical abuse have declined substantially and steadily since 1990; sexual abuse has declined 62 percent and physical abuse 53 percent (p. 3). Neglect rates have also declined by 11 percent, but in a less steady and dramatic manner. The decline in child sexual abuse, researchers hypothesize, has, in fact, declined largely due to the attention and concern paid to the issue.

Fontaine is right and wrong, though. She's wrong in saying that the topic of child sexual abuse is not a subject of concern in society, as it's been an intense topic of focus for decades by researchers, activists, policymakers, politicians, and all our social and legal institutions. Her larger point is correct, though, that most sexual abuse takes place in the home, yet our focus is centered on the far less common but "more palatable" problem of extrafamilial abuse. In 2017, child sex trafficking was added, per a new federal law, as a child maltreatment subcategory, indicating continued concerns of nonfamilial sex abuse (U.S. Department of Health & Human Services, 2022, p. 117). Society, she argues, is not "prepared" to address the "depth and scope" of child sexual abuse within families. Our sex-offense laws certainly reflect the unwillingness she identifies, as they are all premised on protecting children from strangers with prior sex-offense convictions.

One justification for the attention paid to child sexual abuse, as opposed to these other issues, is that child neglect or maltreatment are far less harmful and the effects far less long-lasting. Fontaine points out the real and horrific fallout from child sexual abuse:

> Ninety-five percent of teen prostitutes and at least one-third of female prisoners were abused as kids. Sexually abused youth are twice as likely to be arrested for a violent offense as adults, are at twice the risk for lifelong mental health issues, and are twice as likely to attempt or die from teen suicide. The list goes on. Incest is the single biggest commonality between drug and alcohol addiction, mental illness, teenage and adult prostitution, criminal activity, and eating disorders. Abused youths don't go quietly into the night.

The effects of child sexual abuse are unquestionably profound and can cause lifelong trauma. One understandable reason why social problems such as child neglect and maltreatment receive less attention, while they are far more common, is that the long-term effects are often viewed as less traumatic and consequential. Yet, obviously, child neglect and maltreatment also cause profound childhood trauma. The recent opioid and methamphetamine epidemics, for instance, correlated with increases in these problems; one study, for instance, found that children of parents with opioid use disorder are also at an increased risk of having mental health problems or substance use disorder, winding up in foster care, losing a parent to an overdose, or experiencing neglect during childhood (Winstanley & Stover, 2019). But the causes and consequences of these broader, often structural issues, are more complicated and costly and less politically expedient. In the case of child sexual abuse, it's easy to respond with politically popular calls for more punishment and increased surveillance of sex-abuse perpetrators. The far broader problems of child neglect and maltreatment cannot as easily be addressed via clearly defined, punitive criminal-legal responses.

Prioritizing Punishment

Child sexual abuse receives disproportionate attention from policymakers, while being the least common form of child maltreatment. Similarly, those on registries face disproportionate attention from policymakers, while the most common forms of sexual violence remain largely unaddressed. Legal scholar Eric Janus offers an explanation for this paradox.

In a recent article, Janus observes that despite the harsh registry regime, #MeToo exploded, "revealing widespread sexual misconduct against women, by powerful men, protected by iconic institutions," as did revelations about the nonurgency with which police treated sexual-assault kits (SAK). Janus correctly notes that "this incongruity" is due to "an almost obsessive" focus on sex-offense recidivism at the expense of addressing the most pervasive and routine forms of sexual violence. He argues, in fact, that our sex-offense policies, "are, in a perverse way, designed precisely to protect this aspect of our society—what feminists might call 'the patriarchy'—from taking full accountability and responsibility for its role in sexual violence . . . #MeToo and SAK backlogs persist not in spite of, but in significant measure because of the nature of the aggressive regulatory policies addressed to sexual recidivism" (Janus, 2020, p. 824).

Historian Linda Gordon, in a prescient 1989 article, offers an analysis, related to that offered by Janus, of the reasons for disproportionate attention to stranger sexual abuse. Like Fontaine, she highlights the pervasiveness and hidden nature of intrafamilial sexual abuse. Gordon points out that even in the late nineteenth century, social workers were aware that incest and nonstranger child sexual abuse were a significant social problem caused largely by "male brutality and lack of sexual control" (Gordon, 1988, p. 56). The feminist movement of the time recognized that girls were often least safe at home, and "sympathy for child victims" was "one of [its] major achievements" (p. 57). Indeed, today, we still see that girls and those under eighteen are the most frequent victims of sexual abuse. One study finds that 82 percent of all victims of child sexual abuse are female, with 34 percent under age twelve, and a startling 96 percent of these perpetrators are male (Snyder, 2000); and adolescents aged fourteen to seventeen were by far the most likely to be sexually victimized (Finkelhor et al., 2009).

Gordon argues that the decline of first-wave feminism caused child sexual abuse to be reconceptualized as a problem outside the home and one of "stranger danger," with blame moved toward the child victims themselves or their mothers for not supervising them adequately. Additionally, the problem was traced not to male violence but to "moral neglect" and "removed scrutiny from family and home" (p. 58). Ultimately, Gordon concludes that the absence of a feminist movement led even to blaming the victims of child sex abuse: "Evidence of child sexual abuse means that danger lies in sex perverts, in public spaces, in unsupervised [and] sexually assertive girls" (p. 61). She observes the increasing emphasis on gender-neutral stranger-danger child abductions further confused the issue, leading further away from the danger girls faced within the home from male relatives and nonstrangers. In her conclusion, written in the years just before the vast expansion of registries and other punitive responses to sex offenses, Gordon warns, "Children's sufferings will not be corrected by eroding the due-process rights and civil liberties of those accused. Child sexual abuse needs a political interpretation in terms of male power. But the prosecution of culprits—however necessary—and the breaking up of families that may result do not always benefit the child victims" (p. 64).

Leon: I Want to Do Something, Anything, to Support My Family

Leon is Latino and in his midfifties; he's been on the registry since his release from prison five years ago. He's a physician but is unable to work in his field, as he lost his license because of his conviction. On the public registry website, he's classified as being at "very low risk" of reoffense; it is noted that his offense involved sexual contact with female patients. He claims he is not guilty of the charges, but ultimately took a plea due to the financial cost of a trial, in addition to the potential of a decades-long prison sentence.

Wanting to support his wife and children, he has completed various educational and certificate programs since leaving prison. "I have applied to over forty jobs, and I cannot get an interview. I figured going back to school would open a door for me. I know I can't work as a doctor again, but I want to do something. Anything. My wife supports me, but I need to contribute." Leon came from a poor family and worked to pay for college and medical school. He expresses sadness that he can't pay his children's college tuition and give them a better life as he had hoped. He struggles with clinical depression, and his inability to support his family exacerbates the issue.

The registry, for Leon, is harder in some ways than prison. He says he'd serve another ten years in prison if he could be off the registry and tells me he's met many other registrants who would do the same. His son has special needs, and Leon is not allowed to visit his school or have in-person meetings with the teachers. One of his most painful experiences was not being able to attend his daughter's high school graduation. Security denied his request despite his promise that he would stay with his wife the entire time. He even thought about asking if he could hire a private security guard to accompany him.

Not being able to work, however, is what's most frustrating for Leon. "I can't work. Don't they want my taxes? How can I pay taxes if I don't work?" While he claims he's innocent of his offense, he seems resigned to his status and focused primarily on his inability to support his family. His wife, he says, has a good job, but they desperately need an additional income.

"Prison is better than this. At least in prison, you know where you stand. There is solidarity and respect. Out here, there is no respect. The biggest fear is that you have a record, so if any situation comes up, you'll be accused and found guilty." Leon is now going back to school to earn another professional certificate. He hopes that someone will eventually hire him, but he says he is losing hope.

Empathy and Community

Leon told me he doesn't want to complain and asserts that he has it better than others on the registry. As I've noted, one of the most unexpected comments made throughout my interviews was the clarification so many made about their comparative luck and privilege. They often shared detailed stories of others suffering far more than they did. Leon told me of a man in prison who lost his wife and children after his sex-offense conviction. He says the man is now homeless and doesn't qualify for any social services, and Leon regrets his own inability to assist him with housing or in terms of finances.

I am deeply struck by how the experience of banishment creates both empathy and community. Leon is becoming more active in efforts to help those on registries. Many who tell me their stories state their hope is that the resultant book will help change attitudes and allow them back into society. Even those who claim innocence, like Leon, seem willing to accept the terms of their incarceration and supervision. They consistently emphasized the special registry conditions after their sentences, as the source of their current suffering and the primary injustice they have experienced.

There is a tendency to have empathy toward those in your primary social group. Those on registries share many characteristics of a distinct cohort due to their status as pariahs and their legal and social exclusion. The empathy expressed for others on registries is evidenced by the frequent storytelling about those worse off than themselves, and their engagement in antiregistry advocacy groups and organizations and informal support of those they know from incarceration or group counseling. The empathy and sense of community among those on registries can also be understood as a direct result of the lack of empathy they elicit from society.

Philosopher Thomas Fuchs examines why people who treat those in their own group with compassion and respect can treat others with extreme cruelty. He uses the example of Nazis who were good to their friends and family yet were able to participate in the murder of Jews. His work seeks to understand the process of "compartmentalization" or "dissociation" of empathy, which happens when group members fail to extend concern to others outside their own groups. Mechanisms that lead to separation and exclusion ultimately "define a discriminated 'they-group' within or outside of society and lead to an increasing denial of recognition, culminating in an objectification and depersonalization of its members" (Fuchs, 2019).

To be clear, I am not equating those on registries with the Jews in Nazi-occupied Europe. Those on registries committed crimes that led to their status, and their lot is not in any sense equivalent to religious or racial persecution. The analogy that can be made is that those on registries have become a distinct out or "they-group," placed in opposition to a "we-group" because of easily debunked myths, justifying their legal banishment as well as social and informal exclusion. Fuchs writes:

> This exclusion was implemented, on the one hand, through a definition and radical separation of a "they-group" from the "we-group"; on the other hand, through an objectification and degradation by which the members of the excluded group were refused their recognition as persons and even denied their humanness. These excluding, depersonalizing and dehumanizing ideologies and policies were also able to neutralize or suspend basic empathetic feelings in the perpetrators toward their fellow humans. (p. 245)

This offers one way of understanding of why those on registries have become pariahs. The myth that those on registries are predatory monsters, incapable of change, inevitably destined to reoffend sexually, upholds their status as the "they-group." The view of those on registries as a they-group with the nonhuman characteristic of a "predator" nourishes the "depersonalizing and dehumanizing" ideology that supports their formal policies and social exclusion. This also, inversely, explains the unlikely community of those subject to the branding with the "sex offender" label and the support they have for one another.

Understanding the universal hatred toward those on registries involves recognizing two things. On the one hand, sexual abuse does cause great harm and is a pervasive social reality. On the other hand, one cannot discount the fact that this hatred is driven primarily by myths, including the widespread misconception that all those who commit sexual harm are predatory, unresponsive to treatment, and unable to change even after harsh punishment. Media coverage of the most rare and horrifying cases also reinforces the view that those on registries are irredeemable, subhuman monsters. Thus, those on registries are effectively dehumanized, which leads to their status as pariahs who deserve to be banished. The claim that registries protect children and prevent sexual violence is also a tenuous one, given that there are children on registries, that they expose the children of registrants to direct harm, and that they divert attention from the most common forms of child maltreatment and sexual violence.

Conclusion: Worse Than Murder?

> It means, for one thing, and it's very serious, that people who have had no experience have no compassion. People who have had no experience suppose that if a man is a thief, he is a thief; but, in fact, that isn't the most important thing about him. The most important thing about him is that he is a man and, furthermore, that if he's a thief or a murderer or whatever he is, you could also be and you would know this, anyone would know this who had really dared to live.—James Baldwin (1964)

There are many formal and informal ways that our society expresses that harming someone sexually is a greater transgression, taboo, and harm than taking someone's life. There are endless examples of this, many of which are described in the preceding pages. Some are so cruel that they reach into absurdity, such as laws banning registrants in need of full-time nursing care from residential-care facilities, restricting certain veterans from burial in military cemeteries, and barring registrants from emergency homeless shelters during weather emergencies. In each of these cases, as in the many cited in earlier chapters, registrants are the only group subjected to these laws, and none apply to those convicted of murder or any other past criminal offense.

How can dying, much less dead, registrants pose any threat? Are registrants so uncontrollably and deeply evil that they lie in wait for natural disasters so they can pounce while seeking lifesaving, emergency shelter?

After Hurricane Katrina caused unprecedented mass evacuations of entire cities in 2005, the media decided that of all the issues posthurricane, one of the stories that should be told was that registrants could, like everyone else, face displacement due to a once-in-a-lifetime natural disaster. A persistent theme of these stories was that registrants involuntarily forced from their homes might not update their addresses in a timely enough fashion as registries required. Relatedly, "thousands" would disappear into the ether and flood nearby states, using the opportunity to shirk registry rules. Less than four weeks after Katrina, an NBC story with no clear point beyond stirring fear focused on how even registrants were impacted by the disaster, and that they were part of "everyone": "When citizens of entire cities were evacuated in the aftermath of Hurricane Katrina that meant everyone, including prisoners and registered sex offenders." The story points out that one-quarter of registrants forced to move haven't updated their new addresses within ten days as registry laws require, and "time is up." The message of the story is simply that even in times of extraordinary crisis, registrants are not like everyone, nor are they entitled to any allowance or goodwill.

Those on registries pay taxes and must follow laws, yet they are excluded from the rights available to all others with criminal histories. As one person I interviewed noted, why is he paying taxes and following laws, if he cannot travel or live or visit or be where he likes, and he is ignored by police when harassed and threatened? In what sense, he asked me, is he free? And, as he and so many others observed, if he had taken a life or caused grievous bodily injury, rather than committed an offense deemed sexual, he would endure no such restrictions or such unbearable treatment.

Throughout this book, I've shared the voices and stories of some of the most reviled individuals in our society. A vast web of official restrictions limits their ability to live, work, and travel freely. A government-run list, easily accessible to all online, brands them as dangerous, exacerbating their inability to rejoin society. Informally, they experience social banishment and civil death. These formal and informal sanctions feed off each other. Panic-driven feelings of disgust and fear have created ineffective, animus-based registries, notification, and residency laws; their existence, in turn, offers constant reminders that those listed are dangerous and in need of constant, permanent surveillance.

Offering grace and the opportunity for redemption to everyone after punishment and accountability is fundamental to our humanity. It is, however, daunting to extend this principle to those whom we most fear and detest. Articulating the lived experiences of any invisible and marginalized group is, in most cases, including this one, an effort to raise awareness of our shared humanity. Of course, these stories may also elicit indifference or even satisfaction.

Registry laws reflect how we *feel* and what we *believe* about those on registries. This is not unprecedented, as laws may, at times, reflect hatred toward certain groups who lack political or social power. Yet measures based on attitudes of fear, disgust, animus, or even vengeance, that apply only to special populations, invariably function as punishment. And the punishment is quite well provided via the impacts of the registry, described by those living them.

Registries have been upheld as legal and constitutional because of the high-recidivism myth. Consequently, these laws have been ruled to be civil regulations necessary for public safety. They are, the courts have ruled, essentially the equivalent of vaccine mandates: without mandating certain vaccines, there would be "frightening and high" disease outbreaks, resulting in mass sickness and death. So, the state has a civil interest in mandating vaccines; they save lives while avoiding the high costs the state incurs during epidemics.

Registries, however, have not demonstrated, in over twenty-five years of existence, that they save lives or money. The evidence for high recidivism rates is faulty. Decades of scholarship and the government's own data attest to these facts. In practice, registries function only to punish a targeted subgroup of those convicted of crimes after they've fulfilled their criminal sentences, in what can only be described as cruel and unusual ways.

Registries Are Punishment

The stories in this book offer detailed examples of how, in practice, registries dole out extraordinary and endless punishment to registrants, their loved ones, and their families. Several examples of the insidiousness of the punishment emerged throughout these interviews. While few will be a shock to those living under the registry regime, these impacts are understudied and underacknowledged because of the exceptional marginalization of those impacted. The effects of these unprecedented broad "civil" or "regulatory" measures are thus largely unknown as they apply only to a uniquely reviled group. Here, I summarize the fundamental and nearly universal experiences of punishment faced by those living on registries.

Public Shaming, Lack of Privacy, and Second-Class Status

The public nature of the registry is the most obvious and damaging form of punishment. The formal, government-sanctioned public branding as a "sex offender" is so stigmatizing that it makes reentering society as a full human an impossibility. It also places innocent partners, parents, and children at risk of harassment and targeting, subjects them to housing discrimination, and deprives them of support from family members on registries.

Those interviewed spoke of being targeted by scammers and harassed by neighbors. If they complain to law enforcement, they report being ignored. In theory, those who break laws should fear the police. For those on registries, those who follow the law not only fear the police but receive little protection or concern when victimized by lawbreakers. The listing of personal information and criminal-offense history is, largely, a tacit government-sanctioned nod to vigilantes and scammers. While private registries also extend punishment without enhancing public safety, they do offer some protection from the most blatant forms of harassment and shaming.

Restrictions on Residence, Presence, Proximity, and Travel

The innumerable restrictions of where one can live, work, and travel apply to no other subgroup of tax-paying, law-abiding, nonincarcerated citizens. Residency laws and related restrictions punish registrants by creating enormous barriers to securing housing and work. The inability to travel freely is one of many ways those on registries never regain the rights of full citizenship after paying their debts to society. Limitations on travel also remind registrants that they can never escape their past mistakes, not even when leaving the country.

Social Isolation and Banishment

Those on registries lose their right to privacy, and everyone can see and easily learn of their past sex offense. In a society where such misdeeds are unforgivable transgressions, social isolation is a result of this public branding. Societal rejection is not directly or solely due to registry laws. Those convicted of sex offenses have been the subject of moral panics throughout history, subjected to attitudes of fear and disgust, even before registries. Moral panics and their subjects, theoretically, change, ebb, and flow depending on the changing fixations of media and culture. However, the registry formalized, institutionalized, and bureaucratized a heightened panic, entrenching it in our society and culture. This, in turn, justifies a general willingness to banish and isolate, because, after all, the state itself targets those involved. Politicians who regularly call for more registry laws experience no pushback, as it is among the easiest forms of "punching down" a universally despised group with virtually no political or social power.

Additional Impacts and Themes

In addition to the primary areas of impact outlined above, other unexpected themes and sentiments emerge clearly in the interviews. The reactions summarized below are less universal, but still frequent, and are related to the emotional and psychological toll of the registry. These include self-loathing, fears of false allegations, and the desire for acceptance and redemption.

Self-Loathing and Self-Blame

Many expressed self-blame and self-loathing beyond the expected feelings of guilt and shame about their offense. These feelings were largely due to the impact of the registry on their loved ones. Many commented that they can accept their own punishment but expressed personal torment about how the registry affects their families.

Additionally, many berated themselves for not understanding the extent to which the registry would weigh on their lives. Many said that they would have gone to trial or accepted longer prison sentences if they had fully recognized the effects of registration. Many expressed the wish that their attorneys had fully disclosed the realities of the registry before suggesting they agree to pleas. A smaller number, but more than a few, said they would have likely taken their own lives at the time of their arrests if they'd known the realities of life on the registry.

Assumptions of Guilt

Other common fears I heard, unprompted by my questions, include being falsely accused, unintentionally violating registry laws, and overall awareness of how they will never be given the benefit of the doubt. These fears manifested in different ways. One was an apprehensiveness about being near children. This is particularly sad, for it leads to social-avoidance strategies, such as skipping family and social gatherings where children are present, and eschewing relationships with adults who have children.

This also relates to fears of false accusations, not just by children but also by adults. Some avoided promotions or management positions due to the potential conflicts that can result when in supervisory roles. They feared that angering or firing an employee could trigger a retaliatory response. In turn, many rejected opportunities and were hypervigilant in all social and professional interactions. Many also reported installing video cameras to monitor outside their properties and in their homes. They explained that they believed they would be assumed guilty if they were victims of harassment, vandalism, or false allegations, so the cameras would offer hard evidence of their claims for any incidents at their residence

Desire for Acceptance and Redemption

During interviews, a few people shared fantasies of self-immolation, mentioning the monk who performed this act to protest the Vietnam War. I heard it again when I was a guest on a podcast, after I'd completed interviews. In that case, an audience member asked me if I thought self-immolation by a registrant would be an effective way to raise awareness of the harms of the registry (I told him no). I recognize, though, that this desire shows deep despair. What underlies this impulse is the sense that there is no possibility to change laws or beliefs outside of an exceptional act.

Additionally, such an act would have the possibility of being redemptive. If a registrant died in the hopes of helping others, this would be seen as martyrdom. A related fantasy was that of saving a child's life or rescuing someone in some other way in order to gain reacceptance into society. Many, though, expressed a general wish that if they could just tell their stories, they'd be understood. They desperately wanted to be seen as more than perpetrators of offenses and as more than people who made dreadfully poor decisions. Many believed that they'd be forgiven if given the opportunity to explain why they did what they did and their own experiences of trauma or pain that contributed to the offense.

I could interview only a small number of those who responded to my call, and I could only include a small portion of completed interviews in this book. Part of this willingness to share, I realized, was related to the hope that I'd tell their stories so others would understand their humanity. While many on registries bravely tell their stories and engage in activism, many fear drawing additional attention to their registry status. The potential blowback of being an outspoken registrant makes them particularly reliant on others to speak up on their behalf. One antiregistry organization, Women Against the Registry, was founded partly on this premise, so family members could lead antiregistry efforts while expressing the devastation and harm they, too, experience. It's striking, in fact, to see the number of women leading antiregistry organizations and efforts. These women, often wives and mothers of registrants, but also lawyers, activists, and scholars, share the anticarceral feminist recognition that punitive criminal-legal policies harm everyone—and not only the (mainly) men who are directly impacted—without increasing safety.

Community, Service, and Empathy

Overall, the frustration, anger, and sadness registrants shared were fundamentally due to their lives being characterized by endless and unceasing punishment. The most agonizing aspect of the registry for most is the contradiction of assured swift and harsh sanctions for any violation or mistake without reward for abiding by laws, paying taxes, and being good citizens. Correspondingly, registry restrictions only increase, as new laws and regulations are implemented, with old ones rarely repealed. Registrants are thus subject to ever-increasing punishments, as their time in the community without reoffense grows. Conversely, the risk for reoffense continues to decrease over time, creating an almost-Orwellian scenario.

Still, my conversations with those who live as outcasts revealed an extraordinary ability to persevere without resorting to bitterness or self-pity. I was most struck by the almost universal acknowledgment of their (relative) luck, by the active engagement in service to others on registries, and by the search for community and opportunity despite frequent rejection.

As noted throughout this book, almost all interviewees started and ended with an expression of gratitude for what they have and an acknowledgment of others are far worse off. They shared stories about those they knew from prison or treatment in far direr straits, and I learned of informal networks of registrants supporting each other. Many continue to make efforts to engage in their communities, do service, or participate in religious activities, despite repeated mistreatment. This tenacity was not just to demonstrate to outsiders that they have taken accountability but part of their own wish for self-redemption.

My purpose in writing this book was partly to reveal the reality of the human impact of these terrible, useless, and mean-spirited policies. Hearing what people on registries and their loved ones say is painful because it reflects a deep darkness within our democracy and ourselves. Those on registries sought to be reaccepted into society after punishment.

Indeed, we are starting to address aspects of the maltreatment faced by all those impacted by our criminal-legal system, and particularly those in our jails and prisons. One student of mine, who had spent years incarcerated, was facing homelessness during his reentry process. He regularly reminded those who expressed concern that "the worst day out here is better than the best day in prison." Those subject to the inhumanity of life behind bars without parole or lifetime civil commitment, are even more invisible, tortured, and discarded than those on registries. A related issue, beyond the scope of this book, is how sex-offense panic also infects sentencing decisions and leads to mistreatment during incarceration and supervision.

Worse Than Murder?

Registrants and their loved ones often observe, with frustration, how they are treated as more dangerous and less worthy of redemption than someone convicted of murder. This mistreatment occurs within the criminal-legal system and beyond, and even during incarceration. They are targeted not only by officials but by those with nonsexual offenses; the particularity of their perceived dangerousness is formally represented by their public branding and special web of rules applying only to them, and their status as irredeemable is confirmed by their social exclusion. This observation is also made by activists, advocates, lawyers, and researchers familiar with their experiences.

The stories in the book all attest to how having a sex-offense conviction is worse than having one for murder (or any other crime). All those with criminal convictions face profound barriers to societal reentry. Most will face some extent of employment and housing discrimination and financial stress, as well as experiences of social exclusion due to the stigma of a criminal history. Those convicted of murder and other offenses classified as serious or violent are often ineligible for certain policies and programs for others with criminal histories, However, when exceptions are made to these stringent measures, those with sex offenses are almost always left out. For instance, when states allow the sealing or expungement of criminal records after a certain period, they commonly exclude those having committed serious or violent *felonies*; but misdemeanor sex offenses are often the only misdemeanor category summarily excluded from expungement or sealing (Collateral Consequences Resource Center, 2023).

Also, after criminal-sentence completion (including supervision), no others with nonsexual offense histories, *including murder*, experience the hyperstigmatization and harassment caused by public registration and community notification, or the punishing limitations of residency, travel, presence, and proximity restrictions.

Why are we willing to forgive others who inflict grave harms, *including murder*, but not those who commit crimes involving sex? Few, of course, will say outright that a sex offense is objectively worse than a murder, though some do. Our laws and attitudes starkly reveal, however, that we are more forgiving of someone who has committed a murder. The registry indicates, for all practicable purposes, that we are more comfortable in the presence of someone who killed another human being than we are with someone with a sexual offense in their past. Our laws tell us we don't need to know if new neighbors spent time incarcerated for murder, but we must be aware if they had been behind bars for a sex offense. Our attitudes demonstrate our willingness to accept and even applaud those who attain success and happiness after punishment. We grant others full freedom of movement without restricting where they can live or travel after a criminal sentence, but not someone with a sex offense.

Research has carefully detailed the historical and political origins of the beliefs and emotions that have led to the laws, as well as the impact of the laws on reinforcing these beliefs and emotions. Examining these origins is the only way to understand how sexual harm has been elevated above all other harms—and why those who commit sexual injury are viewed as worse than those guilty of any other misdeed.

One explanation lies in sex panics. A body of research has traced the connection of the first federal sex-offense laws to two interrelated mass fears that first emerged in the late 1980s. One of the panics was based on widespread false accusations of ritual child sexual abuse in day care centers, and the other on wildly inflated claims about the prevalence of stranger kidnappings. While journalists and social scientists debunked both sets of allegations by the early 1990s, the underlying assumptions continue to inform policy and behavior. Thus, we see nearly two generations of fearful children raised by "helicopter" parents who falsely believe that they are at a high risk of being kidnapped by sexually motivated strangers.

These panics had an outsized impact on fears and policies because the few highlighted victims of exceedingly rare but particularly heinous crimes were photogenic, white, and middle-class, with their grieving parents leading calls for swift implementation of untested, emotion-driven policies. At the same time, a powerful political alliance of feminist antiviolence activists with law-and-order conservatives emerged, with both calling for more punishment. While some feminists pointed out that addressing interpersonal violence with state violence reinforced structural inequalities, they were outnumbered by more powerful procarceration voices. Concurrently, a victims'-rights movement emerged, centering the trauma of victims and their families into criminal-legal policy. Similar to feminist antiviolence efforts, victims'-rights advocates first sought to end the mistreatment of women by police and courts when reporting sexual assault. It morphed, however, into demands for increasing perpetrator sanctions and for factoring trauma into sentencing decisions.

The integration of conservative law-and-order goals with those of feminist and victims'-rights activists reveal the unique confluence of bipartisan politics and ideology that led to the centering of the "sex offender" as an embodiment of all social ills. There are no comparable movements against violent nonsexual crime, even though mass incarceration was an adjacent outcome of many of these same factors. For example, Mothers Against Drunk Driving (MADD) emerged around the same time and was also a movement led by grieving middle-class parents who successfully fought to incorporate the role of trauma into harsher criminal sentencing. The success of MADD has influenced parent- and victim-led movements to expand punishments for sexual crime. Similarly, the "war on drugs," and related panics about "crack babies" and "superpredators," have led to calls for longer sentences and mandatory minimums, and also influenced support for increasing sex-offense penalties, while vilifying and dehumanizing perpetrators.

However, these other punishment-driven movements didn't tap as viscerally into now-dominant conservative and liberal core tenets and political goals that relate to sex and sex roles. For conservatives, as Roger Lancaster observes, the civil rights, feminist, and antiwar movements fanned fears about the dissolution of society and the traditional family, leading to an embrace of "culture war" issues such as abortion and gay rights; together, he argues, the result was that "sex panic became the enduring technique of the modern conservative movement—its minimal form, its very essence" (Lancaster, 2011a, p. 41). Liberals reacted to these same societal changes with an embrace of identity-oriented politics and support for policies appearing to redress the grievances of marginalized and minority groups, including carceral approaches to sexual violence to compensate for the historical oppression of women. In other words, in the post-1960s context, specific shifts in conservative and liberal ideologies led both to prioritize issues related to sex.

In his introduction to *The War on Sex*, David Halperin points out that while, "the view that sex *in itself* is bad or harmful is rarely articulated or argued," this is what's most loudly and clearly communicated when sex offenses are treated as the greatest legal and social transgression. The overt claim of a "noble" war against sexual violence silences criticism and, further, as Halperin notes, politically orphans the issue by "unit[ing] feminists and evangelicals, liberals and radicals, politicians and activists, intellectuals and populists, Left and Right" (2017, p. 4).

Expanding criminal-legal responses to sexual violence thus offered the perfect answer to all. They allayed conservative fears that feminism, abortion, and gay rights destroyed families and family values, and appear to protect women and children from the supposed rash of sexually deviant strangers created by unnerving social changes. They also achieved liberal goals of protecting minority group interests while responding to past injustices, and appearing to reverse a history of indifference to women victims and to the tolerance of male violence. The "sex offender," albeit for diametrically opposing reasons, is the unfortunate human casualty of the perfect historical and political storm, playing the role of boogeyman for both dominant ideologies. Punishing him endlessly satisfies some who see him as the embodiment of a dark history of male dominance, patriarchal power, and oppressed and neglected victims, as well as others, who see him as the product of a lawless, decadent, and declining society lacking morality and values.

The political reality, then, of being convicted of a sex offense puts one in a sociolegal position that is worse than someone convicted of murder. With a sex offense, one lacks all defenders and allies and serves as the depository of hateful, fearful, and vengeful emotions from all sides. Rage and fear are far more difficult to temper when coming from all sides, and they easily overwhelm both reason and facts.

Works Cited

Ackerman, A., & Sacks, M. (2018). Disproportionate Minority Presence on the U.S. Sex Offender Registries. *Justice Policy Journal, 16*(2). http://www.cjcj.org/uploads/cjcj/documents/disproportionate_minority_presence_on_u.s._sex_offender_registries_ackerman_sacks.pdf

Alschuler, A. (2003). The Changing Purposes of Criminal Punishment: A Retrospective on the Past Century and Some Thoughts about the Next. *The University of Chicago Law Review, 70*(1), 1–22.

Bellucci, J. (2022, June 6). Personal Communication (Email to author).

Burch, M. (2019). Captive Afterlives in the Age of Mass Conviction. *History & Anthropology, 30*(5), 515–520.

Burch, M. (2021). *Afterlives of Conviction.* https://www.afterlivesofconviction.org/about

Bushway, S., & Kalra, A. (2021). A Policy Review of Employers' Open Access to Conviction Records. *Annual Review of Sociology, 4*, 165–189.

Carpenter, C. (2020a). All Except For: Animus That Drives Exclusions in Criminal Justice Reform. *Southwestern Law Journal, 50*, 1–43.

Carpenter, C. (2020b). Blanket Exclusions, Animus, and the False Policies They Promote. *Southwestern Law Review, 50*, 1–46.

Carpenter, C. (2022). Panicked Legislation. *Notre Dame Journal of Legislation.* https://doi.org/10.2139/ssrn.4179366

Carson, E., Sandler, D., Bhaskare, R., & Fernandez, L. P. (2021). *Employment of Persons Released from Federal Prison in 2010.* U.S. Department of Justice, Office of Justice Programs, Bureau of Justice Statistics. https://bjs.ojp.gov/content/pub/pdf/eprfp10.pdf

Clean Slate New York. (2021). *End Perpetual Punishment.* Cleanslateny.Org. https://static1.squarespace.com/static/5ddd73a9e6903359f16ed36f/t/61d49103fc465b26dea458f1/1641320707426/CSNY+Two+Pager.pdf

Collateral Consequences Resource Center. (2023). *Restoration of Rights Project: 50-State Comparison: Expungement, Sealing & Other Record Relief.* January. https://ccresourcecenter.org/state-restoration-profiles/50-state-comparison judicial-expungement-sealing-and-set-aside-2/

Commission on Judicial Performance. (2016). *Commission on Judicial Performance Closes Investigation of Judge Aaron Persky*. https://amjudges.org/conferences/2019-Annual/SOC-Persky-CJP-report.pdf

Connecticut Office of Policy and Management. (2012). *Recidivism among Sex Offenders in Connecticut*. https://www.ct.gov/opm/lib/opm/cjppd/cjresearch/recidivismstudy/sex_offender_recidivism_2012_final.pdf

Connecticut Sentencing Commission. (2017). *A Study of the Sex Offender Sentencing, Registration, and Management System* [Report to the Judiciary Committee of the Connecticut General Assembly, pursuant to Special Act 15-2, § 1]. http://ctsentencingcommission.org/wp-content/uploads/2018/05/Sex_Offender_Report_December_2017.pdf

Couloute, L., & Kopf, D. (2018, July). Out of Prison and Out of Work: Unemployment Among Formerly Incarcerated People. *Prison Policy Initiative*. https://www.prisonpolicy.org/reports/outofwork.html

Cull, D. (2018). International Megan's Law and the Identifier Provision: An Efficacy Analysis. *Washington University Global Studies Law Review, 17*(1), 181–200.

Dayan, C. (2011). *The Law Is a White Dog: How Legal Rituals Make and Unmake Persons*. Princeton, NJ: Princeton University Press.

Demos, J. (1976). John Godfrey and His Neighbors: Witchcraft and the Social Web in Colonial Massachusetts. *The William and Mary Quarterly, 33*(2), 242–265. https://doi.org/10.2307/1922164

De Orio, S. (2017). The Creation of the Modern Sex Offender. In D. Halperin & T. Hoppe (Eds.), *The War on Sex* (pp. 247–267). Durham, NC: Duke University Press.

Dowty, D. (2021, December 1). *40-Year-Old Syracuse Rape Conviction at the Heart of Author Alice Sebold's Memoir Is Thrown Out*. https://www.syracuse.com

Durkheim, E. (1893). *The Division of Labor in Society*. New York: Free Press.

Efrati, A. (2008, October 23). "Making Punishments Fit the Most Offensive Crimes." *Wall Street Journal*. https://www.wsj.com/articles/SB122471925786760689

eLaws.us. 74-102. Sexual Offenders and Sexual Predators, 102(b) 74 (2006). http://brevardcounty.elaws.us/code/coor_ch74_artvi_sec74-102

Ellman, I. M. (2021). When Animus Matters and Sex Crime Underreporting Does Not: The Problematic Sex Offender Registry. *University of Pennsylvania Journal of Law & Public Affairs, 7*(1), 1–36.

Ellman, I. M., & Ellman, T. (2015, Fall). "Frightening and High": The Supreme Court's Crucial Mistake about Sex Crime Statistics. *Constitutional Commentary, 30*(3), 495.

Feige, D. (Director). (2016). *Untouchable* [Documentary]. https://www.untouchablefilm.com

Finkelhor, D., Turner, H., Ormrod, R., & Hamby, S. L. (2009). Violence, Abuse, and Crime Exposure in a National Sample of Children and Youth. *Pediatrics, 124*(5), 1411–1423.

Fontaine, M. (2013, January 24). America Has an Incest Problem. *The Atlantic*. https://www.theatlantic.com/national/archive/2013/01/america-has-an-incest-problem/272459/

Fritz, M., & Brangham, W. (2016). *Inside Minnesota's Sex Offender Facility, Where No One Has Ever Been Released*. PBS News Hour. https://www.pbs.org/newshour/nation/inside-minnesotas-sex-offender-facility-where-no-one-has-ever-been-released

Fuchs, T. (2019). Empathy, Group Identity, and the Mechanisms of Exclusion. *Topoi, 38*(1), 239–250.

Furby, L., Weinrott, M. R., & Blackshaw, L. (1989). Sex Offender Recidivism: A Review. *Psychological Bulletin, 105*(1), 3–30. https://doi.org/10.1037/0033-2909.105.1.3

Gardner, B. (1987, June 15). Executive Order 89-04. *Establishing the Governor's Task Force on Community Protection*. Olympia, WA. https://www.governor.wa.gov/sites/default/files/exe_order/eo_89-04.pdf

Goodmark, L. (2022). To Free Them All. *Inquest: A Decarceral Brainstrom*. October 22. https://inquest.org/to-free-them-all/

Gordon, L. (1988). The Politics of Child Sexual Abuse: Notes from American History. *Feminist Review, 28*(1), 56–64. https://doi.org/10.1057/fr.1988.4

Gordon, L. (1989, March/April). The Politics of Child Sex Abuse. *Against the Current*, No. 19. https://againstthecurrent.org/atc019/the-politics-of-child-sex-abuse/

Governor's Task Force on Community Protection. (1989). *Task Force on Community Protection Final Report*. Olympia, WA: Department of Social and Health Services.

Gramlich, J. (2020). *What the Data Says (and Doesn't Say) about Crime in the United States*. Pew Research Center. https://www.pewresearch.org/fact-tank/2020/11/20/facts-about-crime-in-the-u-s/

Green, B., & Bazelon, L. (2020). Restorative Justice from Prosecutors' Perspective. *Fordham Law Review, 88*, 2287. https://ir.lawnet.fordham.edu/flr/vol88/iss6/7

Gruber, A. (2021). *The Feminist War on Crime: The Unexpected Role of Women's Liberation in Mass Incarceration*. Berkeley: University of California Press.

Halperin, D. (2017). Introduction. In D. Halperin & T. Hoppe (Eds.), *The War on Sex* (pp. 1–61). Durham, North Carolina: Duke University Press. https://www.dukeupress.edu/Assets/PubMaterials/978-0-8223-6367-5_601.pdf

Hanson, R. K., Harris, A. J. R., Helmus, L., & Thornton, D. (2014). High-Risk Sex Offenders May Not Be High Risk Forever. *Journal of Interpersonal Violence, 29*(15), 2792–2813. https://doi.org/10.1177/0886260514526062

Hanson, R. K., Harris, A. J. R., Letourneau, E., Helmus, L. M., & Thornton, D. (2018). Reductions in Risk Based on Time Offense Free in the Community: Once a Sexual Offender, Not Always a Sexual Offender. *Psychology, Public Policy, and Law, 24*. https://doi.org/10.1037/law0000135

Hawley, J. (2022, March 16). *Twitter post*. https://twitter.com/HawleyMO/status/1504221926662844418

Higgins, E., & Rolfe, S. (2016). "The Sleeping Army": Necropolitics and the Collateral Consequences of Being a Sex Offender. *Deviant Behavior, 38*, 1–16. https://doi.org/10.1080/01639625.2016.1229947

Hinds, T. S., & Giardino, A. P. (2020). Incidence and Prevalence of Child Sexual Abuse. In T. S. Hinds & A. P. Giardino (Eds.), *Child Sexual Abuse: Current Evidence, Clinical Practice, and Policy Directions* (pp. 1–10). Springer International Publishing. https://doi.org/10.1007/978-3-030-52549-1_1

Horowitz, E. (2015). *Protecting Our Kids? How Sex Offender Laws Are Failing Us.* Santa Barbara, CA: Praeger.

Horowitz, E. (2022). *The Real Monsters. Inquest: A Decarceral Brainstorm.* June 3. https://inquest.org/the-real-monsters/

Human Rights Watch. (2013). *Raised on the Registry: The Irreparable Harm of Placing Children on Sex Offender Registries in the US.* May. https://www.hrw.org/sites/default/files/reports/us0513_ForUpload_1.pdf

In re Reed, 33 Cal.3d 914 (Supreme Court of California May 26, 1983).

Jackson, K. B. (1996, May). Prevention versus Punishment: Toward a Principled Distinction in the Restraint of Released Sex Offenders. *Harvard Law Review, 109*(7), 1711–1728.

Janus, E. (2020). Preventing Sexual Violence: Alternatives to Worrying about Recidivism. *Marquette Law Review, 103*(3), 819–845.

John, A. (2014, April 22). A Timeline of the Rise and Fall of "Tough on Crime" Drug Sentencing. *The Atlantic.* https://www.theatlantic.com/politics/archive/2014/04/a-timeline-of-the-rise-and-fall-of-tough-on-crime-drug-sentencing/360983/

Kamorowski, J., Cucolo, H., & Redlich, A. (2017). *International Megan's Law: It's Not about What Works, It's about What Sells.* Common Ground. https://www.researchgate.net/publication/323308904_International_Megan%27s_Law_It%27s_not_about_what_works_it%27s_about_what_sells

Kill Your Local Pedophile Toddler Long Sleeve Shirt. (2022, July 30). *Tee Shirt Place.* https://www.teeshirtpalace.com/products/kyl2011414-kill-your-local-pedophile-toddler-long-sleeve-shirt

Kohan, S. (2020). Registering a Home When Homeless: A Case for Invalidating Washington's Sex Offender Registration Statute. *Washington Law Review Online, 95*, 205–243.

Lageson, S. (2020). *Digital Punishment: Privacy, Stigma, and the Harms of Data-Driven Criminal Justice.* New York: Oxford.

Lancaster, R. (2011a). *Sex Panic and the Punitive State.* Berkeley: University of California Press.

Lancaster, R. (2011b, August 20). Sex Offenders: The Last Pariahs. *The New York Times*, 6.

Landon, L. (2020, July). *Sex Offender Sentencing in Washington State.* Washington State Statistical Analysis Center. https://sac.ofm.wa.gov/sites/default/files/public/pdf/sex_offender_sentencing_in_washington.pdf

Latifi, F. (2022, June 14). Bay Area Drag Queen Speaks Out against Far-Right Extremists. *Teen Vogue.* https://www.teenvogue.com/story/drag-brunch-story-time-kyle-chu

Lave, T., Prescott, J. J., & Bridges, G. (2021). The Problem with Assumptions: Revisiting "The Dark Figure of Sexual Recidivism." *Behavioral Sciences & the Law, 39*(3), 279–306.

Levine, J., & Meiners, E. R. (2020). *The Feminist and the Sex Offender: Confronting Sexual Harm, Ending State Violence.* New York and London: Verso Books.

Lisak, D., & Miller, P. (2002). Repeat Rape and Multiple Offending among Undetected Rapists. *Violence and Victims, 17*(1), 73–84.

Logue v. Book, 297 So. 3d 605 (Fla. Dist. Ct. App 2020).

Maleng, N. (1992). The Community Protection Act and the Sexually Violent Predators Statute. *University of Puget Sound Law Review, 15*(821), 821–826.

Martin, E. (2017, March). Hidden Consequences: The Impact of Incarceration on Dependent Children. *National Institute of Justice Journal, 278.* https://nij.ojp.gov/topics/articles/hidden-consequences-impact-incarceration-dependent-children

McCarthy, A. (2022, March 20). Senator Hawley's Disingenuous Attack against Judge Jackson's Record on Child Pornography. *National Review.* https://www.nationalreview.com/2022/03/senator-hawleys-disingenuous-attack-against-judge-jacksons-record-on-child-pornography/

McLaughlin, D. (2022, March 21). There Are Legitimate Questions about Jackson's Views on Sex Offenders. *National Review.* https://www.nationalreview.com/corner/there-are-legitimate-questions-about-jacksons-views-on-sex-offenders/

Memmi, A. (1974). *The Colonizer and the Colonized*; Introduction by Jean-Paul Sartre. London: Souvenir Press.

Miller, J. A. (2010). Sex Offender Civil Commitment: The Treatment Paradox. *California Law Review, 98*(6), 2093–2128.

Missouri Revised Statutes. (2023). *Missouri Revisor of Statues.* https://revisor.mo.gov/main/Home.aspx#BOTTOM

Navarro, J. C., Knudsen, K. E., & Richardson, C. L. (2022). A Statutory Analysis of State-Level Sex Offender Residency, Loitering, Presence, and Entry Restrictions. *Crime & Delinquency.* https://doi.org/10.1177/00111287221108707

New York Radical Feminists. (1974). *Rape: The First Sourcebook for Women*; Edited by Noreen Connell and Cassandra Wilson. New York: New American Library.

New York State Senate. (2021a). *Assembly Bill A6399C.* https://www.nysenate.gov/legislation/bills/2021/a6399/amendment/c

New York State Senate. (2021b). *Senate Bill S1553D.* https://www.nysenate.gov/legislation/bills/2021/S1553

People v. Barone. (District Court of the State of New York, County of Suffolk, First District 2018).

Pickett, M., Satifka, E., Shah, R., & Wiener, V. (2020). *Labeled for Life: A Review of Youth Sex Offender Registration Laws.* Juvenile Law Center. https://jlc.org

/sites/default/files/attachments/2020-09/Labeled%20for%20Life%20 2020.pdf

Prescott, J. J., & Rockoff, J. E. (2011). Do Sex Offender Registration and Notification Laws Affect Criminal Behavior? *The Journal of Law and Economics, 54*(1), 161–206. Report 156450. https://www.ojp.gov/pdffiles1/Digitization /156450NCJRS.pdf

Przybylski, R. (2017). Chapter 5: Adult Sex Offender Recidivism. In *Sex Offender Management Assessment and Planning Initiative*. U.S. Department of Justice, Office of Justice Programs. https://www.smart.gov/SOMAPI/pdfs/SOMAPI _Full%20Report.pdf

Public Citizen. (2018, November 6). *Twitter post*. Breaking: Florida just passed Amendment 4, restoring voting rights to 1.4 million people with a past felony conviction. Not only does this repeal one of the country's worst Jim Crow laws, it's also the largest expansion in voting rights since the Voting Rights Act. https://twitter.com/public_citizen/status/10599873 87072290816

Redbubble. (2022, September 3). *Pedophile Stickers*. https://www.redbubble.com /shop/pedophile+stickers

Robles, F. (2018, November 7). 1.4 Million Floridians with Felonies Win Long-Denied Right to Vote. *The New York Times*, 14.

Roesler, R. (2007, December 29). Victim Finds Freedom in Forgiveness. *The Spokesman-Review*. https://www.spokesman.com/stories/2007/dec/29/victim -finds-freedom-in-forgiveness/

Rolfe, S. M. (2019). When a Sex Offender Comes to Visit: A National Assessment of Travel Restrictions. *Criminal Justice Policy Review, 30*(6), 885–905. https://doi.org/10.1177/0887403417742948

Rosengren, J. (2022, April 19). Locked Up for Good—Or Forgotten? *Minnesota Monthly*. https://www.minnesotamonthly.com/lifestyle/the-fight-against -minnesota-sex-offender-program-msop/

Russell, D. (1982). The Prevalence and Incidence of Forcible Rape and Attempted Rape of Females. *Victimology, 7*(1–4), 81–93.

Salman, J. (2020, August 11). Sex Offender Loses COVID-19 Contract at VA Hospital after USA TODAY Asks Questions. *USA Today*. https://www.usatoday .com/in-depth/news/investigations/2020/08/11/convicted-sex-offender -got-lucrative-government-covid-19-contracts/3314931001/

Santos, T. D. (1999). Williamson v. Gregoire: How Much Is Enough? The Custody Requirement in the Context of Sex Offender Registration and Notification Statutes. *Seattle University Law Review, 23*(457), 457–479.

Savage, J., & Windsor, C. (2018). Sex Offender Residence Restrictions and Sex Crimes against Children: A Comprehensive Review. *Aggression and Violent Behavior, 43*, 13–25. https://doi.org/10.1016/j.avb.2018.08.002

Scheingold, S., Olson, T., & Pershing, J. (1994). Sexual Violence, Victim Advocacy, and Republican Criminology: Washington State's Community Protection Act. *Law and Society Review, 28*(4), 729–764.

Scurich, N., & John, R. S. (2019). The Dark Figure of Sexual Recidivism. *Behavioral Sciences & the Law, 37*(2), 158–175.

Sheriff, K. C. (2019, September). *Sex and Kidnapping Offender Registration Notification.* King County Washington. https://kingcounty.gov/~/media/depts/sheriff/documents/sex-offender/Notice_of_Registration.ashx?la=en

Siwach, G. (2018). Unemployment Shocks for Individuals on the Margin: Exploring Recidivism Effects. *Labour Economics, 52*, 231–244.

Smith v. Doe, 538,84 (U.S. 2003).

Snyder, H. (2000). *Sexual Assault of Young Children as Reported to Law Enforcement: Victim, Incident, and Offender Characteristics.* U.S. Department of Justice, Office of Justice Programs. https://bjs.ojp.gov/content/pub/pdf/saycrle.pdf

Socia, K. M. (2014). Residence Restrictions Are Ineffective, Inefficient, and Inadequate: So Now What? *Criminology & Public Policy, 13*, 179.

Song, L., & Lieb, R. (1995, February). *Washington State Sex Offenders: Overview of Recidivism Studies.* Olympia, WA: Washington State Institute for Public Policy.

Stevenson, B. (2014). *Just Mercy.* New York: Spiegel & Grau.

Sullum, J. (2020, October 1). Publishing Registered Sex Offenders' Home Addresses before Halloween Is Gratuitous, Unethical, and Reckless. *Reason.* https://reason.com/2020/10/01/publishing-registered-sex-offenders-home-addresses-for-halloween-is-gratuitous-unethical-and-reckless/

Thornton, D., Hanson, R. K., Kelley, S. M., & Mundt, J. C. (2019). Estimating Lifetime and Residual Risk for Individuals Who Remain Sexual Offense Free in the Community: Practical Applications. *Sexual Abuse, 33*(1), 3–33. https://doi.org/10.1177/1079063219871573

Torres, R., & Sobel, R. (2013). The Right to Travel: A Fundamental Right of Citizenship. *Journal of Transportation Law, Logistics and Policy, 80*, 13–47.

Tovey, L., Winder, B., & Blagden, N. (2022). "It's OK If You Were in for Robbery or Murder, but Sex Offending, That's a No No": A Qualitative Analysis of the Experiences of 12 Men with Sexual Convictions Seeking Employment. *Psychology, Crime & Law.* DOI: 10.1080/1068316X.2022.2030736

Uggen, C. (2000). Work as a Turning Point in the Life Course of Criminals: A Duration Model of Age, Employment, and Recidivism. *American Sociological Review, 65*(4), 529–546.

U.S. Department of Health & Human Services, Administration for Children & Families. (2022). *Child Maltreatment 2020.* Children's Bureau. https://www.acf.hhs.gov/cb/data-research/child-maltreatment

U.S. Department of Justice, Bureau of Justice Statistics. (2003). *Recidivism of Sex Offenders Released from Prison in 1994.* https://bjs.ojp.gov/press-release/recidivism-sex-offenders-released-prison-1994

U.S. Equal Employment Opportunity Commission. (2012, April 25). *Enforcement Guidance on the Consideration of Arrest and Conviction Records in Employment Decisions under Title VII of the Civil Rights Act*, Title VII, 29 CFR Part 1601, 29 CFR Part 1606, 29 CFR Part 1607.

Wacquant, L. (2009). *Punishing the Poor: The Neoliberal Government of Social Insecurity.* Durham, NC: Duke University Press.

Walrond, Rev. Dr. L., & Shah, S. (2022, June 1). Op-Ed | New York Needs a Clean Slate Now. *AM New York.* https://www.amny.com/opinion/op-ed-new-york-needs-a-clean-slate-now/

Washington State Institute for Public Policy. (1994, February). *A Summary of Recent Findings from the Community Protection Research Project.* National Institute of Justice

Weisman, J., & Ulloa, J. (2022, March 22). Judging a Judge on Race and Crime, G.O.P. Plays to Base and Fringe. *The New York Times.* https://www.nytimes.com/2022/03/22/us/politics/ketanji-brown-jackson-race.html

Winstanley, E. L., & Stover, A. N. (2019). The Impact of the Opioid Epidemic on Children and Adolescents. *Clinical Therapeutics, 41*(9), 1655–1662. https://doi.org/10.1016/j.clinthera.2019.06.003

Zandbergen, P. A., & Hart, T. C. (2006). Reducing Housing Options for Convicted Sex Offenders: Investigating the Impact of Residency Restriction Laws Using GIS. *Justice Research and Policy,* 8(2), 1–24.

Zraick, K., & Alter, A. (2021, November 23). Man Is Exonerated in Rape Case Described in Alice Sebold's Memoir. *The New York Times*, 15.

Index

About the Author

Emily Horowitz, PhD, is a professor of sociology and criminal justice at St. Francis College in Brooklyn, New York. At St. Francis, she founded and codirects a program that offers scholarships and mentorship so that those with criminal histories can earn college degrees. Her book *Protecting Our Kids? How Sex Offender Laws Are Failing Us* (Praeger, 2015) won an American Library Association Choice Award, and she serves on the boards of a number of organizations that advocate for the end of conviction registries and for rational and just sex-offense policies.